Dear Reader:

The book you are about to read is the latest bestseller from the St. Martin's True Crime Library, the imprint the *New York Times* calls "the leader in true crime!" Each month, we offer you a fascinating account of the latest, most sensational crime that has captured the national attention. St. Martin's is the publisher of perennial bestselling true crime author Jack Olsen (SON and DOC) whose SALT OF THE EARTH is the true story of how one woman fought and triumphed over life-shattering violence; Joseph Wambaugh called it "powerful and absorbing." DEATH OF A LITTLE PRINCESS recounts the investigation into the horrifying murder of child beauty queen JonBenét Ramsey; the author is Carlton Smith. Peter Meyer tells how a teenage love pact turned deadly in BLIND LOVE: *The True Story of the Texas Cadet Murders*. For those who believe slavery is a thing of the past, Wensley Clarkson proves them wrong in SLAVE GIRLS: *The Shocking World of Human Bondage*. Fannie Weinstein and Melinda Wilson tell the story of a beautiful honors student who was lured into the dark world of sex for hire in THE COED CALL GIRL MURDER.

St. Martin's True Crime Library gives you the stories *behind* the headlines. Our authors take you right to the scene of the crime and into the minds of the most notorious murderers to show you what really makes them tick. St. Martin's True Crime Library paperbacks are better than the most terrifying thriller, because it's all true! The next time you want a crackling good read, make sure it's got the St. Martin's True Crime Library logo on the spine—you'll be up all night!

Charles E. Spicer

Charles E. Spicer, Jr.
Senior Editor, St. Martin's True Crime Library

OUTSTANDING ACCLAIM FOR GREGG OLSEN'S
THE CONFESSIONS OF AN AMERICAN BLACK WIDOW

of book—that people will talk about. Gregg Olsen shows us just how chilling it is to realize what might be going on in the house next door."

—Clark Howard, bestselling author of
Love's Blood

"What a combination! God, Mammon, Carnality, all rendered vividly under Olsen's assured touch."

—Stephen Michaud, bestselling author of
The Only Living Witness

"THE CONFESSIONS OF AN AMERICAN BLACK WIDOW is that rare book that is at once a page-turner and an important chronicle of true crime. As Olsen unravels the minister's wife's tale of manipulation and murder it is clear nearly from the start—Sharon Nelson was born to be a black widow killer. An enlightening and devastating read."

—Steven A. Egger, Ph.D., author of *The Killers Among Us: An Examination of Serial Murder and its Investigation*

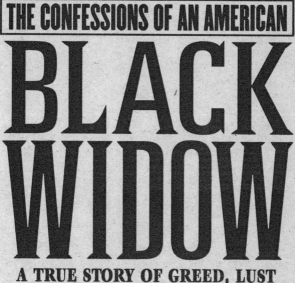

THE CONFESSIONS OF AN AMERICAN

BLACK WIDOW

A TRUE STORY OF GREED, LUST AND A MURDEROUS WIFE

GREGG OLSEN

St. Martin's Paperbacks

For Lorri

THE CONFESSIONS OF AN AMERICAN BLACK WIDOW

Copyright © 1998 by Gregg Olsen.

Cover photograph courtesy Judy Farson.

ISBN: 0-312-96503-6

Printed in the United States of America

St. Martin's Paperbacks edition / June 1998

10 9 8 7 6 5 4 3 2

Dramatis Personae

Sharon Lynn Douglas Nelson Harrelson — Minister's wife, doctor's wife, fireman's wife, murderer

Mike Fuller — minister, Sharon's first husband
Rochelle Fuller (Mason) — eldest daughter of Sharon and lover
Denis Fuller — daughter of Sharon and Mike
Craig — Sharon's lover in North Carolina (*not* the father of Rochelle)

Perry Nelson — Optometrist, Sharon's second husband, victim
Julie Nelson — Perry's first wife
Tammi Nelson, Kathy Nelson, Lorri Nelson (Hustwaite) — daughters of Julie and Perry

Danny Nelson — son of Perry and Sharon
Misty Nelson — daughter of Perry and Sharon

Gary Starr Adams — Carpenter, Sharon's pretend husband (mountain meadow wedding), murderer
Nancy Adams — Gary's first wife, mother of their two children (a grown daughter and a teenage son)

Buzz Reynolds — Rancher, Sharon's lover and pretend husband (pool party wedding reception)

Glen Harrelson — Firefighter Sharon's third legal husband, victim
Andrea Harrelson — Glen's first wife, mother of Todd and Tara Harrelson

Important Others:
Barbara Ruscetti — Perry's office assistant in Trinidad
Judy Douglas — Sharon's oldest sister
Elaine Tygart — Detective, Thorton Police Department
Glen Trainor — Detective, Thornton Police Department

Summer 1996

TWENTY YEARS HAD PASSED SINCE IT ALL STARTED.

Two decades had come and gone.

Seven thousand, three hundred days had become permanently etched in a young woman's memory.

And still the saga of her father's brutal murder had not come to a complete resolution.

Lorri Nelson Hustwaite took a deep breath when she got on the phone to hear the news; the conclusion to a yo-yo of heartache and hope in her family's search for closure. She and her three sisters and brother had filed suit against insurance companies that had paid Lorri's one-time stepmother more than $200,000 in life insurance benefits. Another insurance company had already paid the children $50,000 in an out-of-court settlement.

"The Supreme Court affirmed the decision," said the voice of her sister Tammi over a line stretching from Tammi's house in Redlands, California, to Whitefish, Montana, where Lorri and her family of four made their home. The Colorado Supreme Court had agreed that a consortium of insurance companies had been negligent in making the huge payouts to Sharon Lynn Nelson. The insurance companies had, in fact, gathered enough evidence to make the woman a suspect in the murder of her husband, Perry Nelson. Yet the companies had done nothing with their suspicions. At least, not enough.

"It's finally over," the older sister said.

At 33, Lorri wanted more than anyone to believe that the

words were true. The blond wife and mother of two had been through so much. She dropped the phone and went to hug both her husband and a family friend who was visiting at the time. She felt joy tempered with sadness.

Lorri had never said good-bye to her father.

Whatever labels affixed to her—Black Widow, ambitious gold digger, insatiable slut—she was a killer. Much more, but never less than that. If Sharon envisioned her life as one big movie, in which she was the star, she was mistaken. If she thought she could sweep away the hurt left as a grim remnant of her insatiable greed, she was wrong.

Dead wrong.

Lorri saw it. Others did, too. Yet no one had been able to stop Sharon. No one could even slow her down. From the ranchers, to the deputy, to the office secretary who suspected the worst, none could do a thing to bring the woman to justice.

In the end, only she could do it to herself. It was so fitting. It was almost funny, if it had not been so tragic.

Only Sharon Lynn could screw herself.

In Canon City, Colorado, in a prison that rivals the best the world of punishment has to offer, Sharon repeats her broken-record claim that she is innocent. The frosted-coiffed babe in the orange coveralls didn't do anything wrong. This is a free country. She is an American, for God's sake. She was misunderstood. She made bad choices, but she wasn't a killer.

She asks herself over and over how it turned out so bad for her.

"What good has all of your goddamn wanting to be good and moral gotten you, Sharon? What has it gotten you? I can't answer that yet. Sometimes part of me wants to be the biggest bitch in the penitentiary. When someone is talking at night, go down the hall and say, 'You goddamn motherfucking slut why don't you shut your goddamn mouth?' I can't do that, because my anger and the words would cause that person hurt. There are times when this whole thing gets to me so bad that I want to turn into the bitch that everyone thinks I already am. I don't know how to do it with no conscience. I wish I could. It would make my time so much easier, I think.''

Yet one summer afternoon in 1996, it suddenly no longer mattered what Sharon hoped, wished or wanted. It didn't matter one bit about her at all. As the dust settled on a two-decade-long nightmare of sorrow and dreadful consequences, Lorri Nelson Hustwaite was finally able to rest knowing her stepmother had not gotten away with everything.

She could finally say good-bye.

Prologue

FOR A PLACE WITHOUT AN OCEAN, THERE IS nowhere in the world more lovely than landlocked Colorado. Mountains of unbelievable mass spray upward from spruce-covered foothills with exhilarating force. Stands of birch and aspen shimmer; their leaves moving like silver schools of fish. Snow clings to the tops of the highest peaks throughout the warmth of summer. Rocky Mountain high. John Denver. Coors Beer. The Broncos. Rugged. West. Unspoiled.

Folks who live in Colorado know all of that. Old-timers and newcomers alike know that theirs is the state that holds truest and firmest to the call of the Old West. Colorado is western without the trendy goofiness of California; the granola zealotry of Oregon; the drippy weather of sodden Washington.

And forget Utah, Coloradans opine. Utah, they know, is its own planet.

While those who run other state tourism boards tell postcard printers to "punch up the color," no such effort is needed for the images of the Rocky Mountain State. Skies are sapphire, rich and deep. Look to the heavens day or night and feel a sense of falling up. Foaming rivers hastily run through chiseled chasms like Christo-inspired aquamarine ribbons stretched from boulder to boulder, canyon wall to canyon wall.

Colorado is the place where the great prairies are stopped by the Rockies. Denver, the state's largest urban center, is bunched against the mountains. Like Denver, most of the state's major cities—from Ft. Collins in the north, south to

Colorado Springs, Pueblo and Trinidad, the smallest of the big four—are strung along north-south Interstate 25.

Yet, as is true of any place, after the passage of time the splendor can fade in the eye of the beholder. Mountains can be an encumbrance that forces additional hours from Point A to Point B. Raging rivers overflow in the blink of an eye during lickety-split spring melts. And the trees? They are no longer things of beauty, but disparaged because of a sudden drop in lumber prices. Excitement wanes. Interest falls. Time to move on.

Love can be like that, too.

The man poking through the stinking, smoldering remnants of the living area of the house at 12370 Columbine Court had seen his share of such scenes. Thornton, Colorado, police criminalist Bob Lloyd had personally handled more than 1,000 death investigations. All but what could be counted on two hands had taken place in Detroit.

Detroit. The name no longer brought residual feelings of goodwill and recognition. No more did Detroit conjure the sounds of Motown to reverberate in his head or the smell of a new car inspire him to smile. The Detroit of Bob Lloyd's tenure as an officer there meant only one thing: death.

He kept a black plastic binder of grisly photographs he'd taken over his twenty-year career in the Motor City. He called it his *D book.* If it meant "Detroit" or "Death" it didn't really matter. They were one and the same. Images on the pages revealed dead eyes fixed in lifeless terror, blood-spattered walls and coagulated pools of mahogany . . . all were the reality of the job that took more than it gave.

The veteran criminalist made up his mind that enough was enough when a twelve-year-old girl was shot in the head a couple of blocks from his supposedly safe neighborhood. Drug violence knows no boundaries. The little girl had been riding her bike down her street when gunfire ripped through the air and killed her. Bob Lloyd's daughter was the same age, his sons were fourteen and sixteen. The father and husband knew it was time for the cop to move on.

Suburban Denver was safe, clean, friendly. If none too exciting, then he knew he'd have to buckle down and get used to it. At least he would not need to bring two guns to protect himself during a crime-scene investigation. At least he could go to sleep at night without the worry that the lead spray of a drive-by shooting would shatter his daughter's window and kill her as she slept in her bed. He arrived in the snow-crunched month of February 1986 and the months flew by without a murder. Not several a night nor a handful a week—zip.

"This is the way people are supposed to live," the 46-year-old told a friend.

It was still dark when Bob Lloyd and the others first arrived on the scene, following reports the home had been burned while the owner was away. Arson, they all suspected. It was a good guess. A cursory examination, even in the black of the early morning hours of November 20, 1988, indicated the fire had been isolated to an area off the garage entry into the house. Firemen with beard-stubbled, smudged faces and wet boots told the investigators that charred "pour" patterns around an open pit in the floorboards indicated an accelerant had more than likely had been used by the arsonist.

Criminalist Lloyd walked the perimeter of the residence. It was a one-story, a brick ranch house with neatly groomed landscaping, and, even in winter, a flawlessly clipped-on-the-bias front lawn. Real estate agents love to call such attention to detail as "pride of ownership." He walked along the side-walk noting nothing unusual, with the exception of an iron security grate having been removed from a window well that fed a diffused column of light into the basement level. A drift of curly, brown cottonwood leaves nested in the depth of the well.

A quick round of questions confirmed the security grate had not been removed by firefighters in an effort to make a rescue or to gain access to extinguish the blaze. The criminalist knew, firsthand, that sometimes the very best "clues" turned out to be nothing more than a misinterpretation of what had been done to the fire scene—*before* it was roped off as a crime scene.

7

The beam of his portable light knifed through the air, catching the dusty filaments of a spiderweb.

No one had come in or out of the house through the window well.

Without exception, investigators from all divisions of law enforcement feel the jolting surge of adrenaline when suspicions rise at a crime scene. But it is not a thrill. It is not merely a reaction to the excitement of a discovery. For many, it is far deeper. It is the rush of the hunt. The feeling of pursuit seizes them and propels them. No one who works the scene of a terrible fire or murder is bored. No matter what time a cop is hauled out of the quiet and warmth of a bed or out of the arms of a wife or husband, they readily go. All investigators are hunters.

Bob Lloyd followed his beam of light around the house. The three-car garage had two vehicles parked inside. The largest of the garage doors had been open when the firemen first arrived. A beautifully restored white Camaro and what had become many suburbanites' everyday auto, a pickup truck, sat waiting for their driver.

"Where is Glen?" asked a fireman who knew Glen Harrelson, the owner of the burned home. Harrelson was known to many who had arrived on the smoldering scene. As it turned out, Harrelson was a veteran Denver firefighter.

It was Glen Harrelson's house, for Christ's sake. A goddamn fire had ruined the house of one of their own. A goddamn arsonist had targeted one of their own.

As far as anyone knew, Glen Harrelson wasn't home. The fireman was nowhere to be seen.

Further searching of the smoky confines of the house turned up nothing to indicate he had been home. A firefighter's shield and a packet of photographs were on the nightstand. The bed was made. The clothes in his closet were hung in the starched precision that commonly suggests military training. If he wasn't home, where was he?

A call to his fire station revealed the missing man was not scheduled for duty until 6:30 that morning. He had a good work record and was never late. It was more than likely he was still down south in Trinidad with his wife, Sharon.

A few on the scene allowed themselves a sense of relief when they heard their colleague was not there, and that he often was gone for several days at a time.

Bob Lloyd stepped around a scattering of coins in the living room as he walked through the house.

"Maybe a burglary?" a young officer suggested.

The criminalist, nicknamed "Dr. Detroit" by his coworkers, didn't think so. Beyond the coins, nothing had been disturbed. The drawers in the master bedroom had been left alone. No one had ransacked the closet. No one had taken the firearms neatly arranged on a shelf. The bureau in the guest room was untouched.

The coffeemaker, the smoke detector, the television, everything plastic had been melted into Dali images by the heat of the fire.

In the basement, a chair pushed over to the window with the missing grate indicated a point of entry.

But the spiderwebs are still intact, Lloyd reminded himself. *No one got in or out of here through the basement.*

Whoever set the fire, he reasoned, had come in through a door, and with a house so secure—burglar alarms, window grates with panic buttons for emergency release—it had to have been with a key.

Or an invitation.

If it had been an invitation, then where in the world was Glen Harrelson?

Just inside the garage entrance to the inside of the house was the charred depths of the crawl space. Bob Lloyd knew he would return to that area. He knew most of the answers to the questions police and firefighters were asking would be contained in the blackness of that hole. Since most certainly an accelerant had been used, analysis of the burned-out flooring would yield the answer to what it was. He directed his flashlight through the darkness, but saw nothing but debris.

He had stood in that spot before. *Too many times.* He leaned forward, craning his neck.

"There's something down there," he said, indicating that halogen lights from his truck would be needed. In a few minutes, a power cord from the police generator snaked its way through the garage, past the Camaro, through the entry door and into the area adjacent to the smoldering flooring.

Six halogens blasted into the hole. Eyes focused on the mess below. It took a few seconds for Bob Lloyd to adjust his vision as the white beam eradicated the dark. What appeared to be a seared gasoline can caught his eye. *Of course.* The beam of light plunged deeper, revealing charred fabric, probably clothing and melted carpet bunched up in a pile. Then he saw a twisted figure.

It was a man.

"We've got a homicide," he said. His tone was flat, matter-of-fact. Still, his heart pounded.

It was Glen Harrelson, 45, blackened like a briquette, contorted in the pugilistic position that is the result of incineration of muscle and tendon: his arms pulled up to his chest; his legs stiffened and tight. He was on his back, his head fully intact.

"The skull didn't explode," someone remarked.

Bob Lloyd nodded. He knew it was more likely than not that the man in the crawl space had died from a gunshot wound to the head. Without the piercing by a bullet or the fracture by a hard instrument, the human head almost always explodes in the heat of a fire.

Though not much was left of his face, it was clear that it was still there. Like Edvard Munch's famed painting *Scream*, Glen Harrelson's mouth was open as if to shriek.

But of course it did not. He could make no sound. Never again.

Notifications to the Thornton Police Department were made that the arson investigation at Columbine Court was now a murder case. The victim, more than likely, was the owner of the house, a fireman named Glen Harrelson.

Later that morning, two shell casings were picked up by detectives; one was found by the television set, another closer to the door, near the sofa. After necessary warrants were procured, a fireman went into the hole and gingerly put the dead man's remains onto a board for removal. The victim's bones were so brittle, his skin so charred, that the fireman held his breath so as not to break the corpse into a million pieces. Bob

Lloyd ran his video recorder, providing a calm voice-over to everything he saw.

Everything pointed to an ambush. The killer was lying in wait when Glen Harrelson entered his house. It was probably over quickly. The intruder double tapped—shot—Glen in the head, doused gasoline on his body, stoked the fire with some clothing, scattered the coins and left. It was a classic case of a staged homicide, and it only took the killer a few minutes to do it.

At 36, Elaine Tygart was a six-footer, a woman in a world of size sevens who carried her striking height beautifully and proudly. She had brown eyes and long, frosted blond hair. Bangs framed her face with a feathery touch. She neither looked like a police officer, nor had she ever dreamed of being one. In fact, being a cop had been someone else's dream. Elaine Tygart was in the right place and the right time when, as a college student, her fiancé at the time applied for positions at various police departments throughout Colorado. Almost on a whim, she followed suit and was quickly hired by a suburban Denver police department in the spring of 1976.

A decade later, promoted to a position of investigator, she was one of only a very small number of American women holding such coveted posts. Though she worked property crimes, the new detective found her niche in persons crimes: adult sex crimes, assault and homicide. Elaine liked people and was expert at comforting them while extracting information that would help in the arrest and conviction of a perpetrator. If a victim needed to cry, she'd allow it. If they wanted to talk and talk and talk, Elaine Tygart was there to listen. She was never cold to the victim. She was never easy on the perpetrator.

Elaine was always one to get to the meat of the crime.

Her sheer physical presence had been an asset from the very beginning of her law enforcement career. While not as physically strong as her male counterparts in the department, Elaine's height gave her an advantage over both male and female suspects. Raised with four brothers, she had been a tomboy growing up in Ohio. She knew toughness and bravado were advantages that could not be discounted.

And she could swear. She could let loose four-letter words in sequences that startled. Miss Prissy, Miss Goody-Two shoes, *Charlie's Angels* wanna-be, she was not.

Detective Elaine Tygart, accidental career cop, was as good as they get.

Years later, she told tales of how she proved herself in the matter-of-fact manner one might employ to tell a neighbor over the clothesline, if, indeed, people still had such chats.

She once lifted a belligerent drunk and tossed her down the stairs after she had been spat in the face and kicked in the shins.

"Goddamn you! You're going downstairs! You're going to jail."

Another time when she was called for backup on a theft in progress only to find an officer about to get his head bashed in with a tire iron, she pointed her gun and stopped the perpetrator in his tracks.

"You move, asshole, and you're fuckin' dead."

Word circulated among cops that the six-footer with the frosted hair had real guts. She wasn't afraid of anyone or anything. Even so, she did not hide that she was a woman. She always wore makeup, perfume and did her hair. She never once considered herself one of the guys—even though some treated her that way.

Youth had its advantages as well as its drawbacks. At 28, Glen Trainor was the kind of young detective whom senior, more jaded, investigators like to call "green." That somewhat derisive term was wasted on the young investigator. Although Glen Trainor had only worked two homicides and did lack experience, the tenacity of youth—the hunger for the hunt—more than made up for it. He came to the Thornton Police Department after a four-year stint in the Air Force security police ended in 1983 and became a detective in August 1987.

Glen Trainor also loved his work. It held his interest in a way he imagined no other job could.

I can't believe we get paid for what we do. A lot of people would do this job for no pay, he thought.

Two miles away from the smoldering house, Trainor was reached at the home he shared with his wife Robin and their two-year-old daughter with the request to get over to 12370 Columbine Court. By the time he arrived, officers were canvassing the neighborhood to find anyone who might have seen something that could help determine what—and, more importantly, *who*—caused the fire that killed Glen Harrelson. The arson squad picked through the smoldering ruins and several neighbors gathered beyond the yellow tape. White vapors from the spectators' warm breath caught the light of approaching cars as they talked about how their neighbor had recently married and that he and his new wife divided their time between Trinidad and Denver.

When Elaine Tygart got word there had been a suspicious death involving a Denver fireman in a house fire in Thornton, she was in the middle of the second day of a two-day blood spatter seminar at the Westminster Ramada Inn. Once alerted, the detective packed up her things and immediately went to the station.

It doesn't add up. A firefighter dead in a fire in his own house? Doesn't add up.

At the Thornton Police Department, plans were made to send Tygart and Trainor to Trinidad to make a death notification, and to solve a murder. A sergeant doled out a few bucks from petty cash for meals and lodging. Authorities in Trinidad had been notified Tygart and Trainor were en route and were standing by to render assistance as needed. Glen Harrelson's wife, Sharon, the Thornton police learned through conversations with the dead man's coworkers, lived in a remote mountain home in Weston. They also learned more jarring information: It seemed Sharon's second husband had died five years before, and while there was no murder investigation—that death was ruled accidental, a car wreck—there were some concerns.

It was a little after 3 P.M. when the pair got into their unmarked detective unit, an Impala, for the long drive south.

Their minds raced. There was no red flag larger in law enforcement: The woman they were going to see was *twice* a widow. Her husbands had died untimely, suspicious deaths.

"Wouldn't it be weird if we cleared them both?" Det. Trainor asked as he and his partner merged onto I-25.

"Yeah," she answered. "It would be."

Glen Trainor was three inches shorter than Elaine Tygart, but neither saw themselves as Mutt and Jeff. They were professionals with a job to do. They drove on.

Most longtime Coloradans know of Trinidad and its surrounding environs. The place, in a word, had a reputation. It was an isolated town, a somewhat inbred haven for the alternative and the strange. Of course, the handiwork of Trinidad's gender reassignment surgeon Dr. Stanley Biber and his world-renowned sex-change clinic routinely came up when people outside the community spoke of the town. Some in law enforcement considered Trinidad a postcard-pretty place with a dark side of corruption, mystery, and waitresses with five o'clock shadow.

As one native Coloradan half-joked, "Trinidad has seventy-three churches and eighty bars."

The two detectives chatted about the mountain community as they drove Trinidad's streets in search of the police station and Las Animas County Sheriff's Department. Keenly aware of their outsider-status, they wondered what kind of assistance they'd get from the local cops. Secluded places like Trinidad don't like strangers butting into their business. But to the detectives' surprise, instead of resistance they were greeted with handshakes and offers to help when they arrived in the hand-cut gray stone building that housed both the sheriff and the police.

As the sheriff's deputies began to talk about the woman the Thornton pair had come to interview, an unflattering and unsettling picture began to emerge. Sharon Harrelson had been the talk of the town from nearly her first days in the area. It seemed everyone knew her and no one was surprised the police wanted to talk to her. She was lusty, flamboyant. She was a bed hopper that would give the frogs of Calaveras County a run for their money. It seemed like she'd bedded half the men—married *or* single—in a hundred-mile radius. If you wore pants and were looking for a woman to spread her legs, this lady apparently obliged.

Some of it was gossip. Some of it was mean-spirited; the kind of talk that comes from horny men who didn't get any at home. Sitting in the bar, bullshitting the hours away until closing, talking about the women they'd like to screw . . . the lady in the fancy house on Cougar Ridge frequently came up in conversation.

Whatever the reality of the basis of her reputation, it was doubtful any grass grew under the lady's feet.

The sheriff's deputy told Tygart and Trainor that as far as they knew, Sharon Harrelson was at home. The lack of phone service in the area made it impossible to give her a call to see if she was there. Though it was late, the only way to confirm it was to take the forty-five-minute trip out to Weston, where her home was perched on a mountainside. The Thornton detectives were put into the backseat of an older-than-the-hills Scout and taken to a house where they picked up a young man—the son of another officer—who knew the location of Sharon Harrelson's mountain hideaway.

"Never find it without a guide," the deputy said, as the young man slid into a seat.

Neither of the Thornton cops disagreed. They wanted to get on with it. Even so, Trainor felt a little anxious. As they drove further and further into the blackness of the night, he wondered just exactly where they were headed. All the stories of Trinidad being a haven for crime and the weirdos that flock to such places took hold. It was so remote. It was so Nowheresville. It was the perfect place to bump off a couple of nosy out-of-town cops.

Shoot us up on a hillside and say they never saw us . . .

Glen Trainor chatted nervously about fishing and hunting prospects in the area as though he were really interested. The local deputy promised to take him up to the reservoir, if they had time, to show him the area's best fishing spot.

* * *

The siren of the mountains, the purported sexpot of the Rockies, was puffy-eyed and weary when the detectives and their local law enforcement escort went inside her grand, custom-built home. For all the Thornton police detectives had heard about her, the woman's appearance did not match her reputation. Perhaps it was the terrible circumstances of their visit? At 43, Sharon Harrelson was soft-spoken and devoid of makeup. She was no man magnet. She was tired and wan.

The occupants of the house included two small children—identified as seven-year-old Misty and ten-year-old Danny Nelson—and a young woman named Rochelle and her husband, Bart Mason. None of them mattered, of course. At least initially, all eyes were on the woman who had lost her husband to a terrible fire.

Rochelle scurried the little boy and girl into the living room, while Sharon led her somber parade of visitors to the kitchen.

The flame of her lighter was a tiny torch held by fingers with candy-apple red nails. She put a cigarette to her full, sensuous lips and sucked hard. In a minute, as smoke streamed from her nose, Sharon started from the beginning.

BOOK I:
Preacher's Wife

"*I was a perfect little minister's wife on the outside. I think probably most of our congregational members—except the ones I really let inside me— would have said I was a wonderful minister's wife.*"
—Sharon Fuller

"*So I thought, what kind of a woman is she? She's coming down to Trinidad and she's got two little kids and she's married to a minister. Here she is shacking up with Perry at a motel.*"
—Barbara Ruscetti

1

IT WAS SUPPOSED TO BE A FRESH START. GOD KNEW the preacher's thirty-year-old wife needed one. So did her husband. Four years in Durham, North Carolina, had been besmirched by the unthinkable, the unspeakable. Nerves had been frayed. Blame had been heaped deeper and deeper. No man's shoulders could bear the enormous weight of it all. Seventh-Day Adventist Pastor Mike Fuller knew he had a problem. A pretty one, too. Her name was Sharon.

The family headed west to La Junta and Rocky Ford, Colorado, boiling over the circumstances forcing them from the eastern seaboard. It was the summer of 1976; platform shoes' last stand, the year of the Bee Gees and Donna Summer. For the family in the convertible sliding across the mammoth asphalt belt of the interstate, it was not a happy time. The house they loved had been put up for sale; furniture loaded on a separate moving truck. Friends had been kissed good-bye. The couple's two little girls, Rochelle, seven, and Denise, two, had been yanked from their playmates.

And it was all her fault.

Sharon Fuller had fallen in love with a man in her husband's congregation. It was not the first time and, Sharon knew, it likely would not be the last. Within the embrace of the other man's arms, Sharon told friends, she had found compassion, tenderness, love—emotions she derisively insisted her husband was incapable of offering.

The scenario played in Sharon's mind like a bodice-ripper

romance novel without a happy ending. Tattered dreams. Lost opportunity. Star-crossed lovers. To her way of thinking, such a romantic visage seemed to fit her predicament. Her voice would waver many years later when she would try to dissect what had happened when she had forsaken her husband for a man named Craig.

"It wasn't so much that our marriage was bad at that point. Mike was never a sensitive person. He'd never been one to share like Rod McKuen poems. I'll never forget the first time I went over to Craig's apartment. He had a fantastic stereo system and he had a tape—he had lots of tapes—of Rod McKuen. One of them was *The Jostling of Angels* and it just struck me so," she said, the bittersweetness of the memory bringing a smile to her face. "It was like it was talking about me. The feeling I got was when you're so self-sufficient and self-important and you're walking down the street . . . be careful that your imaginary wings don't jostle the real angels that are the common people."

She could picture her husband walking down the street, his imaginary wings "mashing everybody in his way." She felt Minister Mike considered himself a "legend in his own mind" and did not understand that there were "real people out there that he knocked around emotionally that had real worth."

Her lover had been different. Craig was gentle. Not just during sex, but in everything he did. He had a tenderness that drew Sharon closer than she had been with any man. When little Rochelle Fuller's teddy bear was falling apart, it was Craig who brandished a Band-Aid for the stuffed animal. Sharon felt Mike would have tossed the torn plush toy into a trash bin. Craig had a gentle heart. A man with an easy touch. He was everything she had ever wanted; at least, she told herself so at the time. Sharon always told herself so. Whenever. Whoever. The man she slept with was always the man of her dreams.

Even as they drove across the flat expanses of the Great Plains, thoughts of Craig brought a sentimental smile to her lips, only to be obliterated by Mike's contemptuous comments about the reason the church had sent them packing for the

Rocky Mountain State. Her mind fixated on the day Mike told her they'd be moving.

"We're being kicked out because you're a little slut, Sharon!"

His eyes telescoped from their sockets. The veins on his neck bulged with blood.

"A slut!"

Sharon had hurried to Craig's sister's house in tears. The humiliation had ripped her apart; her nerves were shot, her eyes were red. Though she did not regret the love she and Craig shared, the bliss they had stolen, she could not erase the feelings of guilt and shame.

Craig's sister put her arms around the sobbing preacher's wife.

"Why didn't you tell me about this?" Sharon said.

At first, the woman didn't know what she was talking about.

"They kicked us out because I am a slut!" Sharon ranted.

The woman tried to comfort her. "No, Sharon. No," she said with exaggerated certainty. She told Sharon how church leaders had brought a petition calling for Mike Fuller's removal as pastor of their church. Her husband, in fact, had signed it. Everyone knew about it. Sharon's affair with Craig had not even been mentioned.

"It was to get Mike out because everything had to be Mike's way. You weren't even in it," she said.

In later years, Sharon liked to repeat her version of the truth. She was not to blame for the Fullers ending up in southeastern Colorado. She had not been the source of her husband's downfall in the eyes of the church.

"Once I found out it wasn't me . . . that Mike . . . didn't want to admit nobody liked him, it was extra hard. Because I was having to leave the first place I ever really felt was my home, because people didn't like Mike and his arrogance. His arrogance finally came through. We were there four years. Other churches we were only there for a year or so. Toward the end is when his overbearing ways finally got to people."

There had been no lack of occasions when things could have turned out differently. There always are. There might never have been a long, hot drive to Rocky Ford, Colorado, in Sharon Lynn's life. She had her out the year before. Yet no one would back her up, no one would support her in her quest for love.

Not her mother, not her father.

It was in 1975 when Sharon Fuller made a single move toward freedom from her husband, freedom toward what she felt was a "truer" self. She was entitled to more. She was deeply in love with Craig when she decided she could leave Mike and start over. She drove from Durham to her parents' home in Maryland. She told no one she was going. Not her husband—not even her lover. For all the members of the church congregation knew, Sharon and her little ones went to visit an ill grandfather.

Her parents said she was a fool for leaving Mike. They could still work things out. Marriage was not easy. But a commitment before God cannot be tossed away like so much rubbish.

Sharon was in the kitchen when her mother answered a knock at the door from a floral delivery service.

Her mother, Josephine Douglas, rushed back with a stunning bouquet. A hopeful smile broke over the older woman's face.

"Look, honey, I bet Mike sent you some roses."

Sharon prayed the flowers had been a gift from Craig.

"They are from Mike," Josephine said.

"Trash them."

"Oh, no, honey, they're God's creation. They're beautiful."

"They're ugly and I don't want them."

"I'll put them in a vase and put them in my room."

"I don't want them in the house," Sharon said, seizing the box from her mother's grip and tromping out of the house and throwing the roses on the compost pile.

Mrs. Douglas was furious, but Sharon didn't care.

"You wasted money, Sharon," she said. "You should have let me send them back to the florist!"

Sharon ended the conversation by telling her mother she hated the damn flowers.

"They're ugly," she said.

A day or so later, another bouquet arrived, this time from Craig. Against her mother's wishes, Sharon put the flowers in her bedroom.

"She had a fit," she said later. "She never understood."

In the end, Sharon went back to her husband, partly because of the pull of the Church, a little bit because her mother told her it was the right and sensible thing to do. But she returned to Durham mostly because she figured she had nowhere else to go. When she got back to North Carolina, she learned her husband had been transferred to a church in Colorado. They'd be leaving in a month.

She went to her lover to say good-bye.

"I'm stuck with this," she told him. "There isn't any way out for me. Mike's never going to let me go. I know he's never going to let me walk away."

Craig understood. He didn't try to make Sharon stay. Maybe he hadn't wanted her to stay? Maybe he knew that by her leaving town, less people would be hurt by their messy affair?

Just before the Fuller family left for the West, a letter arrived from Colorado. It had been signed by three elders from the churches in Rocky Ford and La Junta. All three were doctors: Ted Martin, Karl Wheeler and Perry Nelson. Sharon re-read the letter in her Durham kitchen, torn apart by the moving process.

It was a missive welcoming the new minister and his family to their congregation.

"There was something about that letter—about Perry's name that was like a magnet to me. I wondered what this man was like," she said, later trying to convince a confidant the connection between the doctor and herself was predestined, preordained in some way.

Both pitched along the Arkansas River, La Junta and Rocky Ford, Colorado, are like many towns that freckle the somewhat desolate region. With a population base nearing the 10,000 mark, La Junta is by far the larger of the two burgs. Its historic claim-to-fame is its location along the Santa Fe Trail. It is also the Otero County seat. Rocky Ford shares no such distinction. It is a rancher's town set amid the gently rolling terrain that jumps up to the Front Range in a matter of a few miles. It is the home of the sweeter-than-honey Rocky Ford melon. Good schools; scant services. Though only eight miles apart, both towns had congregations of Seventh-Day Adventists. Rev. Mike Fuller would be pastor of both.

Her mouth agape, Sharon stood motionless in the doorway of what her husband had promised would be their new home. Mike poked around the house. Nothing was completed. The builder had gone belly-up. Oak kitchen cabinets were stacked in the garage like children's building blocks. The bedrooms were rib cages of stud walls. The outside of the modest home was raw stucco, neither finished in the final texture nor coated in the wash of beige coloring builders insist approximates the "look and feel" of adobe.

The Fuller family, exhausted and angry, checked into a motel. By 1 A.M. Rochelle and Denise were suffering from severe and seemingly unstoppable diarrhea. While Mike rolled over and slept, Sharon sat up with the girls and made several trips to the front office for clean bedding. It was a horrendous beginning to a new life in a new town. Sand crept into all of their belongings with an insidious grittiness. The girls survived on Kaopectate and cafe meals, their lips rimmed in chalky white from the medicine. Television talk shows passed the time in the room. There were no friends. No phone calls. No nothing. Since Sharon had left her own car in North Carolina, she was stranded in the stinky motel room while Mike went after the builder who had left them without a finished home. The first days in La Junta were not a page out of the welcome-wagon handbook.

Even the church was a disappointment. By anyone's standards, the Seventh-Day Adventist Church in La Junta wasn't much to look at. It stood in marked contrast to the beautiful old church that was Rev. Fuller's charge in North Carolina. Built in the 1930s, La Junta's church was small, holding no more than one hundred in its three rows of pews, nearly black from old layers of varnish.

Sharon bit her tongue. She didn't dare complain. After all, Mike had told her leaving North Carolina had been all her fault.

A day or so later, Mike returned after his work at the church and told Sharon to get the girls ready for a dinner at the home of one of the congregation's elders.

Dr. Perry Nelson and his wife, Julie, had invited the new arrivals for dinner.

Perry Nelson was a superstar in southeastern Colorado. He was handsome, intelligent, head church elder and, best of all, a doctor. In a place big on menial jobs and short on the professions, a doctor was the shiniest link of the profession chain. The optometrist with kind but playful hazel eyes had smoothly planed features offset by a neatly clipped salt-and-pepper beard. He was tall at almost six-foot-three and weighed a trim 180 pounds. His medium brown hair was thinning a bit on the top, and in the fashion of many who just can't let go of youth, he'd let his hair grow a little. Length, he reasoned, was a concealer of the years.

The passage of time notwithstanding, at 43, Perry Nelson seemed to have it all: a loyal wife, three nearly grown daughters, a pleasant—though certainly not ostentatious—home on the corner of Pine and South 12th Streets and successful optometry offices in Rocky Ford and Trinidad. Dr. Nelson was adored by his patients, which amounted to nearly everyone with a need for eyeglasses and contact lenses within fifty miles. He owned a motor home and an airplane. And, certainly among the believers, more importantly than anything, Perry Nelson held a prominent position with the church. So much so, it was a letter written by Dr. Nelson and two others that welcomed the Fullers out to Colorado when their world was crumbling in Durham.

Julie Nelson was quiet, sweet and, Perry chronically whined to friends, cold to him. If in fact she was unresponsive, it was *because* of her husband's philandering. It was not the impetus for it. She was the original stand-by-your-man woman, long-suffering and still vulnerable. Julie helped out in his office, worked as a bookkeeper for another doctor and raised their three daughters, Tammi, Kathy and Lorri. Julie made him a nice home and through her devotion cemented his standing in the community. She had endured her husband's four-year affair with another local woman, and by the time the Fullers came to Rocky Ford, Julie had thought that part of her life was over. She, too, had prayed for a fresh start.

And yet as she readied things for dinner and checked the living room one last time for tidiness, the doctor's wife had no idea that her world would be turned upside down. Who could have known? Also invited to share in the informal dinner were other leading couples from the Adventist church, including dentist Karl Wheeler and his wife, Blanche.

When the new minister and his wife and two daughters showed up, the fate of so many was sealed with a hermetic bond.

Rev. Mike Fuller made the introductions of his family.

"This is my wife Sharon," he said.

"Call me Sher," she corrected. "I like to be called Sher."

After that, nothing would be the same.

"Mike and Sharon seemed like a nice average couple," Julie Nelson said later. "They had two little girls, age two and five, at the time and they seemed like a happy family. I didn't know there were any problems in the marriage. I thought Sharon was friendly. I guess I liked her."

Others weren't so inclined. The Wheelers left the informal dinner party feeling a bit odd about the new woman in town. As they drove from Rocky Ford to their home in the country, Blanche Wheeler tried to put her finger on what it was about Sher Fuller that she didn't like.

"I don't know why," Blanche said, "but I just felt uncomfortable around her."

Karl Wheeler was a serious-minded man, raised on a Nebraska farm with good midwestern values. He had also picked up on something unsettling. He stared straight ahead watching the road, listening to his wife. When she was finished, he blurted an answer.

"She's out looking," he said as he drove on into the night.

Blanche was puzzled. "Looking?"

"You know what I mean. For a man."

When word got out the minister and his wife and children were stuck in a motel because their contractor had gone bankrupt, the invitations to dinner came with regularity. Some called. Some came to the church to offer a welcoming meal. The wife of a dentist found the Fullers' motel unit by tracking down the door closest to the parked convertible with North Carolina plates.

The woman invited Sharon to spend the day baking, sewing, chatting. She took care of the little girls when Sharon and Mike needed to look for a place to live. When the dentist's wife's sister came to stay, she also met Sharon. The sister was a quiet woman, not given to uttering a negative word about anyone. But she didn't like Sharon from the start.

After Mike came to take Sharon back to the motel, the two sisters gathered in the kitchen to talk.

"That woman is trouble," the visiting sister said.

"What do you mean?"

"You just wait and see."

The dentist's wife was surprised by the remark. She probed for more, but her sister didn't have a good answer. She hadn't liked the minister's wife. Not at all.

New blood was needed in Otero County, and Mike and Sharon Fuller had arrived in time for the transfusion. Perry Nelson also needed a boost. He found all of that, and more, in the minister's attractive wife. The woman had a style, a kind of look that had not yet been quashed by the denim-and-boots uniform common among most gals who lived in the outposts of Colorado. Sharon wore her hair long, her dresses tight, her blouses unbuttoned one notch lower than a woman in her position likely had a right to. Even so, she did not overdo her makeup. In fact, beyond a touch of mascara, Sharon Fuller applied nothing more than a coating of lip gloss over cherry-flavored Chapstick. She didn't have to bother.

Her message was in her motion. Sharon moved suggestively. Perry thought he could read something in her walk. Like a cat in heat, dragging herself along the ground for relief. Or maybe it was like a dancer who had been trained to use her body to communicate every nuance of desire? Sharon Fuller sauntered like a woman who held no doubt that all men watched her every move.

Maybe it was also the way she spoke; the way she licked her slickened lips as she contemplated a man from top to bottom, from his eyes to his size. The breathless timbre of her voice was also sweetened with the remnants of a Carolina accent.

That was Sharon. Sherry. *Sher.*

As the weeks passed, the Fullers moved from the Rocky Ford motel to a camping trailer near a local department store, to a little house five blocks from the Nelson residence. By then, the families had become good friends. There were veggie pizza dinners, shared baby-sitting, even camp-outs in the Nelson motor home in the midst of the splendor of the Spanish Peaks. Most of the conversation between the four adults revolved around the church, but even for Sharon that was better than nothing. She was a lonely woman in a town that she had a hard time taking a liking to. Mike had church duties and Sharon had the kids. There seemed to be nothing in between. The Nelson family was a godsend.

When Perry and Julie Nelson invited the Fullers to accompany them on a Memorial Day weekend camp-out in Santa Fe and Taos, New Mexico, it was Sharon who readily accepted. The group departed immediately after church, planning to spend that night at a campground and hiking the next morning. Everyone was buoyant. It was a good weekend to leave Rocky Ford; the temperature was expected to hover just above one-hundred degrees.

Perry parked the motor home along a lazy creek; the air was fragrant with blooming wildflowers and cacti. It was as lovely as any place on earth. The beauty was not lost on Sharon, who found her appreciation for the desert deepen. While it was not North Carolina with its vast green hillsides, she could not deny it was awash with a life of its own.

The next morning, Julie stayed in the RV while Perry, Sharon, Mike and the girls hiked up the mountain. Not long after they departed, Mike became queasy and returned to Julie in the motor home.

While the little girls scrambled ahead on the trail, the two adults talked about their lives, at first disclosing only the most minor of details. Sharon conceded she hated Colorado; hated the fact her husband had been transferred out west. Perry told Sharon of his love for Taos; his passion for flying his plane from place to place. The conversation was warm and lively. Only once did it take an uncomfortable turn. It was Sharon who brought up her past.

"What have you heard about me?" she abruptly inquired.

Perry shrugged. He insisted he had heard not a word. He looked at her quizzically.

Sharon stared into his eyes. "I just wondered if you heard I was the minister's wife who'd hop in bed with anybody."

If the eye doctor was shocked by the candor of the remark, he didn't let on. Maybe he had, in fact, heard a thing or two.

"Why, no," he said. "Haven't heard anything like that at all."

Later, while Sharon was hanging on Perry Nelson's every word back at the campsite, Julie noticed that toddler Denise was missing. She and Mike searched the immediate area and alerted Sharon and Perry.

Sharon didn't seemed concerned.

"I think she was found almost right away," Julie later remembered. "But it still struck me as strange that Sharon didn't care one bit. She couldn't be bothered with her children. Not when she had my husband to talk to, I guess."

Julie made a call to one of her girlfriends from the Adventist congregation when she returned home from the Memorial Day weekend camping trip. She described how she and the new minister had been left to their own devices in the motor home while their spouses had gone off hiking. Julie seemed a little uneasy about the weekend, but she concluded the conversation by telling her friend it was probably just her reaction to having a miserable time. There was probably nothing more to it.

Perry Nelson was the antithesis of Mike Fuller. It would take Sharon an hour to come up with a list of positive attributes about her Bible-waving husband. Negatives, however, came easily. Mike was gruff. He was impatient. He didn't give a hoot about anyone or anything but his precious position in the church. He didn't care one iota about Sharon's needs as a woman or a human being. He was as cold as a Colorado glacier. At least, he was all of that in Sharon's eyes.

Perry Nelson, however, was none of those things. As Sharon saw him, the eye doctor had an intriguing gentleness that resonated through all his actions. He radiated a kind of personal warmth that proclaimed to the world he was a healer. But he was not a mealymouthed do-gooder. He was not a bore. Perry had a playful sense of humor. He could put anyone to quick and welcome ease with a quip or off-the-cuff joke. But, more than anything, Sharon would later insist, Dr. Nelson had caring eyes. His eyes told her that she was special. She was somebody.

"He was so easy to talk to. It was like I'd known him all my life. We just fell into a real easy friendship," she later said.

Perry Edson Nelson, II, had done his Cedar Lake, Michigan, parents proud. They were simple, God-fearing folks who put all of their hope and effort into their children. The times did not make it easy. The oldest of two boys and two girls, Perry was born in 1933, at the height of the Great Depression. The senior Perry Nelson found work in a foundry, as a cook in a sanitarium and later assembled redwood furniture at a local mill. Esther Nelson could stretch a nickel from the icebox to the refrigerator, because she was frugal and because she skimped on herself and her husband. Their children were not spoiled, but they did not go without the necessities. When her kids were older, and money was tight, Mrs. Nelson also worked as caregiver and, later, at the same furniture mill as her husband.

Neither Mr. nor Mrs. Nelson was educated beyond high school, but they saw education as the opportunity for their brood to enjoy a better life. None held as great promise as Perry. He earned good grades, went to church, and when he decided to make a career in optometry, his parents were overjoyed. *A doctor!* He would be the embodiment of the American Dream. Their sacrifice and scrimping had paid off. The day in 1962 when their oldest son—married to Julie and with a growing family—graduated from the Southern School of

Optometry in Memphis, Tennessee, was the brightest moment the family had ever known.

Not long after graduation, the elder Nelsons said good-bye to their prodigal son as he and his young family went west. There was great excitement and hope for the future. At 29, Dr. Nelson was opening a optometry office in Rocky Ford, Colorado.

The Georgia Watkins Memorial Medical Arts Building was in the final months of completion when the Nelsons arrived in the town that would be their new home. Connected to Pioneer Memorial Hospital, the Watkins Building was a simple building with a low-slung roof, utilitarian and undistinguished, save for its decorative use of the multitoned stone mined at a ranch just south of Rocky Ford. A waiting room for the four main offices was shared. It was a good idea for such a small community. Rocky Ford, tiny and out in the middle of nowhere, had done itself proud. Few towns its size had their own hospital and even fewer had such accomplished doctors in private practice.

Over the years, several MDs, chiropractors, dentists and optometrists would run their practices out of the small building. None would leave a lasting mark of greater importance than Perry Nelson. All would remember him and what happened after a sexual cyclone named Sharon blew into town.

2

IF ONLY SHE HAD NEVER MARRIED MIKE FULLER. IF only she had acted upon her own impulses. Sharon drummed her fingertips on the tabletop and remembered there had been an out one time. She had considered the alternative.

The crisply engraved invitations were in the mail and Sharon, then barely twenty, wanted to cancel the November 1963 wedding. She had made a mistake. She sat at the kitchen table with her parents, Morris and Josephine Douglas, in their Maryland home. Sharon pleaded with her folks to back her up, to help her this one last time.

But Morris and Josephine were stone-faced. Crimson came to the old man's ears. Mrs. Douglas fidgeted with a handkerchief and daubed at the shiny surface of the table.

"I don't want to marry him," Sharon said softly. Tears pooled in her eyes.

Josephine shook her head and deferred to her husband.

"You'd be a damn fool to pass up this chance. He's going to be a minister. He's making something of himself."

The volume of his voice increased. Sharon felt herself sinking in her chair, getting smaller and smaller. She was Alice falling into the rabbit hole. Going down, way down.

Later, when retrospection was possible, albeit justifiably suspect, Sharon recalled her thoughts at the time.

"They were reinforcing this little girl in me that marry up, maybe if you marry somebody that's all white and clean and happy, you'll be okay. You won't have to deal with some of the things from your childhood. You won't have to deal with your feelings of 'I'm not good enough . . .' "

Three days after John Kennedy was gunned down in Dallas, Sharon donned a white wedding gown that looked like the yardage of lace used to make it had depleted the world's supply. At twenty, she was a beautiful bride. Her hair was dark and thick, her eyebrows shaped to perfection. Dimples cut into her exquisite, milky skin. If there had been a prettier bride in 1963 or any year before it, none who was at the wedding could think of her.

While her parents looked on, Sharon stared into Mike Fuller's eyes and in a soft voice holding traces of her father's southern accent, promised she'd remain his forever, until death.

And the numbing years flew by. Mike's career as a minister led them from Ohio town to Ohio town. Sharon batted her eyes for the old men in the Adventist governing body. It was all for Mike. Everyone thought she was so lucky to be married to a man with such a future.

Problem was they didn't have to live with him. They didn't have to walk in the rut he created.

It was 1968, and despite the terrible and bloody war in Southeast Asia, for many, America would never be more free in spirit than it was that hot, humid summer. It was inescapable and, in a way, inevitable. The grainy images on television and the ink-smudged front pages of newspapers begat a kind of social, a kind of *gender* consciousness that had been dormant for so very long. It was time for everyone to turn, turn, turn. And while Cleveland, Ohio, was by no means San Francisco, there was still the patchouli-scented promise that the world was changing, and women like Sharon Lynn Fuller were changing along with it. More freedom and more fun. More possibilities. The young wife listened to church-prohibited music on a transistor radio, she went to movies that were forbidden by the church . . . she took it all in. For the first time in her life, Sharon even drank and smoked. And she liked it. As wrong as it all was, Sharon Fuller liked it.

Five years into her marriage to up-and-coming minister

Mike Fuller and still childless, Sharon had once and for all seen the future as her husband and parents had indelibly outlined it. There would be no love, no excitement, no fun. Only mind-numbing work and sex whenever he wanted would mark their time on this planet. Sometimes it would sneak into Sharon's consciousness that only death would bring euphoria. Life had become a predictable bore completely centered around her husband's responsibilities with the Seventh-Day Adventist Church. When she married Mike, she had cemented her lifelong role. She was the dutiful minister's wife, a frozen fixture with a rote smile in a second-row pew. She was to flawlessly type up newsletters, sermons, meeting minutes. She was to serve punch at church functions, help out with the youth camp, teach Bible lessons, lend an ear to the troubled, the confused and the bitter.

Even their fun was tiresome. Saturday nights were reserved for *Mission: Impossible* and big bowls of popcorn made on the stove top and smothered in a cube of melted butter. Sharon, many assumed, had bought into that kind of existence. She smiled with the happy and consoled the sad as the popcorn bowl emptied. But in reality, as the commercials rolled and as conversations with guests waned in the evening, she silently weighed the options of her life.

At 23, Sharon was young and beautiful; and, in time, she began to use those assets. Men's eyes were riveted to her breasts and backside as she came and went from a room. Whether they were members of the church or good-looking passersby on the street, Sharon could feel their eyes as if they were fingers, touching, poking, stroking.

The attention felt good. Sharon was intoxicated by it and wanted more. She wanted to feel the physical embodiment of the rush that lust brought to her each time she smiled at a man who eyed her. She wanted to know how an orgasm felt when excitement and hunger for a man caused it, instead of the mechanical rubbing of her husband.

Sharon was employed as a secretary at a Cleveland printing business typing letters and answering the phone when she gave in to her impulses for the first time. In the beginning, she had not seen herself as a career woman, liberated with bras burning in the fireplace at home. She was earning extra money out in the world and trying to see exactly where she fit in.

Not long after she started at the printer, Sharon began sleeping with one of her bosses, a man of fifty who was old enough to be her father. Even worse, even more taboo, he was married and had two children. The affair went on for months. Sex and companionship were a combination that she craved. It was good and it was safe. While her husband preached, his wife put out. The weeks zipped by without anyone the wiser. But by late 1968, a complication irrevocably altered the balance. Despite a reliance on birth-control pills, Sharon became pregnant by her lover. By then she had marked her twenty-fourth birthday. She lied to Mike and told him that he was going to be a father.

Guilt, shame and hurt, Sharon would later say, nearly got the best of her.

One night after friends arrived at the Fullers' tidy duplex to watch television, a tired Sharon curled up and drifted asleep on the couch. Around 1 A.M. she woke up to overhear her husband telling their friend that he did not love her. *Never had.* The words bit like a taunted scorpion, leaving a welting sting that time would never erase. As long as Sharon would live, she knew the truth would haunt her. From both sides, the marriage had been a terrible mistake.

"I've never loved her. She's like a millstone around my neck."

No one paid much attention to the woman near the concrete steps leading down to the smelly beach that traced the edges of Lake Erie. She was in the last stage of pregnancy, her body gravid beyond belief. So much so doctors had agreed to set a date to induce labor. Even so, the woman had neither the radiant glow nor the Madonna smile most associate with the blessed state. Arched by perfectly plucked brows, her eyes were cold, flat. She made her way quickly and purposefully to the chilly, black water.

One step, then another. In no time, she was breast deep.

The woman was Sharon Fuller. She would never forget that

moment, and over the years, she would tell others of her despair.

"I was just going to do away with me and the kid. That was the only time in my life I have been that ready to just end it. I remember standing in the water, the feel of it. I remember seeing the sunset. If it [the water] had been warmer, I might have kept on walking, but it was cold. It was really cold."

Her desperation turned to anger.

"I wouldn't let Mike do this to me," she recalled many years later. "I wouldn't let Mike put me to a point where I was ready to end it."

Sharon turned around and went back up the steps, the lights of the city of Cleveland looming before her, a trail of water following her. Her clothes clung to swelling thighs and a stomach stretched so tight her belly button had all but vanished. The modified flip that was her hairdo was limp. Her shoes sloshed with each step.

Mixed with the lake water were tears.

Sharon would never forget the night she first wanted to tell Mike about her affair and how the baby she was carrying was not his, but a secret lover's. Two nights after she had considered suicide in the waters of Lake Erie, Sharon and Mike sat on the front steps of their duplex. It was the end of May, 1969. The night air was warm and scented with the heady smell of lilacs. Sharon once again stated she was not happy, that she never could be happy as a minister's wife . . . his wife. She had been living a lie.

"I want you to find me an apartment," she finally said. "I want out."

Mike refused. He insisted whatever problems they had could be resolved.

"You can't leave me. It will destroy our lives. We'll find a way to work it out."

Sharon, she would later assert, knew better.

At 12:30 A.M., June 1, 1969, Rochelle Fuller was born. A day later, Sharon and her beautiful dark-haired baby were settled at home alone—Mike was off at a Seventh-Day Adventist camp pitching tents for a revival. Stranded without a car,

Sharon called her lover to come over to hold his baby. She was playing by her own rules.

By mid-August, heat and the stress of new motherhood had stretched Sharon's emotions to the snapping point once more. The fact that Rochelle was colicky only exacerbated the tensions in the household. There was no nursery in the duplex, so the baby's bassinet was kept in Mike's study. Though there was no other place for his daughter's little bed, Mike was annoyed by the inconvenience. He complained whenever his wife set stacks of clean diapers on the corner of his oak-and-Formica desk. He had sermons to write, church business to conduct. She was not helping matters.

Sharon's blood began to boil and she started to rant.

"You don't want me. You don't want the baby! All you want is somebody that can be a minister's wife. I wanted you to get me an apartment. I wanted out!"

Her husband sat calmly. His unflagging composure inflamed the situation.

So Sharon stabbed him with words. It was all she could do.

"You don't have to worry," she yelled. "I'm going to find a way to get out of your life! Rochelle is not yours anyway!"

Mike was outraged as any man would be. Even so, he betrayed little emotion. He sat on the edge of the bed. He just wanted the facts. He told Sharon that the only way they'd be able to salvage their marriage was for her to come completely clean.

"You have an hour to tell me who this is or I'll throw you out of the house and you'll never see your baby again." His words were flat, cold. "She doesn't need a slut for a mother."

As the clock ticked away the hour of the ultimatum, Sharon finally gave up her lover's name.

"Where does he live?" Mike asked, his voice still calm.

"All you said I had to do was give you a name! You find out where he lives!"

The preacher made a beeline for the telephone book to retrieve the man's address. Inside of two minutes, he was gone on his way to do battle with the man his wife claimed was the father of his firstborn daughter.

Sharon frantically dialed the number of a mutual friend and

begged the man to stop her husband from instigating a dangerous confrontation. A fight would cause a scandal that would taint the ministry. Mike might do something foolish; something dangerous. The friend, a man from the church who knew her secret, agreed. When he arrived at Sharon's lover's address, he talked the irate pastor into leaving without incident.

For the good of everyone involved.

As if her bitterness had not been lessened by the years, Sharon seethed with defiance in her recollection of that terrible night in Ohio. She was trying to liberate herself from the oppression of a husband and a religion. Moreover, she was attempting to free herself from her own guilt. Her own lies. Mike Fuller was a perfect target.

"It was basically . . . like all right, I've had enough of you. You have given me enough digs. You have put me down long enough. This is going to be the ultimate blow, buddy. *She's not even yours.*"

3

ONE LOOK AND IT WAS SELF-EVIDENT. SHARON
Lynn Fuller was more a bouquet of long-stemmed roses than
a shrinking violet. She was one of those women who left an
unforgettable impression wherever she turned up. At the grocery, the filling station and especially at the church office, she
was a lady who could not easily be ignored. Certainly none
of the Coloradans who met her could say she wasn't friendly.
None could say she was introverted or too shy for the role of
minister's wife. Far from it. She was helpful and polite, warm
and eager to please. Nonetheless she didn't quite fit in. Most
figured her sense of style was some kind of a big-city look
from back east. And while they tried not to judge her for how
she looked, it wasn't always easy.

Sharon's dresses were often skintight. Her figure was striking and every bit of it showed. Her tops were fitted in such a
way that the shape and size of her breasts were not left to
anyone's imagination. Often the movement beneath the fabric
and the pencil poke points of her nipples revealed the absence
of a bra. In a religion that did not condone adornment,
makeup, jewelry or overt sexuality, Sharon managed to push
her wardrobe to the very edge of propriety. This particular
minister's wife broke the mold with a sledgehammer.

During the heat of the afternoon, Sharon donned short-
shorts and paraded about town like a woman who knew she
had something to show. And so she did. Ever so slightly, but
always close enough to assert the need for a doubletake, the

round globes of each cheek of her butt peeked from below the crisp hem of her shorts. Make no mistake, for La Junta, Rocky Ford and even five-times-larger Trinidad, Sharon Lynn Fuller was an eye-popper.

Dentist's wife Blanche Wheeler had her own perspective on Sharon's choice of attire. As the daughter of a Seventh-Day Adventist minister herself, Blanche knew that whatever Sharon wore was something she'd never be caught dead in. No decent woman would. Blanche winced at some of the get-ups the new minister's wife sprayed onto her shapely thighs each morning. Given the conservative nature of her faith and her own personal background, Blanche tried to set it aside. Maybe she was too harsh in her assessment? Times had changed. Sharon was younger. When Blanche grew up, pants were considered inappropriate for women.

"Unless you were out working in the field, you didn't put slacks on," she later said.

Sharon Fuller, evidently, didn't see it that way.

Jovial Bob Goodhead thought the world of Perry Nelson. They shared a common history, having been close since optometry school back in Memphis. For many, keeping a friendship viable and strong over two decades is not always possible. People change. Circumstances shift. But Bob and Perry remained close. The two even toyed with the idea of opening a joint practice in Oklahoma City where Bob, his wife Donna, and their growing family made their home. Over the years, the Nelsons and the Goodheads included stops at each other's homes whenever travel brought them within reasonable driving distance.

During one of the Goodheads' visits to Rocky Ford, Perry asked if they'd like to attend church with his family. Bob wanted to go. He wasn't interested in converting to the Seventh-Day Adventist Church, but he was curious. Donna, on the other hand, didn't want to go at all. But what could she say?

Entering the church, Donna noticed a woman in a white dress sitting with two little girls. The pretty young mother seemed to monitor Perry Nelson's every move. She even winked at him. Her behavior seemed inappropriate, even as it related to her own children. She was loudly playing with the little girls while the minister delivered his sermon from the pulpit.

Not one of my six kids would carry on like that, like she's letting them! Donna thought.

After the service, Perry ushered Bob and Donna aside. Julie Nelson was out of earshot.

"What did you think of Sharon Fuller?"

"Who's that?" Dr. Goodhead asked.

Perry pointed out the lady in white who had carried on with her two daughters during the service.

An annoyed Donna acknowledged the woman.

Perry smiled broadly. "She's the preacher's wife. Isn't she great?"

"For a preacher's wife, her kids were sure misbehaving," Donna said, ending the conversation.

It was a secretary with the slight Slavic accent of her parents who was among the first with an inkling something was going on with the eye doctor for whom she worked and the new minister's wife.

A feisty woman with a pinned-up hairdo resembling a lightly golden cinnamon bun, Barbara Ruscetti was a woman who never had it easy. She worked hard for everything she had. Tragically widowed at only thirty-four when her coal-miner husband contracted an unidentified virus that killed almost a dozen, Barb wasn't the type to scramble for a new meal ticket. She didn't set her sights on a new man, though she could have found one easily enough. She was smart, attractive and, as anyone who sat at her dinner table could vouch with unflagging enthusiasm, a great cook.

When her children were young, the mother of four got by on $305 a month—the combined income from Social Security and what passed for a veteran's pension. She supplemented the money by knitting sweaters, baby booties and afghans. She never went on welfare. She never sought a handout. When her youngest was eleven and the financial pressure of college tuition for her older children loomed, she went looking for a job.

On November 11, 1965, Mrs. Ruscetti started employment with a Trinidad optometrist she would come to adore, a man who treated her children with the warmth of a favorite uncle. That man, of course, was Perry Nelson. Over the course of their years together, the two forged a close and enduring friendship. She always called him "Doctor" unless she was angry at him; only then would she use his first name.

Tuesdays and Thursdays were Trinidad office days for Perry Nelson, with the remainder of the work week spent at the office in Rocky Ford. When he was away from Trinidad, Barb Ruscetti ran the office, booking appointments, ordering lenses and repairing eyeglass frames. In time, Nelson's business doubled, tripled and doubled again. At its peak, the Trinidad practice alone was raking in more than $150,000 annually.

Despite his success, outside of his part-ownership in a private airplane, Dr. Nelson was not one to flaunt his wealth. To look at him was to see a fellow who dressed neat and clean, ran two nice offices and went about his business without the gold-chained, diamond-dripping accouterments so many small town docs consider de rigueur. Mercedes? Forget it. BMW? Out of the question. Dr. Nelson had several old cars he was always tinkering with on his days off. In time, one of his favorites would be an old, black VW bug.

No one in Rocky Ford could deny that Perry Nelson didn't dote on his three daughters and that none of them went without. It was true that he cried "poor" whenever Julie took the girls shopping for clothes, but after a fashion show, he'd give in. Dr. Nelson also took his family on trips, often tied to optical conventions. Los Angeles, St. Louis and Las Vegas were but a few of the cities they visited.

Not long before Mike and Sharon Fuller arrived on the scene, the Nelsons purchased a Champion motor home, which made their weekend camping trips as comfortable as staying in a motel.

At various times, Perry also took the family flying in one of three airplanes he owned or co-owned over the years.

When late summer 1976 came, it brought hot days and cool nights. The crisp morning air hinted at fall. Hillsides blazed with the yellow fire of turning aspen. Huckleberry leaves morphed from green to crimson almost overnight. Trinidad had seen another summer tourist season come to a close; another season that had not met the expectations of a town desperate to turn from a mining center to tourism magnet. Maybe when ski season arrived?

There was always the hope.

Dr. Nelson gave Barb Ruscetti a day's warning that he was bringing a "new girl" to Trinidad for office training. He informed Barb it would be up to her to break in the gal for a part-time office assistant position that was opening in Rocky Ford. The new girl was Sharon Fuller.

Barb, then 54, had heard Sharon's name many, many times over the course of the summer. Too many times, she felt, to let pass without comment. Sharon this. Sharon that. A month before the doctor announced his new hire was headed for the Trinidad office, Barb asked about her.

"Who is this Sharon you keep talking about?"

Perry grinned from ear to ear. "Why, Barb, she's our preacher's wife—Sharon Fuller."

Barb's eyes bulged. She was nearly dumbstruck. "Preacher's wife? My goodness, and you're carrying on over her like this?"

Perry shrugged. His lips formed a wistful smile as he thought of Mrs. Fuller.

"Oh, she's a doll. I'd give anything to have her," he said.

Barb, of course, knew Dr. Nelson had strayed in his marriage in the past. She didn't have her head buried in the gritty bottom of a sand trap. She felt Dr. Nelson's interest in the minister's spouse was far beyond any transgression the eye doctor had made in the past. Miles beyond. He was playing with fire in the form of a woman. Sharon Fuller was the mother of two little girls, the wife of a Seventh-Day Adventist minister.

Years later, Barb Ruscetti would never forget her initial impression of Sharon when she arrived for the supposed training.

"She came in and it was all lovey-dovey. There was no breaking in, let's face it. She went into his examining room and she was supposed to take notes. Oh, they just kidded around and everything."

At 11 A.M. that first day, Perry told Barb that she could go to lunch.

"You don't have to come back at one if you don't want to," he added.

Lunchtime had always been from noon to one. Perry Nelson was a stickler for keeping the office schedule. Patients counted on it. Barb was stunned by his words.

My God, I was ten minutes late one day and he ate me up alive, she thought.

Barb canceled appointments, one right after another, planted herself at her desk and fumed. Some help Sharon Fuller was going to be for the business! There was no breaking in this lady. There was no way to teach her a damn thing. The preacher's wife had her own agenda and Dr. Nelson didn't seem to mind one bit. He had his own ideas, too.

That following Sunday, a motel manager stopped Barbara Ruscetti as she was coming out of church.

"I met the doctor's wife," the man said, explaining that Perry and Julie had checked into a room at his motel.

It surprised her. It was not like Julie to do anything like that.

"You did? Julie?" Barb asked as they strolled outside into the brightness of the day.

The man smiled. "Yeah, isn't she cute?"

Something about the motel manager's compliment made Barb feel funny. While Julie Nelson was sweet and kind and not at all unattractive, no one would call her "cute." Cute was not a word that went with Julie. Loyal. Motherly. Caring, yes. But not *cute.*

"What does she look like?" Barb eventually asked, knowing full well her question would spark suspicion. She didn't care.

"She has auburn hair and really nice-looking blue eyes," he said.

That description confirmed for Barbara that the woman at the motel had not been Julie. Julie had dark brown hair. The woman the motel manager was describing was the preacher's wife Sharon Fuller.

What kind of woman is she? She's coming down to Trinidad and she's got two little kids and she's married to a preacher. Here she is shacking up at a motel, Barb thought.

Perry Nelson was a wonderful man, in many, many ways.

But he was not a saint and he'd be the first one to tell someone that fact. Over the course of their years together, Barbara Ruscetti had seen the doctor put his own spin on the concept of a doctor's bedside manner. He had a roving eye for attractive, available women. Barb couldn't count the number of times she had seen "no charge" written on the exam cards of beautiful women, who lingered in the doctor's office and stopped by to say hi. There were other, more concrete, signs, too. When the doctor brought his motor home from Rocky Ford under the pretext of staying the night in Trinidad to catch up on paperwork, Barb had a notion something was going on. She would never forget the time she and her son went to watch a movie and ran into the doctor and a girlfriend.

"Um . . . uh . . . uh . . . Just met here . . . so we happened to sit together. . . ."

The next morning, Barb arrived at the office in time to catch the doctor and the same lady friend climbing out of the motor home.

But Barb could forgive all of that. Though she knew it was wrong, she didn't tell Julie Nelson about her husband's dalliances. She didn't think it was her place to do so. She also didn't think Perry Nelson meant anything by it. Barb never doubted the man loved his wife and three daughters. She never doubted that when the day was done, he'd always return to his family. Barb didn't want to make waves.

Perry Nelson was a man who earned such loyalty effortlessly. He was revered by many in the community. He was trusted. Little old ladies lined up for eye exams with the charming doctor who good-naturedly gibed them. When Barb's daughter wanted a typewriter—an *electric* typewriter, no less—it was Perry who came through with one for a Christmas present.

He handed out more donations to the needy than the local Salvation Army. Until Barb started screening them out, drunks from the Lone Star down the street staggered over for a quick ten bucks and a short lecture on the evils of drinking. Perry Nelson had a heart of gold. He would do anything for anyone. While it was true some of the more desperate took advantage of that generosity, Perry didn't seem to care. He didn't judge. All people were good. Most were trying the best that they knew how.

But the woman from Rocky Ford was a different animal. From the day of their first meeting at the office, Barb Ruscetti could feel it in her bones.

"She's a bitch on wheels," Dr. Nelson's secretary told a friend over coffee one day, after meeting Sharon in the flesh. "She's not nice. You know what I mean? *Not nice.*"

Some old-timers winced at the reality that Trinidad's most famous citizen was Dr. Stanley Biber, a man who'd performed more sex-change operations than anyone on earth. Those who lived there before television and the tabloids discovered Dr. Biber's eccentric, but thriving, practice, wanted the town to be known for Bat Masterson, Tom Mix and its Old West flavor.

It seemed everyone knew one of the transsexuals who had decided that the place where they lost their penis was the place they'd call home.

Dr. Biber's downtown office was on the floor above Dr. Nelson's practice in the First National Bank building. Barb Ruscetti would often ride the elevator with prospective patients, leaving her to wonder exactly what they had left under their skirts.

But she didn't care. She had worries far greater than Annie the Tranny or any of the others.

At least they were honest about who they were.

It wasn't easy, but Barb Ruscetti tried to like Sharon. Barb tried to take Sharon under her wing and show a kindness that she hoped would rub off onto the younger woman. She tried to go along with what she knew was a bad situation. Since everyone but a fool and a hermit had a citizens band radio in the remote canyons around Trinidad, when it came time to give Sharon a handle, Barb ("Spec Lady") dubbed Sharon "Doctor's Doll." Dr. Nelson was "Spec Man."

Sharon always talked of money and how she didn't have any on a preacher's salary. She talked of what she would buy if she was rich. Once Barb offered Sharon a dress that had been hanging in the back of her closet far too long. It certainly wasn't the flashy younger woman's style, but Barb asked if she thought her mother might like it.

"She'd be thrilled to death," Sharon said, smoothing out

the fabric of the garment as Barb presented it to her. "All my mother wears is cotton dresses."

Barb asked her why that was so.

Sharon turned away. She was embarrassed about something.

"Because I come from a very poor family," she said finally, as though being poor meant she should have been ashamed.

Barb was left to wonder if Sharon's moneygrubbing ways had more to do with her childhood than being married to a stingy-fisted preacher.

Julie Nelson was not completely blind. She knew her husband was slipping away once more. The good Lord knew she had been through it so many times that it had almost become a way of life. She had left her husband only once when she could not take it anymore. But after three months of Perry's pleading and the reality of a broken home for her daughters, Julie returned to Rocky Ford. Julie was tired of putting on the happy public face when everyone in town knew her husband was a womanizer. Whenever he found a new woman to romance, Perry would fling compliments around the room. It was as if by building some other woman up, he'd be able to hurt Julie even more.

Perry went on and on about the minister's wife. What a great worker she was.

Right, great worker when she's on her back.

How sweet she was.

Sweet as honey pie dipped in sugar and rolled in razor blades.

How everyone adored her at the office. In fact, Perry said, Sharon and Barb were like mother and daughter.

The woman's a bitch on wheels.

Both parties in the Nelson marriage knew it was hard to change. Tearful promises were made over the phone, in the darkness of a bedroom. Forgiveness was sought. When a man promises his wife he will never stray again, the woman wants more than anything to believe it so. Julie Nelson had bought into her husband's promises more than once. She had tried to keep their marriage intact for the sake of their daughters. And later, she would wonder why she stayed so long, when there

47

had been no chance Perry could really get it right.

But stay she did. For a time, it seemed a miracle had occurred. It seemed like God's hand had touched her wayward husband and brought him to his senses.

Before Sharon arrived in town, other friends saw it, too.

"Perry *had* really changed. He had come around to what's important. He changed. He was a person who did a lot of exercising. He would get up very early in the morning, exercise, read his Bible. He was a Sabbath school teacher and a very earnest Christian," a friend recalled.

Many had hoped Dr. Nelson was one of the rare individuals who knew second chances were gold, both precious and rare.

Sharon Fuller arranged for a baby-sitter after Perry called to see if she wanted to ride down to Trinidad in the motor home. He planned on filling up the rig's holding tanks—the water supply in Rocky Ford wasn't fit to nourish houseplants, let alone drink. After the water was loaded, they'd stop off at the office for "some training" before returning to Rocky Ford.

Much to Barb Ruscetti's chagrin, the doctor and new helper spent the afternoon charting patients and brushing against each other like high schoolers in lust.

Sharon later said what happened next was inevitable.

"I just knew it was going to happen. There wasn't any other way," she told a friend. "By the time we left the office in Trinidad that afternoon," Sharon continued, "there was no mistaking in either his mind or my mind what was going to happen in the motor home."

The signals that had started from the moment they met and lingered over the weeks of the summer had been loud and clear.

The two left Barb to close down the office while they set course for Rocky Ford. Halfway home, Perry guided the motor home off the highway. He parked in a secluded area at the edge of a travelers rest stop. Three trees framed the patch of grass around a picnic table. The sun was low in the sky. In a few minutes, they undressed and made love.

"It was everything I thought it would be. It wasn't hurried. It wasn't rushed. It wasn't forced. It was the most natural thing," Sharon said afterward.

4

TODAY THEY CALL IT THE "GREAT DISAPPOINT-ment." Seventh-Day Adventists trace their church history to William Miller, a New Hampton, New Yorker, who predicted the end of the world and the second coming of Jesus Christ would take place October 22, 1844. His prophecy, first voiced thirteen years before the end was to come, begat the attention of a growing group of followers. Nineteen years later, the sect splintered into what became the foundation for the modern-day Seventh-Day Adventist Church.

Since then, followers have held to the unshakable belief the Bible is the literal translation of the word of God. The human body is the temple of the Holy Spirit. Believers do not smoke, drink alcohol, eat meat or wear jewelry. Church followers share a lifestyle beyond mere beliefs. And they pay for it. Ten percent of a family's income is gifted to the church in the form of a tithe.

Adventists still believe the second coming is imminent. Death is only a sleeping state until He comes. And, of course, they follow a seventh-day Sabbath. Worship services are held in pleasant—though somewhat austere—churches on Saturdays. Being an Adventist is more than following a religion. It is a culture, a way of life.

On July 3, 1945, Sharon Lynn Douglas was born into such an existence.

When the memories of her childhood came so many years later, she pressed her slender fingers, nails lacquered like red

Chinese boxes, to her lips. It was as if by doing so she could stifle the very recollection of what resonated through her mind. The instant it came flooding back, she knew such retrospection had been throttled for decades for good reason. To avoid thinking about what had happened to her was to save herself from being a slave to the past. Sharon Lynn buried her face into her hands, soft curls of bleached blond hair falling past her wrists. She wanted no part of the past, and in fact had spent the last third of her adult life trying to escape it. She was MGM's Dorothy in Oz and her first twenty-five years had been nothing but grainy images in black and white. Color only came when there was freedom.

Her tear ducts rained when she deliberated on growing up inside the impervious shell of fraudulent perfection.

"I had to be the compliant little person, but I got tired of it. So I'd have my little sneaky ways to find someone who would make me feel I was pretty, and I was important. I think I could have been a real good minister's wife/call girl."

When her awakening came as a young woman, it was the result of a desire to cast off the restrictions of the past, to possess everything she saw. Sharon had missed so much. She had been deprived. She would no longer wait.

The red lipstick, the blue of a lover's eyes, the excitement of *feeling* . . . was everything her heart desired.

Sharon Lynn was the middle daughter born to Morris and Josephine Douglas, a hardworking carpenter, and his wife, a homemaker and part-time church bus driver. Though the family was Seventh-Day Adventist, they might as well have been old order Amish, so restrictive was their particular interpretation of their religion. No dancing. No movies. No bowling. Family legend has it that when Elvis Presley swiveled his hips on the *Ed Sullivan Show*, Mr. Douglas went haywire and put an end of television viewing in the tidy household in rural Reisterstown, Maryland.

Morris Douglas was a sandy-haired man with the outward appearance and speaking cadence of a country boy all grown up. He was the type of man who'd stuff his hands deep into the folds of his dungaree pockets, clear the phlegm from his throat and speak his piece. Though it might take him an hour to make his point, when he did, there was no doubt about his meaning. His main message was always: My daughters will be good girls.

Before the Elvis debacle, Josephine Douglas would stand in front of the television set and spread her skirts to conceal the television whenever a cigarette commercial came on the air. Before they had their short-lived TV, the lady of the house would take a tube from the radio when she left to go shopping or run errands in town. She was firm in her resolve: No one would be corrupted by the wrong music when she was not around to turn the radio off.

In her middle daughter's eyes, there was no woman more lovely than Josephine Douglas. Her almost-black hair and dark brown eyes shimmered from across the room. But if she was lovely to look at, Sharon considered her mother somewhat cold and undeniably aloof. If only there had been a pretty smile to go with the rest of her lovely face. When she was younger, Sharon thought her mother was quiet because she had put herself above others, was stuck-up. Later, she realized it was because Josephine was a woman who simply didn't want to draw attention to herself. She didn't want to stand out from the other women of the church. Josephine never in her life wore makeup or jewelry.

Josephine was as serious as she was beautiful. Sharon would grow into adulthood without a single memory of her mother laughing. She never let her hair down. If the woman never had a good time, as Sharon would frequently insist, it was because her singular focus was on her religion.

God's hand was felt on everything the Douglas family did.

When Josephine was upset she would go to the bedroom, shut the door, cry and pray. She would grapple with the pages of a Bible so used that pages literally fluttered to the floor.

Sharon always knew why her mother kept the old one.

Don't get a new Bible! It'd be like saying the old one wasn't any good.

Judy Douglas, on the other hand, never thought their mother was gorgeous. The oldest of the three girls never allowed herself to think those kind of thoughts—not when she viewed her parents as her persecutors. As her enemy.

"My mother beautiful? I don't know," Judy mused later. "I guess there is a picture of her taken when Mom and Dad were first married. She was eighteen. The photographer had her sitting on a post in a fishing wharf scene, her hands were hooked around her knees and she was leaning back. I guess she was beautiful in that picture. But Mom to me was always the woman sitting in the front church pew, all serious, unsmiling. That was my mother."

If Josephine was an unhappy woman, it was no more evident than the time when she marched herself from the house in Reisterstown to the nearby railroad tracks and planted herself in the middle. It was only as an adult that Sharon learned of the incident that took place during the time her mother was pregnant with Joy, the youngest of the three sisters.

"She was just waiting for the train coming along," Sharon recalled of the story. "She didn't want to be there anymore. I've never talked to my mom about it."

And despite her own despair, appearances remained everything in the household over which Josephine Douglas presided. It was supposed to be a close family with no worries, no sadness. Oddly, though Sharon idolized her older sister, she was forbidden to play with her.

"Mom didn't want any fights. She didn't want noise," Judy recalled. "Mom kept us apart. The fact Sharon has no feelings or emotions or can't show them might be based in part on the fact that she was so isolated by our mother."

Bitterness flowed with their mother's milk; it seeped into the air they breathed. In the Douglas household, emotions were expertly hidden. It wasn't that emotions weren't *felt*. They were not talked about; they weren't expressed. The girls were taught that they loved everybody—not that they *should* love everybody. Hate was a four-letter word as ugly as the unseemly ones spoken by those outside their faith. Like most people, members of the Douglas family had a public face, yet for the most part they wore the same mask at home. They were emotional chameleons.

Judy and Sharon became just like their parents. They became adept at keeping secrets.

What others *thought* of a person was far more important

than the truth of someone's actions or character. Lies became part and parcel of creating the most perfect of facades.

"Sharon was taught to be who she is," sister Judy said after her younger sister's world crashed around her, "and she learned her lesson very well. Sharon's deviousness was probably a way to protect herself."

Everything, all the time, was in the name of God. No accomplishments were the result of the person's actions or choices, but a reflection of what the Lord had done. At seven years old, when Judy took the bus from the Maryland countryside to the Seventh-Day Adventist academy in Baltimore, she was proud that she hadn't cried and that she had made her first such trip all by herself.

At the dinner table, her father praised Judy for being so grown-up while her mother looked on and said nothing. It was little Sharon, still in a high chair, who spoke up.

"Oh, Judy didn't go to school by herself," she said. "Jesus went with her."

Everything Sharon and her sisters did that was perceived by their parents as good, God had His hand in it. Everything the girls did that was bad was something they had chosen to do.

They were two little girls in white nightgowns. Judy was almost six and her sister Sharon three when her stomach started to give her pains. Acrid vomit surged from her mouth, diarrhea stained her bedclothes. Judy was in a panic to get herself cleaned up before their mother found out. She didn't like any stink, any disarray. Little Sharon scurried about the room helping her flu-stricken sister clean up.

Judy would always hang on to the image of her little sister working like a crazed beaver cleaning up the wretched results of her sick stomach and bowels. She'd never forget how the little girl told her it would be all right. Their mother would never know and Judy would be safe. She wouldn't get in trouble.

Mrs. Douglas didn't like any messes.

"Lysol commercials remind me of my mother," Judy later said. "We talked on the phone and she put Lysol on it."

And so it went. Year after year. Hour after hour.

God had a place at the immaculate dinner table set by Josephine Douglas. God had a place in the bathroom. The bedroom. There was nothing Josephine did that didn't include her devotion to God. She took care of her children with the idea that it was her sole job in raising them in a manner that prepared them to live in His Kingdom. It was her job to see they grew up with good values, respect for others and love for the Lord. But, even more importantly, to raise them without humiliating and embarrassing incident.

That would have been fine, except for Judy. Morris and Josephine's oldest presented a rebellious streak that reverberated with earth-shattering regularity throughout her adolescent years. She was kicked out of school when she smoked when no others dared. She was chastised when she was caught talking with boys outside of the church.

Judy was a rebel in knee-highs.

Sharon would never forget coming home from school to see a row of police cars lined up outside their rural Maryland home. Her mother told her to be quiet when she wanted to know what was going on.

No one talks about this! No one in this house!

A day later, the police brought Judy Douglas back home. She reportedly had met a boy at a picnic and gone off with him, though that night she had spent with a girlfriend. Judy was not a bad girl, just one in search of her own place. She was sullen and beaten. Instead of talking with her, instead of clueing Sharon in to what had happened, they sent Judy packing for Montrose School for Girls. The gates of the reform school were but a half mile from the Douglas home. No one told Sharon.

"We never had family discussions," Sharon lamented three decades later. "They never talked about why they put her in there. I thought she was pregnant . . . I know later on she had a lot of trouble getting pregnant. Maybe it was a maternity home? I don't know. I still don't know."

As she would wrestle with her own mixed-up life, Sharon Lynn would wonder where it had all gone wrong. In doing so, she often revisited her older sister's troubles.

"Those experiences combined with other things that happened in my childhood . . . I couldn't have told you then, but I felt like white trash. That I lived on the wrong side of the tracks . . . that was the beginning of a stigma for me.''

Like many of their day, Josephine and Morris Douglas believed in the value of corporal punishment. A good spanking or whipping, coupled with some old-time religion, could straighten out even the most ill-behaved, defiant of children. Whenever the oldest Douglas girls misbehaved, they were told to go outside and cut a switch off a bush.

"That one won't do," Josephine sometimes told curly-haired Sharon, as she stood over her, inspecting her selection. "This one doesn't make the right sound," she said as she tore the switch through the air. "Get another."

Punishment in the household was neither swift nor merciful. Though Sharon never felt the full wrath of her father's hand, Judy did many times. But it was more than the beatings, more than the hairbrush, the switches, even the metal grid of an ice-cube tray that had been used as a weapon of punishment against her small body.

Worse than that, strangely enough, was the incessant praying.

"We were sent to our rooms where Mother would pray us to death," Judy recalled many years later. "We'd sit for an hour and a half and were told to think how evil we were and how we had displeased God and shamed the family . . . then Mother would come in and talk about it for an hour. Then we'd pray."

One little incident—speaking out of turn, for instance—could command as much as three hours of penance and punishment.

Years later, Sharon would tell a friend that she vowed she'd "never bring God and a belt into the room at the same time."

Judy's punishment was the most severe. She would later say she had vague memories of being whipped with the buckle end of a belt. Welts and broken skin were common marks on her body. She was desperate to leave, but had nowhere to go.

One time a tearful Judy reportedly went to the police in Reisterstown for help after a particularly severe beating. She begged an officer to take her away from her father and mother, but all the cop did was send her home. By the time she was returned to her parents, the blood on her back had dried. The fabric of her blouse had to be moistened so she could peel it away from her skin. Judy Douglas vowed she'd save every penny she could get her hands on and she'd get the hell out of there.

She was sixteen when she left home.

"If I had stayed, maybe I would have got the education I deserved. Maybe I would not have married an abusive man. But leaving was my sanity. It was the right thing to do. It was not rebellion. It was survival. Sharon and I learned different ways to survive."

Even though she would never say the two of them had forged a close father-daughter relationship, Sharon was her daddy's shadow. She followed him around whenever she could. Mostly she tagged along on errands and when he worked around the house. Morris Douglas was a capable carpenter who put a great deal of emphasis on getting the job done right. He didn't have a whole lot of interests outside of his work and, of course, the church. And while he was not as humorless as Josephine, Morris was not exactly a barrel of fun. Sharon was close to her father, she would later insist, only by default. Her mother was simply too distant.

Among the lessons of good living, Morris Douglas showed his middle daughter that the rules could be bent just a little. Whenever they'd go into town to the hardware or feed store, he'd buy little Sharon a Coke, which contained caffeine, something forbidden by the church.

"Better throw the bottle out before we get home, so your mother doesn't find out," he told her after many such trips.

And if Morris did bend the rules, it was never to the complete breaking point.

One time, when they were school-age, Judy and Sharon found a stack of girlie magazines stashed in their father's toolbox up in the attic. The discovery knocked the wind out of them. Not *their* daddy. Someone else's father—the whiskey-breathed men outside of their faith looked at that sort of material. Not him. How could it be? It seemed as though their father lived in two worlds: the church and the real world.

And though it was as wrong as wrong could be, the girls could not stay away from the magazines.

"We'd sneak up there and look at them. Our daddy didn't do things like that."

When Sharon was in grade-school, she learned for the first time that despite what they preached, many other adults broke the rules to devastating and far-reaching consequence. She was a beautiful little girl then, with gorgeous eyes and thick, curly hair. She was also a target.

Two incidents took place before she was ten.

Sharon had no reason to feel anything but safe sitting in the backseat of the car while a group of Seventh-Day Adventists went out to raise money for the support of the church. As they went from house to house, eight-year-old Sharon sat sandwiched between two men. One of the men put his hand on her lap.

"I'm tired," the church member said. "And my hands are very cold."

Sharon felt his fingers slide up under her skirt and pull at her panties. She pulled her legs tighter together. She yanked at his arm, but said nothing. She didn't want the other man to know what was going on.

A couple of years later, it happened again. This time, the abuser was an elderly employee at the academy. Sharon had heard stories from other girls that the man's hands wandered, but she thought she was safe. She was good friends with the family. She was wrong. One afternoon when she went to get some cleaning supplies from the storage closet, the old man pushed her inside and grabbed her crotch and fondled her.

Years later when Sharon recalled how she told her mother about the fondling by the janitor, she said the old woman insisted she had never heard of the incident. One thing Josephine was certain about, however, was if her middle daughter had been a little older at the time of the alleged abuse, she'd have been less compliant.

"You'd have given him what for, because you were so much like your daddy," Josephine said.

Sharon shook her head and disagreed.

"It wouldn't have mattered what age I was. I don't think I'd have said anything."

5

NEITHER OF THE THORNTON POLICE DETECTIVES
said they were tired or that they wanted to go to the motel
back in Trinidad. But it was getting late. It was also obvious
that while Sharon Nelson Harrelson professed no knowledge
of who might have harmed her third husband, Glen, it was
clear she was not being entirely forthcoming. She talked
around certain subjects, refusing to address much with any real
deal of directness. The emotions stirred by what had happened
had clouded her thinking, she said. Although she made sobbing noises into a crinkley tissue, an action that seemed more
fake than a half-price antique, and dabbed at her eyes, no tears
were evident.

"Where were you when your husband was killed?" Thornton detective Glen Trainor asked with steady, unblinking blue
eyes.

"I was here at home," Sharon hastily replied.

Her speed to answer and her response was startling. Both
Glen Trainor and partner Elaine Tygart knew that by all rights
the woman with the crumbled Kleenex had no way of knowing
when the murder had occurred. How was it that she was so
certain she had been at home? Even the investigators still
didn't know exactly when the fireman died.

Trainor's heart jumped in his chest. He exchanged a quick
glance with his partner. *This was clearly more than a death
notification. This was bigger.*

"Out of everybody that you know," the young detective

asked, "who would be more likely to kill your husband?"

Sharon shook her head. "I can't think of anyone."

Again, her words triggered suspicion. The investigators knew from on-the-job experience an innocent person often can conjure a short list of enemies when it comes to the murder of a loved one. It can be an ex-spouse, a neighbor whose dog barked, a person involved in a failed business venture. There is always someone.

It was nearly midnight; an hour and a half had passed and it was time to leave. A basic foundation of the woman's background had been laid. She had offered an alibi of watching videos the night before at the home of a neighbor. Best of all, she agreed to come into the police station in Trinidad the next morning to make a final statement that would tie up the loose ends.

"I have funeral arrangements to make," she said, "but I guess I can make it down there."

She explained that she'd have to make provisions for the care of her two small children, but provided that could be reasonably worked out, she'd be back for more first thing in the morning.

"Thank you for coming," she said, as if they had been to a dinner party and not an inquisition.

Elaine Tygart left with the feeling Sharon hadn't had a direct hand in the death of her firefighter husband, but she knew more about what had happened at Columbine Court than she let on.

Glen Trainor put it simply: "She killed him or she had him killed."

They got back in the car and headed down the mountain toward Trinidad and their motel.

"You guys didn't let her breathe in there," said the Las Animas County sheriff's sergeant who had accompanied them. "You were firing those questions at her one after another."

The young man who had led them to the house piped up.

"That woman's guilty as sin," he said.

No one disagreed. No one said anything about how people handle grief in different ways. No one said she was innocent of anything.

"We just have to prove it," Trainor said.

The Thornton detectives were on an unmercifully tight budget which left them little in the way of expense money. Meals were not going to be shared at the best places in town, if indeed outpost Trinidad had such an establishment. And insofar as hotel accommodations were concerned, that first night the two shared a double room. The fact they were good friends made the discomfort of the situation easier to bear. That they were on the case of their lives didn't hurt, either. As they organized things for the following morning, they lamented over the fact they had not been able to bring Sharon the news of her husband's death. It seemed Glen Harrelson's mother in Iowa had already been notified and she passed along the shocking news to her son's wife.

Catching her off guard had been their great hope. Unfortunately, Sharon had ample time to frame a story, shore up an alibi and play the tragic widow.

Times two.

Elaine Tygart did not mince words.

"She's as guilty as shit," she said as the two cops discussed their interview strategy for the next morning. "She knows more." They began to write down everything the widow had said in the kitchen that night. They began to sequence each part of her statement. Further scrutiny would come in the morning when they had her face-to-face once more.

And, almost immediately upon their return, their motel room phone rang. It was the Las Animas County sheriff calling, with a name worth checking into.

"Gary Starr Adams," he said.

As he listened, Trainor searched his memory. He said the name out loud, communicating the possible lead to Elaine Tygart. She also drew a blank. It was not a name Sharon had mentioned in her interview. Yet according to what the sheriff was saying, the man was a key individual in the new widow's life.

"Right after her doctor husband disappeared, Adams was living with Mrs. Nelson and driving a brand-new pickup."

The more the investigator and the sheriff talked, the darker the picture of this woman—a former preacher's wife, of all things—grew. It seemed that suspicions around her second husband's disappearance and death had run like a brushfire over a mesa. Everyone voiced an opinion. And all the opinions were the same: Sharon and Gary had conspired to kill Perry Nelson.

"Nobody came forward with information that could prove Dr. Nelson was murdered by Sharon and Gary," the sheriff explained. "But lots of people thought so."

6

AS THE SUMMER OF 1976 WENT ON, SO DID THE GOS-sip and innuendo. The affair Perry Nelson and Sharon Fuller had vehemently denied was the worst-kept secret in south-eastern Colorado. Julie Nelson tried to keep her husband on a shorter leash and Mike Fuller did what he could to see that his wife stayed closer to his side. It was clear, however, that none of that would work. There was no stopping those two.

Sharon, in particular, invited gossip wherever she went.

When she helped out at a Seventh-Day Adventist Bible school, rumors once more wound their way through the canyons.

An upset Sharon was nearly in tears when she told her husband and others how a bunch of hormone-charged teenage boys had attempted to proposition her for sex at the school.

Years later, Blanche Wheeler shook her head at the memory.

"Some women with the school felt it was probably the other way around," she said.

Back at the medical building in Rocky Ford, front-desk assistant Iona Hamilton did her best to avoid Sharon whenever the hot-to-trot preacher's wife was "helping out" in Rocky Ford instead of at Dr. Nelson's Trinidad practice. Though Iona wasn't even a member of the conservative Adventist church, she knew damn well the difference between right and wrong.

Some of the other, the younger, women in the office seemed oblivious to Sharon's actions, and when Iona was unable to bite her tongue, they chided her for being "mean" to misunderstood Sher.

"You just don't like her, because you know Julie," a young clerk said one afternoon.

"No," Iona shot back, no longer able to hold herself in complete check. "I feel there's an evil streak in the woman."

The clerk pooh-poohed Iona's remark, but the strong-minded front-desk assistant stood her ground.

"Someday, you'll see," she said. "She's not the person she pretends to be. She wants everyone to like her, too much. I think there's an ulterior motive here."

And so it went on. Lovers as wrapped up as Perry and Sharon were thought they could keep their rendezvous hush-hush. Some secret. Just about everybody in town knew the two of them were carrying on. The looks. The unnecessary running into each other. They even had a hiding place at the Watkins Medical Arts building in which they squirreled away notes to one another.

Perry showed Barb Ruscetti several of the lovesick missives Sharon had left for him.

"Look what my doll left for me today," he said.

Barb regarded the love note. It was akin to the kind of little message a teenager would write to another to pass the lagging minutes in geometry class. *What was this man thinking?*

"Oh, Doctor," Barb pleaded, "you ought to let this go. It's ruining your life."

Perry folded up the paper and slipped it back into the pocket of his trousers. Barb just didn't understand. He would never give up the preacher's wife.

"I don't want to live without her. I'm going to marry her, Barb."

Barb didn't know what to say. *Doctor's spellbound, bewitched by a big-boobed siren,* she thought. *God help him. God help Julie.*

Mike Fuller was not his sister-in-law Judy's favorite person. He was controlling, selfish and demanding. There was a distance that she could not overcome, even if she had wanted to become closer. He was the preacher, and that alone, given the

Douglas sisters' growing-up years, was a black mark against him. In all fairness, Judy Douglas would later concede much of what she knew of Mike Fuller's character and temperament was from her sister's less-than-glowing accounts of their marriage. Even so, Judy felt guilty, and later a little used when Sharon would drive up to her house in Colorado Springs to rendezvous with Dr. Nelson.

"I knew Sharon played around in her marriage to Mike. Everyone probably knew. I knew that she told Mike that she was coming up to see one of my children who had been very ill with spinal meningitis. It was usually on a Saturday after church. I didn't know the details of Sharon's relationship with Perry. She'd come over, say hello and they'd go off to a motel."

It was no wonder the home owned by Karl and Blanche Wheeler was a beehive of activity in September 1976. Blanche double-checked and triple-checked the foot-long list she kept detailing all that needed to be done for their daughter's September 5th wedding. As if there wasn't enough to do. Blanche pushed up her eyeglasses and let out a sigh, tempered with a smile. Running a dental business and taking care of the responsibilities associated with the forty-acre ranch southeast of Rocky Ford was never easy.

Calves in the summertime, melons and corn to harvest and a wedding, too.

The preparations for the nuptials, Blanche never once had to remind herself, were a labor of love. The other stuff life brought was just work.

When Sharon Fuller called to inquire if she could come to the Wheeler place to practice a song she was going to sing at the next Sabbath, Blanche told the younger woman to come over despite a house full of relatives and her list of things to do. That same day, Julie Nelson expected her husband to bring his RV over so the Wheelers could use it to put up some of their out-of-town relatives for the weekend. Julie telephoned that morning to let the Wheelers know Perry had left and was bringing along a crate of peaches.

Later that the afternoon, Sharon arrived wearing her trademark short-shorts and planted herself in front of the piano. She said she was so grateful Blanche had let her intrude during such a frenzied time. Sharon felt a little more practice and the song, "A Hill Called Mount Calvary," would be perfect.

Less than a half-hour after Sharon's arrival, Perry Nelson pulled up in the motor home. The minute he arrived, Sharon jumped up and announced it was time to take a break. She went outside to greet with Perry.

Blanche felt used. Her blood began a slow boil. The timing of their respective arrivals was too suspect to be passed off as mere coincidence. Perry had left four hours before on a drive that even in the worst snowstorm wouldn't have taken half that long. It wasn't right. The Adventist dentist's wife had put up with Sharon Fuller and her inappropriate behavior and over-the-top attire from the beginning. Blanche did so because Sharon was the minister's wife and, regardless what she did and how she acted, she could be very likable. She could pour on the charm and make even the sourest face light up in a smile. But not this time.

Blanche could no longer look the other way. One morning at the Watkins Medical Arts building where her husband Karl operated his successful dental practice—and where she worked as his assistant—Blanche gathered up her courage.

She first broached the subject with front-desk assistant Iona Hamilton. Iona, an outspoken woman who knew when enough was enough, was in complete agreement. The fooling around had gone too far. Both women knew they were in extremely difficult positions. Julie Nelson worked as Dr. Ted Martin's bookkeeper, and if she had suspected anything, she had not let on. Neither Iona nor Blanche wanted to break Julie's heart.

As they talked in a secluded section of the pine-paneled office, Iona recalled turning a corner in time to see Dr. Nelson and Sharon break what she suspected could have been an embrace.

"It was obvious that they had gotten away from each other pretty fast," she said.

There had been other signs. Iona had seen the doctor and his assistant holding hands, and brushing ever so slightly against each other. Blanche also noticed times when Dr. Nelson's hand lingered on Sharon's shoulder. The relationship between the two—even in the office—was anything but businesslike.

What signaled to Iona Hamilton more than anything that something inappropriate was going on was the fact that many times when she left the front desk to retrieve a patient's record for billing, or to let Dr. Nelson know a patient had arrived, the door would be shut. That was new. In all her years at the medical office, she could not think of a time when Dr. Nelson closed his door, unless he was with a patient. Whenever the door had been shut that summer, Iona would knock and find Perry and Sharon together.

In addition, it also troubled Iona how wherever Perry went into the office Sharon was right there with him. That wasn't normal. No other office worker had ever done that. There was no need for it.

"She always makes it a point to be right next to him. Have you ever noticed that?" Iona said to Blanche.

Blanche had indeed. Even patients with the worst possible eyesight would have seen the same thing.

Sharon Fuller, they figured, was on a manhunt.

Blanche went to her husband with her concerns. Karl Wheeler had thought the same thing. Independently, both had agonized over their suspicions for several weeks. They worried what kind of influence the affair would have on their church and community. How to handle it? What to say?

Finally, Blanche and Karl summoned the nerve to get in touch with Mike Fuller. It was odd, because, in the event the affair had involved someone other than his wife, Blanche likely would have called on the minister for guidance. The minister was the first person a good parishioner should seek out for help. The idea that it was the leader of their church who was being betrayed made the call excruciatingly difficult.

No one blamed Pastor Fuller. No one thought he had been at fault. Yet when the minister arrived that evening at the Wheeler's country home he seemed agitated and defensive. As he listened to the couple's concerns, he did his best to dismiss each bit of evidence. They were mistaken, he said. He batted their words right back at them. Somehow they had misconstrued innocent actions. His wife was a very friendly woman. Dr. Nelson, likewise, was a man who could talk a listener's ear off. The combination of two outgoing people made it only look as though something was going on.

"Nothing is happening, I assure you," he said.

By the end of the hour, the Wheelers were embarrassed they had even brought it up. They knew what they had seen and heard, but there was no convincing their minister that his wife had betrayed him with another man.

Karl Wheeler later remembered how Mike Fuller took the news.

"He was upset that we'd even think of such a thing. He got rather huffy with us."

That night, Blanche and Karl reexamined Pastor Fuller's response. How could they have handled it better? They had not told the man their suspicions in order to hurt him, but rather to spare him the humiliation of a scandal. Rocky Ford and La Junta were small towns. Word was guaranteed to rip through both places like a flash flood.

Then it hit them. The Wheelers felt Mike Fuller hadn't been surprised by the revelations about his wife. It was almost as though his denials were an attempt to cover up for Sharon. Maybe, they wondered, he had been in that spot before?

The preacher was red-faced and angry when he got home. No one could blame him, of course. If he had hoped Colorado would be different, there was no doubt he had been mistaken. He'd left the Wheelers with the realization that not only was Sharon sleeping around again, she was carrying on without one bit of discretion. All of his congregation probably knew by the time the Wheelers confronted him.

"We can't be anywhere, without you sleeping with somebody!" he declared when he saw Sharon and told her what Blanche and Karl had said.

She was backed into a corner, but Sharon was not one to give up a fight—even when there seemed no hope she could win.

"You don't know I've done a damn thing! Nobody saw me do a damn thing! You're taking that bitch's word that something is going on . . . and if you sat in the lobby and listened, you'd hear Perry call ninety-year-old women doll or sweetie!''

Mike threw up his hands. He had been that route before. In Ohio, in North Carolina, and now Colorado. If Sharon was making excuses that night in an effort to placate him, Mike wasn't buying anything she had to offer.

Still, Sharon held her ground,. insisting her husband was wrong and the women in the office were conniving liars, jealous of her friendship with Perry Nelson.

Rocky Ford was the land of in-home sales parties. It was a world beyond Tupperware. Everything from candles to beauty aids to children's toys were pushed over the kitchen table or in the paneled confines of a rec room. Some ladies hosted several such ''parties'' each year. The gatherings were a chance to make a little cash, share some gossip and get to know each other better. On the night of September 27, 1976, Julie Nelson went to a friend's home to learn the wonders of a new face cream. Sharon Fuller, who had also been expected, was a no-show.

When Julie returned home about 10:30 that evening, she was confronted by a shaken figure on the front steps. It was Mike Fuller. The frazzled minister told Julie his wife had left him for her husband. He had been driving around all evening, trying to find where they had gone. He wondered if Julie knew. She had no idea.

Mike proceeded to admit he had been through this before with Sharon. She'd had several affairs in Ohio and North Carolina. He also admitted Rochelle wasn't his daughter, but the offspring of one of Sharon's many lovers. But Denise, born in North Carolina in 1974 during a period of marital stability, *was* his biological daughter. He told Julie they had come to Rocky Ford for a new start, and sadly for him and his daughters, it clearly wasn't working.

Julie suggested calling her husband's secretary.

''Maybe she knows something,'' she said, reaching for the kitchen phone.

Barbara Ruscetti rubbed the sleep from her eyes and reached for the ringing telephone in her neat-as-can-be Trinidad home.

"Barbara, can you tell me where Perry is?" Julie asked.

"Perry?"

"Yes," the doctor's wife said. "He's not home yet."

Barb would have been deaf not to hear the worry that had seized Julie.

"He left the office at five o'clock with Sharon," she said, trying to calm her.

"Sharon?"

"Sharon Fuller."

"Do you know where they went?"

"No, I don't. How would I know where they are?"

"Well, all right, he's not home and it's eleven o'clock and I'm quite concerned."

A few minutes later, the phone rang. It was Perry. He told Julie that all the minister had told her was true. He was, in fact, leaving her for good to make a life with Sharon. He wasn't sorry, not when such a wonderful love was at stake.

"I've never loved anybody like the way I love her," he said.

Julie cried into the phone. "What makes you think you can trust each other with your histories?" she asked.

Mike Fuller looked on and nodded, as if to urge Julie on.

"I'd hate to be her and trust you. How are you going to trust her?" Julie asked once more.

"We love each other," Perry said.

Julie Nelson cradled the receiver against her breast, before sliding it back into the phone. She stopped her tears and let out a sigh. She would never deny that her husband's words and actions had hurt her deeply. Even as the truth of Perry's affair with the minister's wife came to undeniable reality, a strange feeling swept over her. It was relief. The other shoe had finally dropped. Maybe it was for the best?

Maybe she'd get on with her life, too.

The next day, Tuesday, first thing in the morning, Barb Ruscetti picked up the first line at the Trinidad office. It was Perry telling her to cancel his appointments for the day, and reschedule all for Thursday or Friday. Barb said she would. The optometry office stayed quiet that morning; Barb worked the phones and did a few frame repairs. She was a little ticked at the doctor for dropping his workload on to her lap. Sure she was paid to do whatever he asked, but she knew that patients kept their appointments and Dr. Nelson should keep his.

Just before lunchtime, Barb looked up from her desk to see Julie Nelson with a man she had not yet met.

The secretary smiled, but her friendliness was not returned.

"Barb," Julie began, "we're looking for Perry and Sharon. Do you have any idea where they are?"

Barb Ruscetti felt the blood drain from her cheeks. She knew instantly the reason for the visit. Without an introduction she knew that the handsome man with the broad shoulders and a touch of prematurely gray hair was Mike Fuller. *Preacher Fuller.*

Barb stood to face the pair. "No, Julie. I swear to you I don't know where they're at!"

"You know they haven't come home," Julie said. "We haven't seen them."

Barb shook her head. She conceded that she had talked with Perry that morning, but she had no idea he wasn't calling from Rocky Ford. She had no idea what was going on. Not until now, anyway.

She studied the man for a moment.

God, Barb thought, *this minister is good-looking. What does Sharon see in Perry if she's married to this guy?*

Finally, the minister spoke. He indicated in low, careful tones that something "drastic" had happened back in Rocky Ford.

"Sharon left a note saying she was leaving me and coming to Trinidad to live with Perry."

"I don't know a thing about that," Barb sputtered. "I don't know anything. I don't know where they are."

When Julie and Mike left, they took a piece of Barb Ruscetti's heart right out the door. It was such a terrible mess. She felt sorry for the jilted spouses.

"So they drove around Trinidad and dumb fools, Sharon and Perry, had parked down at Prospect Plaza and taken a motel room there," she told a friend about it later. "So what Julie and Mike did was they just went and got the sheriff and they had the sheriff open the door and they found Perry and Sharon in bed together and so Julie said, 'We're getting a divorce. I'm going to nail you to the wall.' And eventually she did," Barb said later.

Julie Nelson remembered the encounter between the minister, herself and the adulterers a bit differently, though no less dramatically than Barb. The spurned pair—Julie and Mike—had gone to the Trinidad police to get seven-year-old Rochelle away from an entirely inappropriate situation. The little girl was trapped inside her mother's motel love nest and Mike wanted her home with him and her little sister, Denise. Though Rochelle was not his blood, she was never anything less than his daughter.

"The police went in with Mike and he told Sharon that he was there to get Rochelle and take her home so she could go back to school," Julie recalled. "Perry was taking a shower at the time and Mike walked into the bathroom and ripped open the shower curtain and just stood there. I don't know what he said. I don't know if he said anything. He just wanted Perry to know that he knew he had taken his wife from him and his girls."

Later, when Mike sought a restraining order against Perry and Sharon prohibiting unsupervised contact with his girls, he told Julie it was because Perry was shameless and Sharon was a neglectful mother.

"I asked Rochelle if Mommy slept with Perry and she said she did. Right there in the motel," the minister said.

No matter his or her age, it was a child's most terrible nightmare. It came to thirteen-year-old Lorri Nelson one night and it grabbed her like the bogeyman. She woke up with a start, her eyes wide, imprinted with what she had seen in her sleep.

Her dad was not smiling. Her mom was sputtering cries and tears in the way that people do when nothing can soothe them. Outside the door of her dad's dressing room were a pair of packed suitcases. Her mother said nothing as he gathered his belongings . . . it was over. All over. In the instant that her father would step from the house, the girl knew that

*the family would never be the same. Lorri stood in the hall,
the scene frozen in her memory.*

Later, when she was at a girlfriend's house, the phone rang.
It was her mother telling her to come home right away. There
were no questions asked. No pleading to stay fifteen minutes
longer. Lorri went home knowing what she was about to face.

Her bad dream had come true.

"My parents told me Dad was leaving . . . my dad told me
that I'd always be his 'favorite youngest' daughter. He was
crying, my mom was crying, we were all crying. We gathered
to pray. My father knelt down and asked God for His protection. 'Please help our family through this,' he said."

Then he left. Sharon's name had never been uttered, yet her
shadow had been cast over everyone at the house on the corner
of Pine and 12th. The cheery white dwelling with the green
shutters was no longer a safe haven, no longer a happy home.
The family inside had been shattered.

A few felt sorry for Sharon Fuller, though most knew her
misery was self-inflicted. Sharon had her new man, had scored
the husband-hunter's brass ring—a doctor. Sharon had youth
and beauty. She had a nice body. She had money and, at least
she hoped, all that comes with that. She had everything but
what many women hold the most dear. Sharon no longer had
her children. Her daughters were with her estranged husband.

When Mike Fuller came over to commiserate with Julie
Nelson over the whole sordid mess, he said he doubted Sharon
really loved her kids. His wayward wife loved to sew and she
never seemed to make anything for her girls.

"It was all for her, all of the time," he said.

Before he mentioned it, Julie had never given it a thought.
But it was true. It had to be. Whenever she saw Sharon traips-
ing around town she was wearing some snug-fitting jumpsuit
that she had made herself. Her daughters never had anything
new.

Barb Ruscetti was another who could not imagine a mother
leaving two little girls behind. *What kind of woman could
leave her children? The pain Sharon must be feeling had to
be devastating,* Barb thought.

Sharon told her of seeing Mike drive the girls past the Watkins Medical building to the baby-sitter's house three doors down. Sometimes she would see them walking by, skipping along. Even laughing and having a good time. Two little girls without their mother. Two little girls without Sharon. She was unable to talk to them or hold them.

"I just can't handle it," she said. "It's tearing me up."

The strain on Sharon was evident. The source of it, however, was not fully clear to Barb or anyone. By then, most had heard Sharon had had extramarital affairs in the past, and that had been the reason for her husband's transfer. Others had heard Mike Fuller had suspected the affair between his wife and Dr. Nelson for months, and had, in fact, caught them in bed together long before the Wheelers voiced their concerns.

It was not her husband who wore her down, though Mike did try to get his wife to come home, despite all that had transpired. It was not her own sense of what was right and moral. It was Rochelle and Denise.

Sharon said she couldn't give them up.

Not long after the affair became public, Sharon began to waffle on her decision to ditch her husband and children. Guilt had taken hold. Sharon called a family friend, a counselor, in Fort Worth. She thought she was slipping off the edge of sanity. It hadn't turned out as she thought. Everyone else was fine, while she was a victim of viciousness. It was unfair. It was unjust. Julie was still billing out insurance and helping out at the office. Mike was seen as a saint. Sharon, however, was talked about all over town as the tramp who wrecked two marriages.

The counselor told her to get in her car and drive down to Texas. Sharon agreed. She needed help.

The Seventh-Day Adventist Church in La Junta, Colorado, was not going to be the same. While it was true that everyone among the parishioners knew what had transpired between the elder and the wife of their minister, few spoke about it. It was there, however, underneath the surface, behind the message of every sermon. While other folks outside of the congregation gossiped about it more overtly, the Adventists kept a lid on it the best they could.

They were strange and sad days.

"It's like everybody knows what's going on, but nobody talks about it. We were so disappointed. I think disappointed that Sharon didn't have more respect for herself and for her husband. To do something like this. Disappointed in Perry for the same reason," Blanche Wheeler said.

Long after it was all over, Mrs. Wheeler reiterated what had been the consensus of many who knew the sordid details of the affair.

"When Sharon left for Texas we all hoped she would get help and do the right thing by Mike and her little girls. We hoped and we prayed."

7

JESUS, IT HURT. PERRY NELSON FELT HE HAD BEEN dumped. Sharon had gone to Texas to get her head together with some Christian counselor. It was obvious a therapist of that particular ilk was not going to condone a woman's illicit relationship with another woman's husband. It was, of course, adultery, for crying out loud. Adultery times two. To make matters worse, word around Rocky Ford had it that Mike Fuller had either gone after her or was planning to do so. He wasn't going to go away easily. The preacher was mad at his wife, disgusted by her, but he still wanted her. A Christian counselor, Perry figured, would push for a mending of the broken family.

About that time, Perry's and Julie's twenty-fifth high school reunion loomed. Perry told his wife he would still accompany her back to the event in Cedar Lake, Michigan. He was neither happy nor particularly interested in the reunion with his wife or their classmates. It was almost as if he had nothing better to do. The estranged couple had little to talk about on the flight to Michigan. More than once, Julie dabbed at her tears with a wadded tissue as she fought for composure.

Her handsome, charismatic husband was stone cold whenever he bothered to speak with Julie. When he looked in Julie's direction it was as if she was made of glass. His eyes skipped over her; looked through her. All he cared about was Sharon. Sharon this. Sharon that.

But I'm right here, Julie thought.

When they arrived, Julie tried to act happy around relatives and old classmates, but inside, her heart continued to crumble. Perry had nothing to do with her. He barely even pretended they were together. He didn't talk to her. He didn't even walk with her. He walked ahead, or several paces behind.

On the return flight to Colorado, Julie sat alone and cried most of the way. It was only at one point that she saw a glimpse of compassion for her suffering.

Perry turned around in the seat in front of her and put his hand out.

"Don't cry," he said, "everything's going to be all right."

By then it didn't matter. Sharon Fuller could have him. Julie had made up her mind that she would be moving on.

I'm out of here, she thought.

Julie kept her distance in Rocky Ford. If Perry was merely going through the motions, then Julie would not over-compensate for his lack of love for her. She wouldn't prepare him special meals. She certainly wouldn't sleep with him at night. Why should she? He didn't love her. He was with her by default. Julie spent most of her weekends in Denver with the former wife of another local doctor. As the empty days passed, she told herself she would build up her mental and emotional strength and move on.

Sharon Fuller was falling apart. And while she confided in many, few had any sympathy for her. If ever there was a case of making your own bed and being forced to lie in it, Sharon was the perfect example. She drove to Fort Worth in a car Perry had bought for her. The fog was thick and her eyes were bloodshot from ragged emotions and sleepless nights. Sharon had left two men in Rocky Ford: a husband and a lover. She told people she didn't know which one she should choose.

Mike Fuller, however, couldn't let go of his wife. Though there were times when she had tested him to the nth degree, he still wanted to keep his family together. He still told friends he loved Sharon. If only she would come home . . . if only they could start over.

Maybe in another place, another town.

Sharon saw the Texas psychologist almost daily for two

weeks. She was, as she explained, "trying to sort out who I was . . . what my feelings were. Where my life was going. Do I need to slit my throat and end this or what?"

The Seventh-Day Adventist counselor encouraged her to call Mike. Despite the wanton infidelity, despite her fragmented loyalties, the counselor insisted that her marriage still had a chance. It was, he said, worth saving.

Sharon recalled the man's words: "You really want Mike to love you more than anything. You're testing him . . . to see if he'll still take you back after you've been such a naughty girl."

Sharon bought into it. She told herself that her affair with Perry Nelson was an offshoot of unresolved issues in her marriage. It was not because she was so in love with Perry. No, not at all. She told the counselor she would give Mike another chance. She would give up Dr. Nelson.

"Perry's got to go," she said, firmness in her voice growing with each word. "Perry has disrupted my life. I've destroyed his life. Maybe if Mike and I can rebuild, Perry and Julie can rebuild?"

It was after 11 P.M. when Preacher Fuller's jet from Denver finally touched down at the Dallas airport. Sharon's stomach was crocheted into knots. It was an emotionally raw reunion. Tears fell on both sides as they held each other. Both agreed they wanted to save their marriage. Even so, the bitterness was not completely forsaken. Sharon vented her anger over why her husband's shortcomings had forced her into another man's arms once more. It was his fault, too.

From his suitcase in their motel room, the minister withdrew a see-through nightie.

Sharon's eyes popped and she hit the ceiling.

"You flew down here for a piece of tail! That's all you did!"

Mike tried to persuade Sharon that she was wrong. She had jumped to the wrong conclusion. He had come to Texas because he wanted to save their marriage. And, as even Sharon would later concede, he must have been telling the truth. Mike Fuller sat up all night, stiffly, uncomfortably, while she berated him about everything from their sex life to the manner of his day-to-day attire. He took it all, one shot after another and for good reason: He had two little girls at home who needed a mother.

After four days of "couples counseling," endless talking, and a wading pool of tears, the Fullers drove back to Colorado. Beyond pulling over for gasoline and food, they made only one stop on their way up north toward Denver and suburban Arvada, the city where Mike had been relocated to a new church. Mike parked in the Nelsons' driveway in Rocky Ford and went inside the house while Sharon stayed slumped in the car, embarrassed and anxious. She had promised never to speak to Perry again. A few minutes later, Mike returned.

The preacher scooted back behind the wheel and announced he had had it out with Dr. Nelson. He warned the doctor to back off, that Sharon had made up her mind to put her family back together. Sharon was going to be a mother to her two little girls. Sharon was going to be a good wife once more.

When they arrived at Mike's rented house in Arvada, two elderly women from church were up waiting in the front room. The women had been employed to baby-sit Rochelle and Denise while their father went after their mother.

Sharon tried to make pleasant conversation, but she knew what they were thinking.

"As I walk in . . . these two little old spinster ladies are judging me. It was all over the church. Everybody knew that I'd left Mike . . . that we'd reconciled . . . that God had brought us back together," she said later.

The Arvada church had an enormous congregation, the largest of Mike Fuller's hopscotching ministerial career. Two thousand members, give or take a hundred or so, knew Sharon Fuller by her reputation. Most knew that Rev. Fuller's wife had an affair with a church elder down in La Junta. A few heard it was not the first such affair for the striking, albeit mixed-up, woman. When Sharon took the second pew with her children for church services, she did so amid dagger stares and catty gossip. Sharon made her own vow from that pew: She wasn't going to put up with it . . . not for long.

To escape the tedium of her world, Sharon took a job at a Denver area hospital as staffing coordinator. The hours were long and the work stressful as she made sure personnel were in place whenever sickness or snow left the hospital without some staff. The job kept her busy, but it didn't stop her thinking about Perry Nelson. Occasionally she called Barb Ruscetti in Trinidad for an update, but she didn't break Mike's "no talk with the doc" rule. She passed phone messages through Barb and even sent a few notes in the mail. At night, she drank a six-pack of beer. By day, she drank vodka mixed with fruit juice.

When Perry Nelson sent her a little silver music box that played "Somewhere My Love," Sharon made up her mind. She quit her job and told Mike she was moving out. This time for good. He could have everything but her final paycheck, the sofa and her sewing machine. She said she was getting an apartment in Denver, maybe later returning to Rocky Ford. Who knew? No one was going to dictate the rules of her life. Not anymore. First off, she went to visit her sister Judy in Colorado Springs.

She did not say she was going back to Perry, but, of course, that was her plan.

She called Perry and he drove the Buick LaSabre convertible to the Springs. He knocked on Judy Douglas's front door one evening with an excited knock, an impatient rap. But the man was all smiles when the door swung open. Sharon, who had been sipping brandy with her sister, was elated. Judy thought she had never seen a happier couple.

That night Perry took Sharon to a motel in Manitou Springs and they made love all night. Just as she promised they would every night. Every day. All the time.

Sharon tried to sort out her life and she needed time and support to do so. Instead of returning to Rocky Ford right away, she alternated her time in the Denver area and at one point she asked Judy if she and her daughters could stay at her place for awhile. Mike had not wanted Sharon to take the girls, but at least in the eyes of the law, Sharon was their mother. Judy, who was struggling through her own marital problems, was glad for the diversion that houseguests could bring. Judy bought a second hand bunk bed and turned her downstairs into a bedroom for Rochelle and Denise. Sharon planned on working for a Colorado Springs Pearle Vision, and though Judy had her own four kids to raise, she said she would help her younger sister with the little girls.

Sharon, for the first time in a long time, seemed happy. Maybe she would make something of her life, after all. Maybe she had pulled herself together and was finally going to do the right thing.

The hope was short-lived.

Mike Fuller had made no bones about it to anyone who would listen: Sharon was an terrible mother and he'd raise the girls without her rotten-to-the-core influence. There was no way he'd have Rochelle and Denise live in sin with their mother. The woman was unfit. When Karl Wheeler heard of Mike's plan to take the kids from Sharon by court order, he offered to accompany him on the task. Mike knew Sharon was hiding out at Judy's place in the Springs. Karl Wheeler considered himself the voice of reason. If the minister was going to spout off, then Karl would be there to listen and calm the jilted husband.

"Mike was a feisty sort of guy for a preacher. It didn't take much for him to double up his fists and take a poke at someone," Karl said later.

The two men drove from Rocky Ford to Colorado Springs in the Wheelers' brand-new white Lincoln Continental with a maroon top. They stopped at the El Paso County Sheriff's office and explained the situation. A deputy agreed to escort them to Judy's residence to enforce a custody order.

Karl remained in the Lincoln while the deputy and the preacher went inside to settle the issue of custody. As Karl waited, he wondered how things could have turned so ugly.

Perry, how'd you get in such a mess?

Sharon, stunned at the intrusion, claimed it was *she* who should have the girls. She was their mother. Rochelle and Denise needed her.

No one bought it.

In the end, custody papers in her face, she gave in.

"Let him have them," she said quietly.

Judy thought her sister didn't fight that hard to keep the little girls. Not really.

Not as hard as she would have if *she* had been their mother.

*   *   *

When Sharon Fuller returned to Rocky Ford for good in December 1976, it brought an unexpected sense of relief to Julie Nelson. She had been unable to eat or sleep decently for weeks. Julie knew her marriage was over and her husband had wanted to be with the preacher's wife. She even suspected they had met during one of his business trips to Denver, though she couldn't prove it. She longed for the day when she wouldn't have to prove anything. When she wouldn't have to worry she would stumble on a motel-room receipt or a bill from a jeweler for something given to the Other Woman. When Christmas came and went, it was clear the family would never be as it was before Sharon Nelson had crept into their lives.

The preacher's wife had a hold on the doctor that was tungsten.

When Perry told Julie that he and Sharon were once again going to make a life together, he said that she could stay on in Rocky Ford and even keep her old job in the medical office.

Julie didn't think so.

"I'm going to California," she said. "I've already made up my mind. No matter what happens here."

Mother and youngest daughter packed what they could load into an old Pontiac on January 2, 1977. Julie knew she was not coming back. Lorri halfway hoped that her parents would work it out eventually. She didn't want to leave her father. She didn't see why she had to go.

When Perry came out to wish them a safe trip, he put his hand on his wife's shoulder and whispered, "Julie, everything's going to be all right."

Julie said nothing. She had heard that before. Ten thousand times.

"I meant to get you a better car," he said.

Julie didn't care one whit about the car. "It's fine," she answered.

"Maybe, if things don't work out," Perry continued, "you'll want to come back and we can start over."

His remark stunned Julie. "I won't," she said. She couldn't imagine why he would even suggest such a thing. "And if I ever did," she said, "I would not want to start over here."

Not with you.

She stopped herself from saying more. It was a reflex, not a true assessment about how she felt. She wondered how Perry and Sharon thought they could start over in Rocky Ford. They had stirred up a scandal the likes of which no one had ever seen. And they believed they could act as though they had done nothing wrong? Incredible.

Still crying as she put the car into gear and drove out of town, something came over Julie and stopped the tears. Almost in an instant, she started laughing with Lorri. All of the hurt of her marriage was gone. All of the pain she had endured left as suddenly as the sun dropping behind a cloud.

She knew everything would be all right.

"I had a promise from God," Julie said later. "I couldn't have shed another tear from that moment on."

When her mood was foul, Sharon had the demeanor of an executioner. When she started back to work in the Trinidad optometry office, she picked up where she had left off. She would make no doctor's employee of the month, even if the office had a staff of one.

Some of Dr. Nelson's patients tolerated Sharon, but many found her to be snotty, impatient and downright rude. A well-to-do family from up the river was one of the first to bail out on Dr. Nelson's practice because of Sharon's rotten attitude. The family's youngest son planned on getting contact lenses as a wedding present for his 17-year-old bride. Since Barb was mired in a mountain of paperwork, Perry asked Sharon to dispense the lenses to the girl.

Out of the corner of her eye, Barb watched as Sharon showed the girl how to put the hard contacts in. The girl winced in pain, as many first-time wearers do. She started to shake and cry.

"This hurts," she sobbed. "Please get them out! Take them out!"

For some reason, Sharon just sat there. So Barb got up and helped the girl.

"I don't want these," the girl said, tears still running down her cheeks. "They hurt."

Sharon stood up like a rocket.

"You're nothing but a damn baby! I won't even bother with you." She turned on her heels and advised Barb that if she wanted to dispense the lenses, it was fine with her.

"I'm not even going to bother with her!"

Then she disappeared into a back office.

The young husband shot a glare in Sharon's direction and told Barb they didn't have to take that kind of abuse from anyone.

"Mrs. Ruscetti," he said, "this doesn't pertain to you, but none of my family will ever come back to this office as long as she's here."

And they never did.

As much as she enjoyed the full freedom of the office, at least as it had been in the days before Sharon, Barb Ruscetti began to hate to leave her desk. It seemed that every time she did, she'd return to find Sharon rifling papers, going through files and generally poking her nose into every piece of paperwork she could get her hands on.

As the guerrilla attacks on the office files continued, no matter how often Barb asked Sharon to cool it, she'd laugh it off. Tension increased. Sharon was pushing Barb's buttons with reckless abandon.

"What are you looking for?" Barb asked, as Sharon bent over and fanned out some files from a bottom drawer. Caught, Sharon stood up, her skirt still clinging halfway up her thigh.

"Nothing," she said.

"Then get the hell out from behind my desk or I'll throw you out the damn window!"

Sharon smiled and moved out of the way.

Barb wished she *had* pushed her out. In the long run, it probably would have been an act of mercy for so many.

8

SHARON'S EYES HAD TURNED FROM BLUE TO red. Her prettily painted mouth was a taut gash of lipstick and anger. If she was a bitch on wheels, as Barb Ruscetti had characterized her during their first encounter, that morning in Perry Nelson's Trinidad office she was running the Indy 500. She had heard more bad news: Now Mike was seeking full, *permanent* custody of Rochelle and Denise in Otero County Superior Court. When she arrived to tell Perry about it, she stomped her heels like a petulant child and flung obscenities about the room like boomerangs welded of steak knives. One after another sliced through the air. Sharon seemed to pay no mind that patients could hear her tirade. She cared nothing about anyone. Sharon Fuller was, as Barb could see, the center of her own universe. And she was fit to be tied.

"That fucker! That fucker can't do this to me!"

Barb was aghast. This was Dr. Nelson's office, not a miners' pool hall. She tried to understand Sharon's bitterness. She tried very hard. Each time she went to the place in her heart where she could retrieve sympathy for others, she came up with nothing for the woman slamming things around the office and using every dirty name in the book against her husband. The minister's estranged wife was not going to get any support from her. She had done her husband dirtier than any woman Barb had ever seen, heard about, read about. She was vile and evil. Sharon had lost her children because she was a neglectful mother. The two little girls were better off without her.

"Perry, call the goddamn judge in La Junta and put a stop to this. You know him! Call him now!"

Perry stepped back from Sharon's screaming mouth and slowly shook his head.

"No," he said, quietly but with considerable firmness. "This is between you and Mike. I'm staying out of it."

Sharon grabbed for the phone. In a minute she was on the line screaming at the top of her lungs to the unlucky court employee who picked up the line.

"Don't fuck with me and my girls!" Sharon raged into the mouthpiece. "They're my girls! Mike can't have them!"

After she vented her anger for what had to be only a few seconds, but seemed much longer, the line went dead. Enraged at being disconnected by some two-bit clerk, Sharon threw the phone halfway across the back office. It clattered against the floor.

"I'll show that son of a bitch! If he thinks he's going to take my girls away from me! I'm not going to lose my daughters! They're mine! *Mine*!"

A few weeks later, Perry pulled Barb aside in the office to tell her what had happened when Sharon went to court to hammer out a final joint-custody agreement with her former husband.

"Oh Barb, it was something else," Perry said one afternoon when Sharon was not around.

"Well, what happened?" Barb asked.

"Mike got up and said what she did—she didn't even get to talk—the judge just said, 'I declare you a whore, and I am taking your two daughters away from you! You will not even have visiting rights until they turn thirteen years old! When they turn thirteen years of age they can make up their minds if they want to stay with their so-called mother or go with their father.' "

Barb couldn't imagine a judge saying such things. No man of the law talked that way. But then she couldn't have dreamed up a woman like Sharon Lynn Fuller, either.

Sharon hated living in another woman's house. Signs of Perry's life with Julie were evident everywhere she looked:

the wallpaper, the carpet, the way the dishes had been put away. All were reminders of her man's life with another woman. She couldn't stand living there one more minute. They put the Nelson place in Rocky Ford up for sale. Sharon sold the convertible Mike had left her, and she and Perry bought a tiny gray "dollhouse" further down 10th, between Pine and Locust Streets.

The instant their divorces went through, Sharon wanted to get married. She had given up so much for Perry Nelson that she damn well would not tolerate a long engagement. Perry readily agreed. In reality, he had no choice. He had been the focus of such derision since leaving Julie for Sharon that a happy ending would be his only salvation.

Sharon made her own wedding dress, not because she had to, but because she could and she wanted to. It was a Gunny Sax pattern that flowed full and long to the floor with a cinched bodice that accentuated her full breasts. She selected a light, wheat-colored material, though it was more a preference than an acknowledgment that white fabric would have been inappropriate for the bride. She also fashioned the flouncy brim of a straw hat with silk flowers and lace. She picked out a beige leisure suit for Perry.

On July 1, 1977, the pair that had scandalized Trinidad and Rocky Ford exchanged wedding vows in a private ceremony at the St. Francis of Assisi Mission in Taos. It had to be Taos, for Sharon. The place had seemed magical from that first weekend trip during which she'd gotten to know Perry. The couple honeymooned over the next couple of days, spending their last afternoon in Santa Fe.

When they returned to Colorado, the local gossip line percolated with the latest.

He married her. The eye doc married the minister's wife!

For many in Rocky Ford, the news that Sharon and Perry had tied the knot brought more resignation than joy. When they came back as man and wife, few marked the occasion with a gift. It just didn't seem appropriate.

Nor, to some, did it seem genuine.

"I felt like the whole marriage was a show," said a woman who knew all parties in the sordid and tragic Nelson saga. "It was like they were trying so hard to portray that they were so happy. They were trying to prove to the world they had done nothing wrong, that their love was good and right. It didn't matter about Mike and the kids or Julie and the girls. Their love was higher than that. Sharon was always a big one for appearances. She wanted everything new and perfect in her home. But it was just for looks. Her marriage was the same way. There was no heart to anything she had or did.''

Living in California with Lorri, Julie, for one, was surprised when she got word of the July union. She checked with her lawyer and he confirmed that though the divorce was pending, it had not yet been made final at the time of the Taos wedding. Julie let it sit. She didn't want the man anymore.

Those two deserve each other, she thought.

Sharon Nelson could spit tacks. She had never been so angry in all her life; at least, she couldn't think of a time when she had been. At the end of a visit, Rochelle Fuller informed her mother that her daddy was moving her and her sister to Ohio the next morning. Since Mike had legal custody, Sharon saw no way of stopping him.

"I saw them drive away," she told a friend, "and I didn't know when I'd see my girls again."

Three weeks later, a letter arrived addressed to Sharon. In the missive, Mike indicated that even though he had moved to pastor a new church out-of-state, visitation with their daughters could continue. Sharon and Perry would get Rochelle and Denise for Christmas vacation and two weeks in the summer. They'd have to arrange for transportation to and from Ohio.

Sharon considered waging a legal battle for her daughters, particularly Rochelle, whom she knew was not Mike's biological daughter.

"I didn't know how to do it without tearing [Rochelle] up, totally. How do I drag [Rochelle] through court without screwing [her] up more than [her] mother?" she asked.

Sharon did what she did best when it came to her children. She let them go. She let Mike have them.

* * *

Sharon was supposed to pay the bills at the office. It was such a joke. Sharon paid nothing. All the money that came into the business was hers. She was now the doctor's wife and she was entitled to all the bucks that come with the title. She certainly wasn't helping matters. Whenever there were two nickels in the till, she'd liberate the funds. She had made a practice of shopping in the mornings and coming back to the office to show Barb what she had purchased before leaving for lunch with her husband.

One day Barb got a nasty surprise when she got on the line to place an order for contact lenses with a Dallas manufacturer that had been doing business with the Nelson practice for years.

"Barb," the account manager said before they could barely exchange the pleasantries that cross-country vendors and clients often do, "we can't send you any more lenses until your bill is paid."

"What do you mean? It's paid the first of every month."

"No, it hasn't been paid in almost three months."

Barb was at once embarrassed and angry. She knew the problem was that short-skirted woman with access to the office checkbook. She told Perry what the lensmaker had said.

Perry bristled at the implication.

"Barb, you're out of your mind."

"No, I'm not."

Later, Barb learned Sharon had tired of paying the bills. It bored her. Rather than eat crow, Perry secretly took over the responsibility for the payables. He didn't dare ask Barb to do it, though she would have. He didn't want an "I told you so."

Sharon continued to help herself to the daily receipts. A few times when Barb went to cash her paycheck, the teller apologetically informed her that there wasn't enough money in Dr. Nelson's account to cover it. Money, Barb knew, was tight. Dr. Nelson had alimony, child support and a staggering debt load that needed major cash flow. If all corners were cut to a circle, maybe they'd get by. But not with what Sharon had in mind. It blew Barb's mind when Dr. Nelson showed up with a thousand-dollar ring that Sharon had "bought" for him. For one thing, members of his church didn't wear jewelry of any kind. With Sharon by his side, everything had gone out the window. When Sharon whined for a new dining-room set, three thousand dollars that the doctor didn't have was somehow found to buy it.

Anything for Sharon.

Barb Ruscetti could see Dr. Nelson getting sucked in deeper and deeper and she knew the reason why.

"She was gorgeous. She was very busty, had a nice figure and this reddish-brown hair and she's got blue eyes. Very beautiful and she really manipulated her men. She got whatever she wanted."

Then the news came at the height of a hot August summer: Sharon was pregnant.

Around Christmas 1977, Julie Nelson returned to Colorado to help out with her daughter Kathy's wedding at a church in Thornton. The former optometrist's wife held her head up high and focused on the task at hand: making the wedding day perfect for her daughter. The fact that a very pregnant Sharon was there with her husband—just six months' divorced—was a difficult pill to swallow. But Julie bit her tongue and did her best to keep any bitter feelings to herself.

"I've been so busy getting this wedding together," Sharon told a Rocky Ford couple who had driven up to Denver for the occasion, "I didn't have time to get out any Christmas cards this year."

Poor thing, and pregnant to boot!

When the remark made it to Julie's ears back in the church's basement kitchen, she tried to come up with an excuse for her rival.

"Maybe she meant she had been so busy making her dress or something," she said.

Blanche Wheeler didn't think so.

"She wore that dress at the office Christmas party."

"Well, maybe I should just take it as a compliment. Maybe she wants to take credit for it because it turned out so nice."

Three months later, in the first week in March, Sharon gave birth to a beautiful baby boy. A few who did the math, including Julie, were certain the baby was no preemie. Sharon had probably been pregnant when she and Perry married.

Had to be a reason for that quick-draw wedding in New Mexico.

Sharon didn't care about the rumors. She simply crowed over the obvious.

"At least I gave Perry a son. Julie only had daughters," she said.

Baby Danny Nelson quickly became the apple of his father's eye.

"There was no man prouder or happier than Perry when they brought that little boy home. I'll tell you, I thought the marriage just might work out. They seemed so thrilled," said a friend of the family.

Stuck in Paradise, California, and bitter as a peach pit, Lorri Nelson blamed her mother for ruining her family. If only Julie Nelson had been more of what her husband had wanted in a woman. Prettier, sexier, more fun . . . all the things Sharon was, all the things Perry had been denied. While the ex–Mrs. Nelson cried her evenings away, she got little real compassion from her youngest daughter.

Later, Lorri would berate herself for the way she treated her mother.

"I was young and selfish. I blamed her over things over which she had no control. Here she was working in a new job, trying to get on her feet and she had a daughter who made it clear that I wanted to be with my dad—not *her*. I'm sure I hurt her very much."

In the spring of 1978, Lorri's nonstop prayers were finally answered. She was getting out of Paradise and going home to Colorado. Her folks agreed that she should spend the summer back in Rocky Ford. When fall came, she would enroll in Campion Seventh-Day Adventist Academy in Loveland, Colorado. She'd be with her father again.

For Lorri and her father, the happy times returned. When Perry laid out the itinerary for a summer vacation, Lorri could hardly wait to go. But even if the trip hadn't included such destinations as New York City, Niagara Falls, Washington, D.C., and Colonial Williamsburg, Lorri would have been enthusiastic just the same. Traveling with her father, Sharon and baby Danny would be a blast.

Sharon was so much fun. She'd make up silly little road songs, she'd join in when they had their "Big Mac Attacks" and sought the famed Golden Arches of the hamburger chain. When a stateline came into view, Sharon, Lorri and Perry would stretch their limbs to the very front of the motor home to see who could lay claim to be the first one in the new state.

When they stopped at Sharon's parents' house in Maryland to show off the new grandson, everyone had a great time.

"They were really nice people," Lorri said later of Josephine and Morris Douglas. The elderly couple did not appear to be as controlling as Sharon had portrayed during her monologue about her youth.

"I was expecting them to be a lot more strict, but they seemed very kind."

The first time Lorri Nelson ever drank enough to get drunk was New Year's Eve, 1978. She was fifteen. Her drinking partners were Sharon, Perry and a would-be boyfriend named Luke. Sharon started things off telling the teens that it was better for them to drink at home than off on the road somewhere. She poured sickly sweet tumblers of Tom Collins mixer and vodka, as well as flutes of champagne, as if the kids could drink like an adult with poor judgment. As the midnight hour approached, Lorri munched on dried-out Christmas fudge as she watched the walls begin to move.

Sharon made it seem so fun . . . until the booze got the best of Lorri.

"I was never so sick in my life," Lorri said later. "I think that's what my father had in mind when he let me drink, though it was Sharon that was really pushing. Back then, I thought it was cool."

It was shortly thereafter that Sharon started buying alcohol for Lorri.

"Don't tell your father." She flashed a conspiratorial smile. "He'd go through the roof. He's loosening up, but not that much."

Sharon showed Lorri how she could hide peppermint

schnapps in a mouthwash bottle so she could drink whenever she wanted back at the academy in Loveland.

"I thought she was great," Lorri said later. "I thought she was a buddy. I really, really liked Sharon."

In reality, Sharon was no one's buddy. It wasn't until many years later that Lorri discovered just how wrong she had been when she had thought of her stepmother as a friend. Lorri met up with Campion Academy's girls' dean in Bozeman, Montana. The dean had sent word she wanted to see how this hellacious young girl—the former thorn in her side—had turned out. By that time, Lorri's life was proof positive that people really *could* turn their lives around. She decided to go.

"I felt so sorry for you," the woman began. "With what you had going on at home and what your stepmother was doing behind your back."

Lorri was startled by the remark.

"I don't understand. What was Sharon doing?"

"She kept calling up telling us to search your room. She said she had reason to believe that you were smuggling alcohol into the dorm."

Lorri's heart dropped. She could feel her face grow warm. Sharon had set her up. Sharon had tried to destroy her. No wonder her father had sometimes seemed aloof. It had been Sharon. Sharon had said something ugly to him as well.

Lorri's mind flashed to the image of Sharon sitting at the kitchen table, drinking coffee and smiling. Smoke curled from the ashy end of a thin, long cigarette.

"If you want to call me Mom, I'd consider it a great honor," she had said. "Of course, I understand you have a mother already."

Lorri tried it out in her head a few times, but was never able to call Sharon mother. Instead, she chose the nickname Sharon preferred above all others: Sher.

Before the disclosure made by the girls' dean had stunned her into a silent disbelief, Lorri had believed a terrible lie. She had been oblivious to the nature of the woman who had infected their lives like some kind of insidious disease. She had not heard the sarcasm in Sharon's voice when she talked about her sisters or her mother. She had not seen how really snotty

Sharon was when things irritated her or when she didn't get her way.

"I thought she was so wonderful. I thought she gave me so much freedom. I thought she really liked me. But she didn't, did she? I guess she didn't like anyone but Sharon."

Lorri had wondered to herself what it was that kept drawing her toward trouble. Sometimes she chalked it up to the scabbed over hurt of her parents' divorce. Occasionally she blamed her religion. Other times she was more pragmatic, and knew she made her own choices—and frequently they were poor ones.

In the late summer of 1980, only four weeks into her senior year, she was in a patch of trouble once more. As she had done before, she was drinking and being defiant and irresponsible. The dean at Campion wanted her to shape up, pull her act together, get with the program. *Or else*. She could concede she was a problem, but no more so than many other teens. She wasn't running away. She was going to school and partying.

Perry had been notified and he and Sharon, along with toddler Danny, made the trip up to Loveland to straighten out the girl. Lorri had never seen her father so angry as he lashed out at her for making a mess of her life, making a mess of his life. Sharon held Danny and smiled smugly.

Though Lorri was nearly grown at seventeen, a frenzied Perry threw her across the bed, pulled off his belt and whipped her. Lorri had been spanked before, though it had been awhile. But she had never been spanked so hard in her entire life. Sharon egged her husband on. Lorri needed to be taught a lesson.

"This has been going on too long. She can't keep doing this to us!"

As Lorri thrashed on the bed, she broke some blood vessels in her nose and started to bleed. Blood stained the bedsheets and pillow.

After the whipping, Perry told Lorri to clean herself up. Sharon had wanted to go to the movies and that's where they'd go—as a family. The film was *Caddyshack*.

Lorri sat stonily, glancing at her father and his wife. Sharon was no longer the best friend, the older girlfriend. She was no longer the woman to whom she'd confide. The woman laughing out loud at the antics of the gopher on the golf course was no one she wanted to know.

While the Nelsons were watching *Caddyshack*, Lorri's roommate discovered blood on the bed and notified the dean. The school administrator flew into action, nearly ready to report a terrible crime, until Lorri returned and explained what happened.

Two weeks later, Academy officials expelled Lorri Nelson. No one wanted a repeat of what had happened. No one wanted to see the violence escalate. Without her father's knowledge, Lorri was sent to her mother's. By then, Julie Nelson was living in Walla Walla, in the very southeast corner of Washington state.

"At the moment I saw her smug face while I was being spanked, I knew that she didn't really care about me," Lorri later explained. "She had convinced my father that I was no good and that I deserved everything I got. I'll never forget the look on her face. Even through my tears, I saw her smile."

Long after the sharpest of the memories associated with the beating at Loveland had faded, Lorri Nelson talked with Barbara Ruscetti about what happened in that dorm room. The doctor's daughter was still mystified.

"Mrs. Ruscetti," she said, "why do you think he did that?"

Barb didn't mince words. "Because Sharon told him to do that to you. I heard her."

Lorri pressed for details and Barb recounted something she heard Sharon tell Perry.

"Perry, I think you ought to take your belt off and just beat the holy hell out of Lorri. Teach her a lesson!"

As Barb saw it, Lorri's father was under Sharon's spell.

"I bet if Sharon said, 'Perry, we're going down and rob the Trinidad National Bank tonight,' he would have gone. He wouldn't have asked any questions."

Not everyone was blind to Sharon's modus operandi when it came to Lorri. Blanche Wheeler would hear of things Sharon had done to Lorri through her daughter, Kerry.

"She was almost conniving," Blanche said later. "She almost seemed to make trouble for Lorri."

Shortly after she packed her things for Walla Walla, Lorri received a letter from Sharon. She wrote to request the return of "everything I bought you to get you set up for your dorm." She listed some director's chairs, bedcovers, a curtain she had made. She wanted it returned right away. Lorri boxed it all up and shipped it to Colorado, even though she knew that it was her father who had paid for the stuff, not Sharon. She did so because she knew that no one could win an argument with Sharon.

Lorri enrolled in Walla Walla Senior High with the understanding that most of her credits from her Adventist schooling would transfer over and she'd be able to graduate with her class. As it turned out, many credits did not carry over. Bitter and disappointed, Perry Nelson's "favorite youngest" daughter quit school to work full-time for an accounting firm. She didn't know it then, but she was pulling herself up from an abyss so insidious that she had not even known it had consumed her. Eventually, Lorri earned a GED.

That same year, she wrote to her father. It was a long letter, full of remorse for the pain she had caused over the years. She had never been so sorry in her whole life.

A reply came postmarked Trinidad. Lorri recognized the handwriting as her stepmother's.

"You have some nerve even writing to your father after how you've treated him!"

Lorri cried as she read Sharon's bitchy string of hateful words. Sharon made it clear Lorri was not welcome and if she knew what was good for her, she'd back off. Once and for all.

"You used your father. Like the boy who cried wolf . . . you were always in a crisis! Help me! Those days are over. You've hurt Perry for the last time."

A door had been slammed shut; a wall had been built. The father and daughter who had once shared a precious closeness would remain estranged for two years.

Sharon Nelson, once more, got what she had wanted.

9

MONEY FOR JULIE. MONEY FOR UNCLE SAM. MONEY to keep the business afloat. Money for Sharon. The outstretched hands were everywhere. Perry was close to busted and he knew it. As if she needed to do so, Sharon reminded her husband daily of their escalating financial troubles. And though the tax bills and business expenses were choking the life out of their bank account, it was Julie Nelson's old charge accounts that made Sharon's blood boil over. The way Sharon saw it, Julie, in a fit of justified spite, ran up bills all over town—all over Colorado for that matter. The local ladies' shoe store, the Fashion Bar in Denver, a dress shop in the Springs. Sharon urged Perry to file bankruptcy so they could start over, but he wouldn't hear of it.

"I was raised to pay my debts," he said.

"I was, too," Sharon scoffed. She reminded Perry that *she* was his wife now. She shouldn't be saddled with expenses rung up by the first wife. She knew there was no way out of the alimony and back child-support payments. The other stuff, forget it.

"I was not raised to pay debts that you and this woman incurred over a five-year period of time and didn't disclose to me," she said.

And still the money drain ran unchecked.

Rochelle Fuller called her mother from Ohio one morning before Sharon arrived at the Trinidad office. Barb Ruscetti took the call and promised the girl that she'd have her mother call her back as soon as she got in. When Sharon finished speaking with Rochelle later that day she made a beeline for the check register.

"I'm sending Rochelle four hundred dollars for a stereo," she announced.

Barb couldn't hide her exasperation. "Sharon, you can't," she said. "We don't have the money."

"Well, I'll be goddamned if I'm paying the bills! I'm sending my daughter four hundred dollars."

Perry emerged from examining a patient, and put the kibosh on the stereo.

"Let Rochelle's dad buy her one," he said.

Sharon stomped her feet. Her face went red with anger.

"I'm not doing without money anymore," she said as she stormed out. "I'm sick and tired of it."

As Barb saw it, Sharon was trying to win back her daughter's affection. The only way she knew how to make herself feel better, make her daughters feel like she cared about them, was to buy presents to send.

"I don't think her little girls loved her anymore," Barb told a friend.

And despite the lack of money, her strained relations with her daughters, Sharon would still have her dream. She wanted to feel good about herself. She wanted a fancy new custom house.

If Weston, Colorado, wasn't so isolated, no cartographer would bother inking it on any map. But as luck would have it, the village located thirty miles of scenic roadway from Trinidad was always the perfect dot on the map. Nothing around it but a long, lonely, winding stretch of road. Snowcapped mountains brushed against the horizon where asphalt sliced through rocky outcroppings along the highway as it drops down the canyon where the little town was bunched up. A small green-and-white sign advises travelers not to blink: WELCOME TO WESTON.

The town's most well-known business was Weston Supply, a general store that had been the purveyor of miners' goods and supplies for more than a century. Locals who need something, and don't want to make the drive into Trinidad to get it, can usually find what they are looking for at the store/post office.

Wet Canyon was a deep chasm, cut by the Purgatoire River over a millennium of pelting rains and avalanches of snow. It was rugged and breathtaking. Sharon had fallen in love with thirty-five acres above the canyon. The views were stunning: twenty miles away Chuchara Pass could be seen, as could the snowy beauty of the Spanish Peaks. On a clear day, Mt. Baldy in New Mexico fractured the horizon with its stately, though simple, form. Sharon told Perry that they would build a magnificent home, the finest in the county, right there on a tree-studded spot along Cougar Ridge. Perry, as always, agreed.

For the dawn of a new decade, the mountains would be a good place to live. Sharon cajoled and begged. She used everything in her considerable arsenal of feminine skills. In 1980, the family had grown to include an infant daughter Sharon named Misty.

The mountains would be the perfect place to raise the perfect family.

The 1980s had begun with a land rush. It seemed more people were moving into Wet Canyon as the decade started than in the twenty years prior. While it was true the region was still sparsely populated, more folks were showing up. For old-timers there were new neighbors; for the new people there was an unspoiled beauty that they hoped their numbers wouldn't eradicate. Ray and Candis Thornton were among the newcomers to the Canyon. By late spring of 1980, the real-estate developer and his kindergarten-teacher wife, were living in a log cabin, staking out a meadow that would be the site of their new ranch home.

One afternoon a Champion motor home pulled off to the side of the road. Both Ray, 38, and Candis, 35, had seen the rig before. The owners had bought a sizable tract of land not far from their place.

The wife carried an infant daughter while a little boy shadowed his father into the grassy expanse of the field. They introduced themselves as the Nelsons. They were living in the motor home until their house was completed.

"I instantly liked Dr. Nelson," Ray later said. "But I didn't like her. She was wearing extremely short shorts. She seemed loud, a little mouthy as she talked about her plans for her house."

As the time passed and Ray and Candis Thornton got to know their neighbors better, they marveled over what it had been that brought the two of them together.

"Dr. Nelson was a real likable guy," Ray said. "We often wondered how he could get involved with someone like Sherry. Their personalities were so different. Perry Nelson was a real professional type person. She was not. Not at all."

The Weston store owner was another who would never forget Sharon Nelson during those early days. She was a friendly woman with a comment for everyone. Whenever she came in with her husband, she made sure everyone knew how much in love they were.

"Whenever I saw them they were lovey-dovey," the store owner recalled. "She was hugging him and kissing him. That was Sharon."

For some, an inspiration for a dream house is torn from the glossy pages of shelter magazines or culled from the cherished memories of their travels. That's how Tudor homes get built in Boise and how adobe-style homes find their way to Virginia. More bad ideas are built from dreams than good ones. Sharon Nelson had tired of living in the little houses built by someone else; she wanted her own place. She wanted it to be big, grandiose, one of a kind.

Just like she saw herself.

The focal point was a six-sided great room that soared to a cathedral ceiling; a freestanding, double-flue fireplace would be put in place to provide warmth and ambiance. A wraparound deck, eight feet wide by 120 feet long, would provide all the outdoor living space anyone could ever desire. The master bedroom, also with a cathedral ceiling and outside entrance, was enormous at sixteen feet by twenty-eight feet. If the kitchen and the children's bedrooms were less grand and seemed almost incidental, the house only reflected the priorities of its designer. This was a love nest and a place to show the world what she had. The fact water had to be hauled from a neighbor's well only confirmed it. Who needs water when you have love?

Sharon even gave the place a name. And why not? Tara, the Biltmore, San Simeon . . . all were homes so distinctive, so important that they had been dubbed with a nickname. Sharon called her creation Round House.

Some considered such the house "Doctor's Folly," built in a place without running water and phone lines for a woman few trusted. Others reflected on the woman who had been replaced.

Blanche Wheeler for one felt a twinge of sorrow for Julie Nelson. The house her ex-husband had been building for his home-wrecker of a new wife was, by all indications, a showplace.

"Poor Julie," she told her husband Karl one evening. "She waited five years to get her kitchen remodeled and Sherry gets everything she wants all at once."

The Robinson name was synonymous with Wet Canyon and had been for generations. Albert Robinson was the third generation of his clan to run the sawmill four miles up the canyon. Al and his wife, Melanie, made their home in a red-brick home—added on to as children were born—next to the mill. Tiny frame houses dot the edge of the right-of-way across from the mill: homes of millworkers.

In his sixties, Al was as tall, lanky and determined as he had been in his youth. He was the type of man who refused to ask his workers to do something he wouldn't do himself. Melanie Robinson ran their home with military precision. The cupboards were always stocked. Melanie didn't want Al to make the drive to Trinidad in snowy conditions because she had let the larder run low.

Al didn't like Sharon Nelson, from the first time he laid his eyes upon her.

Perry and Sharon had stopped by the Robinson place to talk about supplies for their new house. Perry had been driving; Sharon was asleep in one of the bunks of the motor home.

Just as Perry reached out to shake Al's hands, a loud voice came from the motor home. It was Sharon.

"You son of a bitch!" she yelled. "You let those damn flies in there and woke me up!"

"I didn't mean to," Perry said, obviously embarrassed by the outburst.

Al Robinson said nothing, but he knew right then and there that he didn't care much for Sher Nelson, his new neighbor.

Many years later, the old man remembered how he felt about his first encounter with Sharon.

"Here was this guy—a helluva nice man—busting his butt to build this woman an expensive home in the mountains, and she was treating him like that."

The passage of time did little to lessen Ray Thornton's distaste for Sharon Nelson. When Sharon invited the Thorntons for dinner, Ray balked. He couldn't stomach the idea of mealtime with that sleazy woman. Candis, on the other hand, wanted to go.

"But you'll be able to talk with Perry. You like Perry," she said, reminding Ray invitations don't come every day in the mountains. There were few neighbors, and many of those were hermit-types.

Ray finally agreed.

"Guess we better go," he said.

Candis was awestruck by the spread Sharon set out on her beautiful dining table. Linens, crystal, china; it was as beautiful as anything Candis had seen in one of those women's magazines that tell ladies that they can do it, too! The meal itself was superb. Sharon was a fantastic cook, even Ray had to admit that.

Sharon told the Thorntons about how pleased they were with Weston, how they had come to the mountains to start over.

"This is a new beginning for us," she said.

As the meal was finished, little Danny Nelson emerged from the back bedroom carrying a photograph.

The boy, almost three, chattered excitedly as he brought the photograph to Candis.

"This is when I got borned," he said.

Candis looked down and froze her facial muscles in what she hoped was not too alarming a manner. It was photo of Sharon, legs spread wide, pushing her son from her womb. The image startled Candis. It wasn't that she didn't think the birth process wasn't beautiful; it was just such an explicit picture of her hostess. She thought the photo should be a private, family memento.

"Very nice, honey," she said.

After dinner, the Thorntons left with an eyeful. The doctor and his wife were a couple of those liberal types that probably fit in better in the city than out there in Weston.

In time, everyone would see those photos. Sharon, it seemed, was proud of her body. She never let an opportunity pass in which she didn't comment on it. When friends from out of town came, Sharon showed the photos Perry had taken of her when she was pregnant. The shots showed her as she stood in the doorway, her belly enormous, her breasts full as honeydew melons.

Another time, when the subject of a doctor's visit came up, Sharon again turned the subject into a self-compliment on her fantastic body.

"I disrobed and the doctor took one look at me and said, 'Why, Sharon, you don't have a tan line!'

" 'No, doctor, I sunbathe in the nude.'

" 'Just beautiful,' he says."

Sharon was the kind of woman who could say anything. At times, it seemed as though she lacked the ability to censor herself. Even with her husband in the next room, she'd go on about local men she found particularly attractive. Men she thought might make good lovers.

She wasn't too off-color. She wasn't too descriptive. But there was no doubt she was interested.

She said of one neighbor that "he could eat crackers and put his boots under my bed anytime."

Another time, word got around the canyon that Perry and Sharon had another couple over and played strip poker. By the end of the night, no one had on a stitch.

And if something happened, Sharon never said one way or another. She'd simply laugh it off . . . and make folks think that something did.

Even though she had begun to see her husband's point of view when it came to Sharon Nelson, Candis Thornton continued to enjoy a casual friendship with the neighbor from the mountaintop. Yet the more she got to know her, the more she found disconcerting. Sharon seemed to have no shame, no understanding of propriety.

While the two women visited over iced tea at Candis' place, Sharon told her the story of how she snagged Perry.

"You know, I was married to a minister before Perry," she said.

Candis admitted she had heard something about that.

"Well, we had been transferred out to Rocky Ford from North Carolina. Candis, it was a bad marriage. Very bad. I was very unhappy with Mike. He didn't treat me right at all."

The schoolteacher nodded, sipping her drink, wide-eyed while her neighbor described her soap-opera life.

"You know, my husband had records on all the members of church, how much money they had, what they owned and whatnot. I just helped myself to the records. Looking through the tithes I found Perry's name. He had daughters in private school, he had an airplane, a nice house. Best of all, he was a doctor."

Candis hung on each word, but instead of being entertained by the story of the beginning of Sharon's pursuit of Dr. Nelson, she became uneasy.

It seems kind of calculated, she thought.

"I went after him. Based on the records, I decided I would have Perry Nelson. I set my sights on him. And I got him."

When Candis told her husband about the conversation, Ray Thornton wasn't surprised by Sharon's confession. Perry Nelson wasn't the first man to be snagged by a determined woman. He could easily imagine Sharon scouring the church books in pursuit of the man with the most money. She had a lust for money and material things—anyone who spent ten minutes with her could see that. The Thorntons knew Sharon was the type of woman who could use her charms to get what she wanted. All of her charms, they figured, involved sex.

Sharon had a lovely singing voice. People who heard her sing often remarked that she could perform professionally. Others thought her voice was a gift from God, and as such, belonged in the venue of a church. It was only after time passed and folks got to know Sharon that such comments were made with less frequency.

Though to the outside world it appeared they had everything stashed up at Round House, one thing was absent. Sharon had longed for a piano so that she could practice songs for the occasional wedding and for the community church she and Perry sometimes attended after the Seventh-Day Adventist leaders in Trinidad told them they were no longer welcome. One day, a Weston neighbor invited Sharon to practice on her old upright piano.

Another local woman remembered the story of an incident resulting from one of Sharon's practice sessions. It involved Sharon's interest in the neighbor's husband.

"The first Saturday Sharon showed up she was wearing slacks and a sensible top. The next Saturday she had on short-shorts. The next time, the lady told Sharon that she had to go out of town, but Sharon could practice anyway. When she got there the woman's husband was sitting on the front porch reading the paper. Sharon was wearing short-shorts and a revealing blouse. When the lady left the house, she had a funny feeling and she decided to come back. There was no husband on the porch. No Sharon at the piano. She found the two of them on the couch all over each other. The lady picked up a broom and beat Sharon top to bottom all the way out of the house. Later, I heard Perry asked her how she got those bruises. Sharon said she fell down."

During a trip to look over some Colorado real estate, and to visit with old optometry school buddy Perry Nelson, Bob and Donna Goodhead from Oklahoma City tried to adjust to the new wife. Donna was very uncomfortable around Sharon. Everything Perry's second wife did and said seemed to relate to sex.

"I could really be happy with you, Bob," Sharon said in her innuendo-dipped way of speaking.

Mike took it as an innocent comment, a compliment that Perry's wife thought he was a good-hearted man.

Donna Goodhead didn't take it that way.

"She really wants you in bed," she told her husband later when they were alone.

"She didn't mean that at all. You have to be kidding. That's Perry's wife you're talking about."

Donna felt like laughing out loud.

"Boy, are you naive. That woman has eyes for any ball-bearing mammal that walks the earth. Let's get realistic, Bob. The woman has no shame."

BOOK II:
Doctor's Wife

"The reason Perry stayed with her was purely sexual. Sharon gave everyone the impression she was a real hot number. She was one of those little tarts with a round ass and large bust that comes around in short-shorts that show her crack. But there was something lurking beneath the surface with Sharon. You wanted to be real careful around her."
—Terry Mitchell, Trinidad chiropractor

"Everyone, lock up your husbands! Sharon's coming around."
—Medical-office assistant

"She led Perry around by the penis."
—Donna Goodhead, friend of Dr. Nelson's

10

IT WAS A SNOWY MONDAY MORNING, NOVEMBER 20, 1988. Icy air swirled over the roadways, filling ditches with white powder and forcing even the most seasoned mountain driver to take it a bit slower around the curves. Bundled-up kids pulled clothing tight to their bodies as they puffed "smoke rings" of hot breath while waiting for the bus to round the bend and take them to the warmth of a classroom. Snow splattered and drifted from Weston to Trinidad like seven-minute frosting flung off the ends of beaters by a sloppy cook.

It was as cold as a merry widow's heart.

Sharon Nelson drank cup after cup of tepid coffee and smoked cigarette after cigarette, her ashtray resembling a stinking scrub brush of yellowed butts, ends dipped in the red of a lipstick. As she sat with her grown daughter, Rochelle Mason, in her Trinidad home, Sharon agonized over the horrific events of the night before. The terrible news relayed by her heartsick mother-in-law, the police interrogation, her distraught young children, all of it seemed to hit Sharon quite hard. Her face was puffy and pale, and she jumped to her feet several times to run to the bathroom.

Nineteen-year-old Rochelle expected her mother to be broken up over Glen Harrelson's death, but she had not expected such an extreme reaction. She could understand such a response if her mother had been married to Glen for fifteen years—but the two had been man and wife for less than one. Sharon's oldest daughter tried to put whatever it was that was eating at her out of her mind. People grieve in their own way. No two survivors of a tragic loss acts the same. No one knows how a broken heart feels, unless, Rochelle knew, it is their own.

Thornton police detectives Glen Trainor and Elaine Tygart fueled themselves with coffee as they waited for the woman to come down off the mountain. They did not know Sharon Fuller Nelson Harrelson had gone to her daughter's home in town in preparation for her interview. Neither did they know what would happen when she arrived or if she would have a change of heart and change her mind about coming at all. At least this time, they'd be in control of the environment. At the mountain house, Sharon was in her own element, able to get up and move freely about whenever the questions became too "painful" or too uncomfortable. She could go to the counter for more coffee. She could check on her children. She could leave for the bathroom. At the sheriff's department, she'd be a visitor, not a hostess.

Accompanied by Rochelle, Danny and Misty, Sharon arrived right on time, around 10 A.M.

She wore a sweater and honey-dipped-tight jeans with high-heeled boots balancing lovely legs that gave her the tottering gait of deer on cobblestones. She wore little makeup and had fluffed up the wiry curls that came from her head like a Barbie doll with a ten-year-old girl's curling iron makeover. In the harsh fluorescent light of a police station, Sharon was less attractive than she had been the night before.

Anyone who reads fashion magazines targeted at American women like Sharon knew: The warm light of an incandescent bulb is a tonic for middle-aged skin. *Fluorescents show every wrinkle, every flaw.*

Though she had willingly come to give her statement, Sharon arrived with slight bitterness. She had flirted with the idea that she would tell the cops off for subtly suggesting she might have had something to do with Glen Harrelson's tragic death. She was going to set the record straight right then and there: "Now I've lost a husband, my *second* husband . . . and what in the hell are you doing? Why don't you go look for the person?"

With the kids waiting outside the room, Sharon was motioned to a chair behind a mammoth antique oak conference table in the Trinidad Police Department, the law enforcement office on the other side of the building from the Las Animas County Sheriff.

The widow sat at an angle, her back to the door, her legs crossed. She was offered the seat by the open door for a reason. The detectives wanted her to maintain a sense of freedom, to think that she could come and go as she pleased. The more comfortable she was, the more she'd likely stay put and talk. Almost from the start, it was clear that though the woman had been gossiped about as a man-eater she didn't seem anything of the sort at that moment. She was sweet. Nervous. Demure. She even focused her attention on the female detective, refusing to live up to a reputation which made her out to be an insatiable flirt.

Trainor turned on the little tape recorder.

"Okay, Sharon," he said, "uh, before we get started I just, I want to let you know that you're here of your own free will, okay? You understand that you are not under arrest or anything like that?"

"I know," she said, her eyes again meeting only Elaine Tygart's.

They spent the next few minutes reviewing Sharon's personal background. She told them who her parents were; when she was born. She listed the Adventist schools she attended. She told them how she was a young bride when she married Rev. Fuller. Over the next couple of hours, the investigators simply allowed Sharon to speak. It was easy. Talk, she did.

Sometimes Sharon was blunt. Other times she was evasive. And always, she let the investigators know that she was a good woman, though she had to admit she didn't always do good things. As Tygart and Trainor tried to sort out the story of her involvement with Dr. Nelson and how it had led to the breakup of her marriage to Preacher Mike, it became obvious there was plenty between the lines that she didn't want to bring up.

They pushed her gently.

"Did you have a relationship before Perry, before you got, you guys got divorced?" Trainor asked as he continued treading a fine line on a question that might put Sharon on the defensive.

Sharon didn't bat an eye, however. "No, I was separated. Yes, yes. Um."

"What year did this, what year did you meet him?"

"Seventy-six, seventy-six."

"When were you divorced from him? From Mike?"

"Seventy-six."

"And then when were you married to Perry?"

"Seventy-seven."

"Within a year's time?"

"Seventy-seven, yeah."

As the three continued to talk, Sharon's two young children became somewhat anxious and loud. The little boy and girl wanted their mother's attention.

God, they wanted anyone's attention.

Det. Tygart stepped into the hallway and suggested to Rochelle that it might be a good idea to take Danny and Misty to her house until the interview had run its course. Though Sharon's oldest daughter seemed concerned about her mother, she readily complied. What choice did she have? The kids had been through a great shock. Taking them home would get them out of the emotional fray.

When the subject of extramarital affairs during her marriages to her second and third husbands was more directly broached, Sharon conceded she hadn't been perfect. But she wasn't a cheat, either.

Yet once more she failed to mention Gary Adams.

Det. Trainor leaned closer and fixed his gaze on the woman with the hopelessly crumpled Kleenex. He did not bark out his questions, but he was firm.

"I asked you this once last night, and I'm gonna ask you again, just to put it on tape. As far as you know, did Glen have any extramarital affairs?"

"No."

"What about yourself?"

"No," she said unflinchingly.

"Is there anyone that could, that other people might have misconstrued a relationship going on with either you or Glen?" Tygart asked.

Again she answered in the negative.

"Someone that would appear to be extra friendly, or just a little more fond than normal?"

Sharon's resolve stayed intact. Her arms tightly across her breasts, she shook her head.

"No."

Outside of son-in-law Bart Mason, Sharon continued, there

was no one who helped out with chores or house maintenance while Glen was gone during the week. Sharon did admit, however, that she did have male visitors up at the house.

She named a man who had come up to see her from time to time, but once again, it was not Gary Adams.

"Did your relationship ever go beyond just a . . . a friendship?" the detective asked, again treading so gently.

Sharon hesitated, hunting for an answer. She said she had strayed only once. A fling took place when she came back to the mountains after breaking up with Glen, but that was *before* their marriage. She also mentioned a brief love affair with a man named Harry Russell, but that happened *after* Perry had died and *before* she met Glen.

Still, no mention of Gary Starr Adams.

Even though she could have ended the interview there, her soiled virtue still intact, she continued to talk. As she spoke, she became visibly upset. Nearly two hours had elapsed and with each minute, the woman with the two dead husbands slowly began to tighten up.

"Sharon, there's something you're not saying. I've been listening to you talk and I don't know the reasons, but you're not telling us the truth."

Sharon feigned shock.

"What do you mean?" she asked.

"Sharon, you've got to tell us the truth."

Trainor patted Sharon's arm. It was a gesture meant to comfort her and continue the interview.

"And the most important thing in your life now is finding out who killed Glen Harrelson. Okay? Sharon, you're covering up for someone, okay? You don't need to be a part of that. You didn't kill your husband."

"No, I didn't."

"But you know who did. You absolutely do. You don't need the kind of trouble that can cause you. And it's just—and it's going to prey on your mind and it's going to get worse and worse and for your children's sake so that they can get on with their lives and so that you can get on with your life, you need to tell us everything you know. You're not doing that."

Like a skewered water balloon, tears flooded down her face.

She kept her head down, her hands clutching a tissue to her eyes. And she sobbed and sobbed, muttering something about knowing what happened and how she had not been a part of any of it. She had been a victim, too.

"What can you tell us, Sharon?" Tygart asked.

She didn't respond. Glen Trainor continued to push, telling her that it was time for her to get on with her life.

"Were the kids getting in the way?"

Sharon didn't answer, so Tygart asked once more. "In your relationship with Glen?"

Finally, Sharon said no. She said she and Glen were happy. His mother, his coworkers could vouch for that.

Det. Trainor pushed once more. "Look, Sharon, I've been looking at you and you've been doing this for a real long time and you're a troubled woman."

"Yes, I am."

"You're absolutely about to fall apart at the seams and I know why. What happened up there wasn't supposed to happen that way. And I don't know what happened, okay? And that's what we're trying to find out."

"It's not gonna go away. It's not gonna change, only for the worst."

"Sharon, tell us what you know. Look, it's obvious you're scared of something. We'll protect you. We'll put you in a hotel room and guard you if necessary. Tell us what you know."

She regained her faltering composure and nodded.

"I will, but not here. These walls have ears."

"Then we'll go."

"I want my kids."

"We'll go get them from your daughter's place."

No one said another word. Not to the sheriff's department or to each other. They simply picked up their belongings and left. Glen Trainor had it in his mind that by acquiescing to her requests, they'd be able to maintain her trust and learn whatever it was that she was holding inside. Beyond picking up Danny and Misty, the Thornton detectives knew nothing about what they would do next or where they would take Sharon, the lady of the canyon with two dead husbands.

Once again, Glen Trainor and Elaine Tygart were driving

around Trinidad with no idea where they were going. After the cops stopped to pick up her squirming kids, Danny and Misty, Sharon instructed them to get on the highway and drive.

No one said much. Sharon and her children huddled in the backseat, making small talk and chatting about nothing of consequence. The detective drove north on I-25. And they drove. Every once in awhile, the two partners exchanged looks. Again, the reputation of Trinidad had reared its questionable head.

Where are we going? Is this a setup? Trainor thought.

Both officers had their guns out and on their laps, just in case Sharon was leading them into an ambush. Her remarks at the sheriff's department had somewhat perplexed and slightly worried them. Why had she said the walls had ears? Did she mean that local cops were somehow involved in the murder of Glen Harrelson?

But why?

"What's going on, Mom?" Danny asked, interrupting the steady silence of the drive.

Sharon gently patted her son's blond head and forced a smile. "You'll see when we get there."

Glen Trainor wasn't impatient, but he didn't like the idea that they were all out on a Sunday Drive. It would, he thought, be nice to know where they were going. Finally, he met Sharon's eyes in the rearview mirror and asked.

"Are we just going to drive to Denver or are you going to want to stop? We can drive to Denver, if that's what you need to make you feel safe."

Sharon shook her head. That wasn't what she had in mind. She suggested they continue a bit further north to little Walsenberg, Colorado.

"I know of a Pizza Hut where we can talk privately," she said.

Pizza Hut. The venue seemed ideal. What could be more cozy and safe than a pizza restaurant? It was the ideal locale for Sharon Harrelson to spill the rest of her story. Whatever it was that she was going to say. It was the place she wanted to go to sort out what had happened and how none of it was her fault. Not really.

The cops drove on.

11

FOR ALL SHE HAD BEEN THROUGH, SHARON
Nelson stayed steadfast in one regard: She didn't give a hoot
what anyone thought or said about her. Everything was someone else's problem. *So what? None of their beeswax.* She left
the minister. She dumped the doctor. *BFD.* She could have slept
with half the high school football team and not batted an eye.
But she didn't do that. Instead, as her marriage to Perry crumbled, Sharon took up with a man named Buzz Reynolds and
moved into his house on a gorgeous spread of Colorado ranch
land. So what if she left her husband and shacked up with Buzz?
She didn't care who knew about it. Sharon was living her life as
if her actions had no effect on anyone. She was a woman unfet-
tered by convention. She was no longer the Stepford Wife that
she had felt was her destiny. She told friends she wanted a divorce. As if to rub salt in Perry Nelson's considerable and gap-
ing wounds, Sharon had added the betrayal of a decade-old
friendship to the mix. Buzz Reynolds, a self-made rancher with
vast holdings, was one of Perry Nelson's best friends. Buzz
Reynolds was a friendly man with a kind word for everyone, not
a home-wrecker, not a Don Juan. Ten years older than Sharon,
Buzz was more pleasant-looking than handsome, and, like
Perry Nelson, he was ripe for the picking.

Buzz had money.

Folks around town wondered if Sharon Nelson could have
found it within herself to exercise a bit more discretion by
dropping her skirt for a man her husband didn't know so well.

Did the men who fell for Sharon's charms take stupid pills, or what?

One morning not long after she left Perry and their kids for money and madness with Buzz, Sharon arrived at the Trinidad optometry office to pick up a check for hours she had supposedly worked at the clinic. When she asked to see her estranged husband, Barb told her to wait a minute.

"He's busy with a patient," she said.

A little later, the patient gone, Sharon and Perry got into a heated argument over money, their marriage and Sharon's wandering ways. Barb could hear the two of them scream at each other. She expected everyone else in the building could, too.

A few minutes later, Sharon stomped out of the back office and went over to Barb.

"I'll tell you what. If that son of a bitch doesn't give me a divorce, I'll blow his fucking head off. I'll kill him."

Barb tried to calm her by making a joke of the remark.

"Oh yeah?" she kidded. "What would you do with the body?"

Sharon didn't laugh.

"I'll stick it in the freezer. Nobody will find him there."

And so the war went. Sharon would say this. Perry would do that. Bless his heart, Barb thought, the man was no match for his bitch-on-wheels wife. If they didn't have the two kids, Dr. Nelson would have been a smart man to just let her go. But, of course, that was not an option. Perry was mad, but against all reason, he was still in love.

One afternoon, Barb rolled her eyes as she handed Dr. Nelson the telephone. It was another Sharon sneak attack. A Trinidad grocer was on the line asking for payment of $150 worth of groceries. Sharon, it seemed, had told the checker to bill her husband, "Dr. Perry Nelson."

An irritated Perry balked at the charge. He wasn't going to pay a dime to support Sharon while she flaunted her affair with Buzz. The woman had no scruples whatsoever. Perry had reached his limit. Sharon had traipsed all over town buying things and dropping his name like ticker tape in a parade.

"I'm not sleeping with her. Bill the guy who is," he said tersely. Though the words were meant to jab, there was something in Perry's voice that suggested the effort had been wasted. Barb could hear it: Perry still loved Sharon.

The dreaded F-word. Like most everybody else, Barbara Ruscetti had heard the word more often than she cared to. But never in almost two decades of employment had she heard Dr. Nelson utter such coarse vulgarities. When he came in the office swearing a blue streak, peppered with "F this" and "F that," she stood her ground.

"You don't use that word around me," Barb said, feeling glad that despite everything, she could still tell the doc what was on her mind. "Maybe you use it around Sharon, but you don't use it around me."

Perry shot her a classic "who me?" look.

His disinterest in her feelings irritated Barb even more.

"Just knock it off," she said, brushing the wisps of her cinnamon-bun hairdo from her reddened face.

"Don't get your tits in an uproar," Perry said, when he finally got the message the woman he had depended on for so many years was not enjoying the new and improved Dr. Nelson.

"I will. You're not talking to me like that." Barb shot him an uncharacteristic glare. "I'm not going to stand for it."

Perry shrugged an apology, but didn't clean up his act. He had never been a saint, but Sharon's influence had dragged him down lower than a sewer line. Barb hated what she saw, but there was nothing to do about it. She was torn. She not only loved her job, she *needed* it. She could only hope that Perry would shape up. She couldn't quit. Barb Ruscetti was stuck.

"I never heard him say one bad word until Sharon. And then, I mean it was like he was full of the devil," Barb said, trying to come to terms with her beloved boss' dark transformation. "He just did a Dr. Jekyll and Mr. Hyde, you might say. He turned from good to bad."

Perry, no longer the occasional-beer Seventh-Day Adventist that he had been when he was with put-upon first wife Julie, took to the bottle as his fortunes and personal life began to snowball into the biggest mess in southern Colorado. Who could blame him? His new wife—the cause of his ruin in the eyes of so many—had left him for his good friend, Buzz

Reynolds. Yet many were left to wonder: What had he expected when he married Sharon? Did he really think that she would be true to him? Or he to her, for that matter?

The doctor sought solace from the bottle.

One time Barb pulled Dr. Nelson aside when she detected the boozy odor coating the slurred words of his speech.

"Perry," she said, calmly masking her horror, but being as direct as she could be, "you can't come in here like this. Patients won't like it. They can smell it, too."

He shrugged and turned away.

As the optometry business continued to fall off, Barb's paychecks were often delayed. With only the Trinidad office open, Perry had expected patients from Rocky Ford to make the trip to town to see him. They didn't. One week Barb collected only $14 in receipts. There had been no glasses to dispense. No exams to give. No nothing. People just didn't want a thing to do with the Nelsons. Sharon once insisted that if Perry's office offered Visa and Mastercard as a billing option, more customers would come.

But, of course, plastic money made no difference. The problem had never been with Dr. Nelson's patients and their pocketbooks.

Mixed in with the anger and bitterness, Barb couldn't help but feel a measure of sorrow for her employer. She frequently overheard Dr. Nelson talking with his banker as he sought to delay loan payments. The figures were staggering to the woman who put her children through school on crocheted booties and a small salary. Dr. Nelson owed $120,000 on the mountain house. The IRS was due more than $100,000; the State of Colorado, $80,000 in back taxes and penalties. Various lens labs around the country were due between $5,000 and $10,000 apiece.

Perry Nelson was in so deep he needed a snorkel to breathe.

One morning, not long before his Bronco was about to be repossessed by the dealership because he could no longer keep up on the payments, the doctor came into the office looking disheveled and wan.

Barb met him at the door. "What's the matter, Doctor?"

"Oh, Barb," he said quietly, "I'm going to end it all."

"You don't mean that, do you? You remember what my grandmother would say."

The comment brought a smile to his haggard face. Barb Ruscetti was always talking about the advice her grandmother had doled out.

"What's that?"

"You die, Perry, you go straight to hell."

Perry let out a weak laugh. "I'm going there anyway," he said.

The rest of the morning Barb kept her eye on him. He wasn't stable and she was worried. At lunch, she closed the office and went to see a friend of Perry's. She told the man that she thought Perry might be considering suicide. The friend said he'd go see his pal as soon as he finished his work.

"No," she said somewhat desperately, "you ought to go now."

The friend found Perry Nelson in his Bronco with a loaded revolver. Tears had striped shiny tracks down his face and his hands trembled.

But he had not pulled the trigger.

"Perry, you gotta hang in there. Things will get better. They really will," the friend said. "I promise. Things will get better."

Though the kind words seemed to calm the eye doctor and avert tragedy, the friend was dead wrong.

Things would never get better.

It was the kind of Christmas surprise no husband wanted. Perry Nelson looked shell-shocked. Sharon had hit him with an announcement that sent him deeper into the bottle. He had invited her up to the mountain house for Christmas with Misty and Danny, some gifts, some dinner, and if he was lucky enough, a chance at a reconciliation. Sharon, however, had another agenda. She told him that she couldn't come back to him. She was carrying Buzz Reynolds' baby.

She cried how it was not her fault. Cross her heart and hope to die, it was an accident.

Perry called his estranged wife every name in the book. He told her she was a whore and a slut and if she wanted to have

Buzz's baby so damn bad, she ought to get a divorce and get on with it. If she ever wanted to come back into his life, she'd better get an abortion.

"I'm not raising no one else's child!" he yelled.

A couple of days later at the office, Dr. Nelson was in another of his fit-to-be-tied moods. He didn't have a nice word for anyone. He had three pairs of glasses that needed to be repaired, and instead of working on them himself, he threw them in a tangled mass on Barb Ruscetti's desk. His abruptness startled her. She looked up from her work.

"You send these out to get fixed," he said loudly.

Barb studied the glasses. "Whose are they?" she asked.

The doctor's face went red. Barb could see the thermometer that was his anger threshold rise twenty degrees.

"You don't have to know whose they are. I just said for you to send them in and fix the damn things."

Barb stood up, her tiny stature dwarfed by Perry's six-foot-plus frame. "Pardon me for breathing," she snapped at his back as he retreated to a back room.

Dr. Nelson's attack was so out of character; even when he'd been boozing at the tavern, he wasn't a mean drunk.

She asked what was wrong.

Again, Dr. Nelson's tone was off-putting. He was loud and harsh as he spat out his words. "Just don't bother me. Just leave me alone. Don't even talk to me!"

Barb backed off. A couple of hours later, the optometrist slumped himself onto the lobby couch. It was time to talk.

"What in the hell is eating you?" she finally asked. "What did I do for you to holler at me like that?"

Perry Nelson buried his handsome, salt-and-pepper bearded face into the palms of his big hands and started to cry. Barb reached over to him, feeling sick to her stomach that her words had set him off.

"Barb," he said, "tell me something. How would you feel if you found out that your wife was sleeping with your best friend and she was pregnant?"

His words knocked the wind out her.

"Who?" she asked.

"Sharon's pregnant by Buzz."

"You're kidding," she said, feeling her words fall flat.

Perry didn't care. He'd said the same thing to Sharon that morning when she dropped the bomb.

"No lie, Barb, you could have knocked me over with a feather."

He told Barb he'd thrown the rest of Sharon's clothes out on the porch that morning and told her never to come back.

"What is she going to do?" Barb asked.

"I really don't care," he said.

After the Christmas holidays, Sharon begged Perry to let her come back home to the mountains. Things had not gone as well with Buzz as she had hoped. In fact, when she told her rancher/lover she was pregnant, he booted her right out the door. Sharon whined how well-to-do Buzz Reynolds didn't love her. *Poor Sher.* Her oldest two children were living in the Midwest with their minister father; her two youngest in Round House with their father. Perry had told his round-heeled wife to get lost. Sharon had no money. No one liked her. She hit rock bottom and moved into a seedy apartment in Rocky Ford.

"The rent's around ninety dollars a month," Perry told Barb one afternoon when he gave her the latest Sharon Nelson Update.

"What kind of place does she have that only costs ninety dollars a month?"

Perry made a face that slipped into a slight smile. "It isn't in a very good part of town."

"I didn't know Rocky Ford was big enough to have a bad part of town," Barb said.

The doctor nodded. "Oh, yeah, it's not very nice."

Those who remained close to Dr. Nelson knew that when he said he didn't give a hoot about daughter Lorri's wedding, he was the biggest liar in the Rocky Mountain State. His youngest daughter by Julie had been nothing but trouble and just because she had gotten herself pregnant was no reason to break out the brass band and dance at her wedding. Though he seemed adamant in his refusal to go to Montana, most suspected another person was the real reason. Sharon had never made a secret of her disgust with Lorri since the incident at the Adventist academy in Loveland:

"She's no good. She's got no respect for anybody!"

Barb Ruscetti couldn't believe Perry was in his right mind when he said he wouldn't attend the wedding.

"This can bring you back together," Barb insisted. "If you don't go, you'll regret it the rest of your life."

Perry was nearly moved to tears when he finally agreed to go. His life had been full of regrets. He had given up so much . . . but despite the brainwashing by his knocked-up-by-his-former-best-friend estranged wife, he still loved his "favorite youngest" daughter. He took almost four-year-old Danny, leaving Misty with Sharon and he drove north to Montana. It was a Rocky Mountain soap opera in southeastern Colorado and he was glad to get away. His relief was short-lived. When he arrived in Billings, he was stomping-feet mad at himself—he had lost his wallet and $500 at a rest stop on the way.

The reunion between father and daughter exceeded both their expectations. As the two got reacquainted, it was evident to Lorri that her father was still deeply troubled by his shattered second marriage. He still loved Sher, he said, but he could no longer look the other way and forgive her. As Lorri probed, her father told her about Sharon's pregnancy by old pal Buzz Reynolds.

"It's over," Perry said bitterly. "This time, I swear to God it's over for good. I kicked her out and I want nothing, nothing to do with her ever again."

As he walked Lorri down the aisle on February 21, 1982, in one of those godawful rented taupe tuxes, Perry Nelson smiled warmly and proudly. And while the moment could not have been happier for the pretty young bride, she saw something in her dad that she had never seen before: sadness in his eyes.

Judy Douglas had always been pro-choice when it came to abortion and a woman's right to take responsibility for her body. Yet in Judy's estimation, her younger sister's repeated abortions made Sharon the poster girl for forces seeking to restrict the procedure. Sharon had terminated at least five pregnancies that her sister knew about, maybe more during the years when the sisters were estranged.

"She used to stop by on her way to Denver, on her way to get an abortion. It was very casual for Sharon," Judy recalled several years later.

At the time of Sharon's pregnancies from her myriad Colorado lovers, Judy knew better than trying to convince her birth control might be a good idea, given her history of promiscuity and obvious fertility. Sharon *wanted* to get pregnant.

"She had some strange romantic idea about pregnancy and her affairs. I never understood it. I never will."

Sharon's attitude about her abortion repulsed Barb Ruscetti when Sharon told her about it back in Trinidad. She was so perfunctory about it. It was nothing at all. *An inconvenience.* Sharon told Barb that she was almost five months pregnant when she aborted Buzz's baby up in a Denver clinic. She confided to Barb that she told the doctors the baby's father had serious heart trouble.

As Sharon rambled on, Barb could feel her pulse quicken.

Oh, my God. People would die to have a baby and look what she did.

Springtime in the Rockies is the kind of magnificent season that inspires weekend painters to bring their easels alongside creek beds flanked by mountains still dipped in white. Green shoots bust through the crust of crunchy snow, reminding observers winter finally has been shoved aside by the forces of a sweeter-tempered Mother Nature. Colorado springtimes are times for renewal.

Sharon Nelson bought into that; at least, to many who knew her, it seemed that she did. After unleashing every ugly word she could conjure, about everything from their sex life to his table manners to his undershorts, she finally took a breather and stopped bad-mouthing Perry. After seven months of sleeping with her estranged husband's supposed best pal, Sharon set her sights on returning to her beloved Round House. She told friends she had tired of Buzz Reynolds, of living off and on in the fleabag apartment in Rocky Ford. No one knew how she did it, but somehow Sharon charmed her way back into

Perry Nelson's good graces. Whatever it was that she did to win men over, it had to be pretty good. Dr. Nelson acted as though he had never stopped loving her. It was as if she had been on a vacation or out of town nursing a sick relative back to health. The pregnancy, the betrayal, the bile-coated words had never taken place.

Outwardly the doctor was all smiles.

Sharon's return to Perry, however, only brought additional heartache to the doctor's daughters and friends. All they had seen when Sharon first entered Perry's life was the ruin of everything he had built, everything the man had stood for. No one, not even his daughters, considered the man a saint, but they knew him to be caring, honest and trustworthy. All of that had changed when Sharon Fuller came into his life. God, they hoped, *they prayed*, the woman would be gone for good. In time, the man would come around. In time, Sharon's spell would fade. In time, Perry would stop drinking, stop smoking, stop carrying on like some lust-crazed teenager whose zipper was forever stuck open.

The prayers went unanswered. Sharon made her move toward reconciliation with her husband on their son's fourth birthday, the first week in March of 1982.

When her father answered the phone he put up a brave front, but Lorri could tell something was wrong.

"Dad, what is it?" she asked.

"Guess you'll find out," he said cautiously, as if confessing to a capital crime. "Sharon and I are working things out. We're getting back together. The divorce is being called off."

Lorri could barely believe her ears. She had rejoiced a dozen times since her wedding that Sharon was now another man's problem, had been so sure Sharon was gone for good.

"Dad, she got pregnant by another man! By *your* friend!"

Perry explained all of it had already been handled. He'd paid for an abortion and Sharon's pregnancy was no longer an issue.

"She's the mother of my children, Lorelco. I let one family slip away. I'm not about to make the same mistake twice."

Lorri tried to get him to see the light as he had so clearly demonstrated at her wedding when he said he was through with Sharon, but there was no arguing with him over the phone. Lorri pressed the point as hard as she could without angering her father. She didn't want to risk another separation over Sharon.

"I love her," he said, almost sadly, before saying good-bye.

Lorri hung up the phone in shock. She slumped her numb body into a kitchen chair while reason ran a merry-go-round in her head.

Why, Dad? Why are you going back to her? What makes you so blind to what other so clearly see—what you had seen yourself? she thought.

Not long after the Nelsons reunited, Sharon accompanied Perry back to Cedar Lake, Michigan, to help celebrate his parents' fiftieth wedding anniversary. And though Perry told friends he was happy that things had worked out, Sharon was not so happy. She complained bitterly that Perry only wanted her back in his life "to be his maid." He didn't love her, Sharon raged, he only wanted to use her.

Funny thing, up and down the spring thaw–swollen canyons others were saying the same thing about *her*. Some scratched their heads at the motivation of the doctor's reconciliation with his wife.

"Don't underestimate the power of pussy," one wise old-timer remarked. "Nothing on this earth can compete."

Sharon Fuller Nelson understood the power better than any-one and as the warmth of the Colorado spring moved to the scorching heat of the summer, she put her secret weapon to good and frequent work.

There was a method to her madness.

For Candis Thornton, being friendly with Sharon Nelson was both easy and hard. It was easy, because Sharon could be so much fun. She was quick with a quip, always up for doing something with a group, eager to fit in. No matter what was said about her, there were times when she was easy to like. During the time when Sharon had left Perry, the two saw each other infrequently. But when Sharon came back into her es-tranged husband's life, she seemed to try to foist herself back on the people of Weston. She wanted to be a part of the community. She seemed to crave the connection between herself and the others of Weston. Sadly—at least, for her—she didn't really fit in.

There were times when the doctor's wife and the school-teacher would get together and Sharon would say something downright disturbing.

When a group of Canyon neighbors had a get-together that included a hayride, Sharon and Candis had the occasion to spend one trip alone.

At one point, Sharon stared at Candis. Her eyes were fixed and her expression seemed serious.

"What is it?" Candis asked.

"I envy you," Sharon said.

Candis was surprised by the remark. How could Sharon Nelson, the woman who had a wealthy doctor for a husband, two beautiful children, a mountain top house with a six-sided great room soaring to a cathedral ceiling, envy *her*? She wondered what it was that she had that Sharon could possibly want.

It turned out it was something Candis *didn't* have that her neighbor had coveted.

"I wish I could be footloose and fancy-free like you and your husband," she said. "No children. No one to tie you down."

Candis made some comment about how lucky Sharon was to have children. Though they were a handful, they were bright and beautiful. Her son and daughters were a wonderful blessing.

Sharon shrugged off the compliment. "I wish I never had my kids," she said.

The words shocked Candis. She didn't know what to say. *What kind of mother would say something like that?* It wasn't that she didn't want a break from her kids, like so many parents do. The way Candis took the remark, Sharon didn't want her children at all.

When Candis thought about it, she wondered how well those children really fit into their mother's life. *Maybe they were an afterthought? Maybe she didn't really have strong maternal instincts.* She hardly spoke of the children. She hardly gave them a second thought. It seemed that Sharon put great emphasis on her own personal appearance, forsaking her son's and daughter's well-being.

"She would come out looking like a New York model," Candis said later. "The kids would look all grubby and unkempt like they had come from String Town in the south."

Sharon, her back against the wall many years later, discounted Candis Thornton and her comments.

"I've always felt Candis had a real strong envy of me . . . that I had the kind of life most people dream of . . . on the outside."

The door to Round House opened and the beautiful woman smiled. It was a few weeks after the woman and her husband patched it up after a messy separation. Her long hair was pulled back, cascading against her shoulders, and though it was a dark color on that particular day, it caught the light like a blonde's. Her blouse was opened at the neck, past the first button, and the second . . . revealing breasts that were full and, Gary Starr Adams figured, meant to be seen. He knew she was a doctor's wife. He had seen her around Weston, and despite the fact that he had been the roofer on the mountain house, they had never met. He asked if he could borrow a wheelbarrow for a job he was doing along the Wet Canyon road. They talked for a few minutes. She was friendly and interested, asking questions and remarking how great it was that as the crow flew they were practically next-door neighbors. Gary, his wife Nancy and their young son lived in a mobile home at the bottom of Cougar Ridge. The Adamses also had a daughter, but she was grown and living near Denver. By the time Gary Starr Adams met up with Sharon Lynn Nelson, his place was nothing more than a ramshackle dive, added on to willy-nilly like a dozen good intentions fallen flat.

Maybe it was right then and there. Maybe it was later. Neither could be sure. But no doubt about it, there was a little bit of magic there. Little bit of fire.

12

THE HANDWRITING HAD BEEN ON THE WALL SINCE the day Sharon-the-preacher's-wife sashayed into the optometry office and set her sights on bewitching the member of the Adventist congregation with the most money. Barb Ruscetti had hoped Perry's separation from his social-climber wife had meant she also would be free of Sharon. But when the Nelsons patched things up, Barb knew her days at the office were numbered. Sharon wasn't the type that would share her man—or his office. Sharon had made it clear time and again that the business could not support two optical assistants. One of them would have to go.

So though it still broke Barb's heart, it was no real surprise when she was laid off the end of June 1982.

Perry left her a note with her final check:

> *"Barb, you know I wouldn't do this to you for nothing in all the world. You know I don't have much of a say-so in this anymore."*

After seventeen years working for Perry Nelson, Barb Ruscetti held no doubts that she was about to face a challenge that would test her. She was glad unemployment insurance would help her through the rough spots until she found a new job. A month after she made her application, however, she received a letter indicating that she was ineligible for benefits.

Unemployment taxes, the letter indicated, had not been paid by her employer for more than a year.

Barb was still fuming when she found Perry in his office.

"Tell me something," she said, waving the letter in his face. "Why haven't you paid into my unemployment for me?"

Perry was startled. "Barb, I have," he said.

"You're a damn liar! If you did, why did I get this letter?"

He studied the page and shook his head. "They don't know what they're talking about."

Barb challenged him to call the unemployment office to get it straightened out and Perry immediately went for the phone.

"Hey!" A voice cut through the office.

"What the hell is going on here?" The voice belonged to Sharon.

Perry put the receiver down and Barb spun around to answer.

"Nobody's paid into my unemployment! You took it out of my check, but you didn't pay it."

Sharon stiffened. "That's a lie!"

"You mean the unemployment office is telling us we're liars? That you did pay it?"

"Yes, I did!"

Perry dialed the unemployment number again and spoke with someone for a few minutes about the letter, about the funds. Embarrassment replaced his outrage. Barb Ruscetti's unemployment tax had not, in fact, been paid for thirteen months.

He gently set down the phone and turned to Sharon.

"Haven't you been paying into her fund?"

Sharon shrugged. She had been caught and she knew it.

"Why should I?" she retorted.

Barb felt herself lunging. She wanted to slap the smug look off her mouth. Instead, she pulled herself together and made her way toward the door.

"You bitch," she called out, hating that she had been provoked to use such language. Sharon always brought out the worst in her. She brought out the worst in everyone.

Perry ran after Barb, telling her how sorry he was for what

his wife had done. He had never meant for things to turn out that way. Barb, as angry as she had ever been in all her life, let her good sense take control once more. As she put the useless letter back into her purse, she shook her head and let out a deep sigh.

She knew the answer before she even asked the question: "Oh, Doctor, what did you get yourself into?" Barb knew the answer was the she-devil in a tube top with an attitude that the world was hers for the picking sitting back in the doctor's office, scratching her claws on a tabletop as she ranted about Barb Ruscetti as if *Barb* had been the one who'd done something wrong.

"Yeah, I know," was all the man could say. "I know."

It had been Sharon's idea. She had wanted to preside over a party in her beautiful new home for months. She had wanted to show the locals that despite all that had been said about her, they would love her. They *had* to love her. She invited about twenty friends and neighbors to a Halloween costume party. Perry was a guru in a long robe. Sharon wore a long ecru dress and a big, wide-brimmed hat that made her look like some kind of Scarlett O'Hara of the Rockies. Her accent dripped southern hospitality. She even hired Sam Bachicha, a local legend of a one-man band, to perform for the evening.

Sharon set out a beautifully frosted cake, decorated with the words *Play it Again, Sam.*

And while neighbors and friends gathered to dance under the high ceiling of Round House's living room, the hostess had her eyes on the man she had wanted from nearly the first day she saw him at her front door asking to borrow the wheelbarrow. His blue eyes called to her.

Gary Adams was the man of the hour. A man, Sharon told herself, whose time had come. Gary dressed as a mountain man, in a fringed leather shirt, leather pants, hat and a fake beard. He chatted with Perry for a while as Sharon played hostess with the mostest. A few rum and Cokes later, Sharon "borrowed" Gary from his wife, Nancy, and asked him to dance.

"Oooh," she said, her breath warm against his ear and

neck, "I love the smell of leather." As the music played, as it became more apparent that no one was paying much attention to them, Sharon pressed her breasts against Gary's chest.

"Why don't you come in the office on Thursday and get an eye exam and we'll get to know each other a little better?" she asked, her words slipping deeper into a sexy, southern accent.

Gary Adams knew Thursdays were days when Sharon left her husband at Round House with their son and daughter while she presumably did some office work. No eye exams were given on Thursdays. Even so, Gary planned to go. He was intrigued.

"At first [her advances] kind of embarrassed me. My wife's right there. My wife's dancing with a friend. They're dancing one way and Sharon and I are dancing very close. I thought maybe it was just the liquor. She'd been drinking. I'd been drinking some, too," he told a friend.

The Robinsons and the Parsons were among the group at the Halloween party. None of them would leave with any indication that there had been any romantic sparks between Sharon and Gary. Maybe it was that Sharon was discreet? Maybe it was that everyone was having too good a time to notice?

Dr. Nelson was among those who paid no mind to his wife's attentions toward the leatherclad guest. As smart as he was, when it came to his wife the eye doctor was blind. Especially when it came to other men. Men liked the doctor's wife and she knew it.

"I think she intimidated a lot of people, especially women. She was gorgeous. She could get a man. Just walking into a room men were attracted to her. They were intrigued . . . the way she carried herself. The way she walked . . ." one of Sharon's admirers later recalled.

The following Thursday, Gary Adams found Sharon sitting at her desk in tight black pants and an orange, red and white long-sleeved sweater. Her outfit covered her form without leaving anything to the imagination. She looked good. Gary smiled and said hi.

"Hello," Sharon said, looking up with a warm smile. "How you doing?"

Before he could give much of an answer, Sharon invited him to come into a back office where they could talk and "get to know each other."

Sharon closed the door and moved close.

Long after it happened, the memory of the encounter brought a smile to Gary Adams. He'd never forget what happened and how surprised he was that it had.

"I thought she was going to give me a big hug and she gave me a kiss and that's when she started really rubbing her crotch on my leg. At first her arms were around my back, and then she went down to my butt and just pulled me in tighter to her."

After a few minutes of fooling around, a patient who needed to check on eyeglasses for his wife brought an abrupt halt to the pair's passion. Sharon left for the front office to talk to the patient. In a few minutes, she returned.

"Why don't you go get a motel room?" she said.

Gary called from the Trinidad Best Western around five o'clock and gave the doctor's wife the room number. A bit annoyed, she told him that next time he should rent a room on the other side of the motel.

"Someone might see my car," she said, the voice of experience.

A few minutes later, Sharon was surprisingly talky and nervous as she tried to get comfortable in the motel room. She had been so hot-to-trot back at the doctor's office that if he had put as much effort into it as she had, they would have had sex right then and there. At the motel she looked around as if she was worried someone might see her or that Perry would find out from his friend and handy neighbor—Gary Starr Adams.

"Do you have some protection?" she asked.

Gary told her that he had a vasectomy. Sharon thought for a moment and frowned.

"I have to go to the bathroom," she said. "I got pregnant from Buzz and he said he had had a vasectomy."

When Sharon emerged she wore nothing but a black bra

and black panties. Her tan was all over. No lines. No imperfections. As far as Gary Adams could see, she was a *Playboy* centerfold minus the staple. The woman was a knockout.

Yet something was wrong. Under the covers, no matter how beautiful she was, nothing was happening. Gary's penis was a limp noodle and no amount of stimulation from Sharon could make it stand to attention. God, the woman tried. God, she gave it her all. But nothing. Zip. Gary grew more anxious. Impotence had never been a problem before. Never in his entire adult life.

"She was trying to get me aroused," he recalled later, "I just couldn't do it. Right then, it should have been a warning . . . saying my body knows more than my brain. It is not right."

The two hugged and kissed for awhile under the sheets, but it was useless. Gary said how sorry, how embarrassed he was. Sharon was nice about it. She said it didn't matter.

She even asked to see him again.

Whether he knew it at that moment or weeks later, Gary Adams could never be sure. But after that first afternoon with Sharon Nelson in the motel room, he was hooked. He was hers.

"Let me think on it," he said.

When it came to roofing or carpentry, everyone in Wet Canyon knew that Gary Adams was an expert. He was fast, dependable and affordable, and most everyone in the community had used his services, or knew that if they needed something done, he was a good man to call.

Whenever Ray Thornton looked out at the road and saw Gary Adams drive his little blue import pickup up the hill to the Nelsons' house, he figured the friendly carpenter was doing some work for the doctor and his wife. When the trips became more frequent—almost daily—Ray began to wonder. Perry was never home when Gary drove up to the house on Cougar Ridge.

After a while, it became obvious something was going on, though it brought little comment.

"We minded our own business and didn't get involved," Ray later said.

Poor Perry. The price of being the talk of the town continued to be higher than the optometrist had likely considered when he decided his lust for the minister's wife should not be bridled. As word continued to ricochet from Trinidad to Rocky Ford and back that the eye doctor had stolen the preacher's wife, even the most loyal remainder of Perry Nelson's long-time customers drifted away, canceling appointments and never calling back. Sometimes the excuses were lame, but more often than not, patients were disarmingly direct. Perry begged many to reconsider, but time and time again, patients who had once been delighted by Dr. Nelson's jokes and friendly ways would be charmed no longer.

"You don't steal a minister's wife and do business as usual in Trinidad."

Even when Perry went into a restaurant or made a visit to the store, formerly friendly folks were cool. He'd go out of his way to strike up a conversation, but many chose to turn a deaf ear.

While Perry struggled to save his professional life, his wife continued to sleep with the carpenter from the bottom of the canyon. The first few times, sleep and cuddling was all they really could do. Gary Adams still couldn't maintain an erection.

He went to the office one Thursday, not really sure why he was trying so hard to consummate an affair when, at least physically, it wasn't working right.

"I'd like to be with you," he said one day, "but I don't have any money."

"That's okay," Sharon replied, getting her purse and fishing through it for some bills. "You paid last time."

"I don't feel right about taking your money."

She handed him thirty dollars. "That's fine."

But again, under the sheets of a motel bed, nothing worked.

Sharon didn't act as though she minded much. She nuzzled with Gary and tried like an Olympian to get him aroused.

"Perry doesn't hug me or kiss me like you do. We don't have sex."

* * *

Gary Adams lost his wet noodle on a plateau above Trinidad Lake one unseasonably warm afternoon in the spring of 1983. Finally. After several attempts at intercourse with the beguiling woman of his dreams, Sharon's mountain man finally rose to the occasion. The two had spread out an Indian blanket out of view, in the midst of some of the country's most spectacular scenery, and closed their eyes to make love. They came to the lake for that singular purpose. They came for a singular reason: there were no motel fees to be paid; they could have sex for free. And it worked.

Sort of.

"I didn't please you," Gary said, rolling off of her. Even though he had finally maintained an erection, he felt like a failure. Gary was certain Sharon had not experienced an orgasm. She had not moaned, groaned or writhed in the kind of ecstasy that he had hoped she would when his mission was finally accomplished.

"Oh yes, you did," Sharon said. "Just hold me. Perry doesn't even touch me anymore."

Gary put his arms around her, and despite the fact he had done his best, he felt utter shame. He had cheated on his wife only once before. He had been a virgin when he married Nancy. He had wanted the kind of sex he had seen in pornographic movies. He'd wanted it so badly that when it finally came, and Sharon hadn't, it hurt his pride. It made him want her more.

Over time, he discovered what it took for his lover to be satisfied. He shared his information with a friend.

"A lot of times," Gary explained matter-of-factly, "she has to grab a man's dick and actually move it herself and position it and move it and rub it the way she wants it. And once I found that out, I was able to do it real easy with her. She had to be in control, I guess."

When Sharon finally climaxed she would let out a scream that Gary Adams was sure carried across the mirrored surface of the lake. She'd stiffen her body, and pull him in tightly against her torso. She was frozen as if she could hold the moment longer.

Gary also craved oral sex with Sharon.

"She tasted so good," he told a friend, "I always called it her 'special sauce'. She'd get real wet and it was almost like an addicting drug. Once I had it [oral sex] with her, I just had to have it."

Sometimes they'd arrange to meet in the timber between their homes at a place where Gary had stashed a couple of sleeping bags to make Sharon more comfortable when they made love outdoors. She was a real lady, and she needed to be treated just so. No screwing in the brush like a couple of dogs in heat.

Whenever they met, wherever they met, it was always about sex. By a lake at a ski area near Raton, at a motel in Trinidad, at Round House when Perry was gone; it was always about sex.

"Perry's getting suspicious about us," Sharon said as Gary slid down past her ample breasts. "If he catches us, he'll kill me. I swear he will."

Gary tried to allay his lover's concerns. They had been very careful. No one knew they had been sleeping together. Perry would never know for sure.

The days turned into weeks; weeks into months. The yellow deck lamp that was Sharon's signal down to the Dude Ranch that the coast was clear for a tryst flickered like a strobe light whenever struggling Perry was working late or on a trumped-up errand for his wife.

For Sharon and Gary, it was sex and promises—the kind that only leads to trouble. Some would say the subject was inevitable. Sharon wanted out of her marriage, but she didn't want to be penniless. She was entitled to the Good Life, a big juicy slab of the American Dream. The fact she was unhappy with her doctor husband had not been her fault. If he had amassed the kind of fortune she had expected, she might have felt differently. Some thought so, anyway. But as the affair with Gary increased in intensity, their talks took a darker turn. Sharon told Gary how Perry had slapped her and was abusive to the children. She even showed a bruise that she insisted Perry had left on her during one of his drunken inquisitions.

"I'm afraid of him," she said tearfully.

Gary felt sorry for Sharon. He wanted to put her up on a pedestal and protect her. Though he never thought Perry was a violent man, no one really knew what went on behind closed doors.

"Have you ever thought of him having an accident?" Gary asked after one of their trysts.

Sharon nodded. She had. She said she had thought of getting rid of Perry for years. She reached out and held Gary close. She was glad her mountain man had come to the rescue.

"He doesn't have that much insurance on him," she said, pulling Gary closer.

He kissed her, the smell of her "secret sauce" still on his mouth.

"Think about it and see what you want to do about it," he said.

In time, their lovemaking escalated to the kind of fever-pitch reckless abandon that Sharon had always said she dreamed about. Perhaps the element of danger, the thrill of the kill was part of the ecstasy. Perhaps it was merely the combination of those two particular people?

Sharon was in love with the man.

"He had a body like I'd never seen before on anyone," she said, once she tried to put into words her deep attraction for the man. "Not really muscular . . . but there was not an ounce that he didn't know how to use. For whatever he chose to use it for. I'd never had anyone in my life who accepted me so totally, in any state, any stage. I could have been working out in the garden with sweat running down my neck, dirt between my toes . . . and never detracted."

Gary Adams liked to think locals called his place at the foot of the mountain "the Dude Ranch" because in the 1930s it had been one. Fat chance. Most called it what it was: an added-to shack, the type that in a Warner Bros. cartoon would have an outhouse with a moon cut in for ventilation. But to Gary, wife Nancy, and their youngest of two, a son nicknamed Skip, it was home, sweet, home. While Gary roofed houses up and down the Canyon and earned less than twelve thousand a year, Nancy rolled up her sleeves and went to work as a waitress or cabin maid for local motels and cafes. It wasn't a particularly generous lifestyle—not like the Nelsons up the mountain. But Gary Adams didn't have any bills and he figured that work was a means to pay for food and gas. Nothing more. He didn't see the need to push himself to a better job. Things were just fine in Wet Canyon. Just fine.

A wartime baby, Gary Starr Adams was a one-year-old when his mother and carpenter father moved from Missouri to Colorado to settle in Denver. His family was small, only his parents and a brother, four years older. There was no hardship. No unstable childhood. The Adams family didn't move around much. They ate meals together. No one drank. The Adams, by all accounts, were close.

Gary was always a standout. He was handsome, bright and more than a bit stubborn. He wanted to do things his own way. When he was a junior at Jefferson High he let his hair grow just a tad longer than what school officials considered appropriate. It wasn't outlandish for 1960. It wasn't even noticeable to many, but the fact was most other boys were having their hair buzzed into flattops.

"The vice principal told me either get a haircut or don't come back . . . so I didn't come back," he once told a friend.

Instead, a few months later he joined the Marines and *they* shaved off all his hair.

In 1962, Gary married Nancy in California. His stint in the Marines as a tank mechanic over, the Adams family returned to Denver. Gary quickly followed in his father's footsteps and found work with a hammer and nails as a roofer for Arrow Roofing.

By then, Gary Adams was an average Joe. He liked hunting elk and deer. He liked tipping back a few beers, shooting the breeze with his buddies and imagining his life would go pretty much as his parents' had. And that was just fine with him. He wasn't looking for anything better.

But that was before Sharon.

Gary was a man with odd loyalties. He was able to compartmentalize his actions to keep his guilt in check. That he was screwing Perry's wife made no difference as far as the two men's friendship was concerned. When Perry Nelson needed help with a project, it was more friendship than guilt that brought Gary Adams to the eye doctor's aid. When he helped Perry pour the driveway slab for Round House, Gary was rewarded with a pair of brand-new designer sunglasses.

"Real nice," he recalled.

13

AS HIS PRACTICE GASPED FOR SURVIVAL, PERRY Nelson was in a desperate search for ways to save money. The rent on his office space in downtown Trinidad was not outlandish, but when he saw space for rent on Country Club Drive that cost less money than what he was paying, he jumped on it. The owner of the medical building was chiropractor Terry Mitchell. The space was nice, albeit smaller than what he had been used to over the years. It also needed to be remodeled and finished up, but Perry said he'd take it. The reason? The rent was a paltry $35 a month.

Dr. Mitchell liked Perry from the first day they first met to discuss the rental. He was outgoing, friendly and enthusiastic. He had plans for the office space. If he was down on his luck, he didn't complain about it much. When he consummated a deal, which culminated in the sale what was left of his Rocky Ford practice, Dr. Mitchell loaned Perry a truck to move his equipment to Trinidad.

From the beginning it was clear the Nelson finances were in shambles. Dr. Nelson was late on his rent and apologized profusely for requiring a couple of extra days to come up with what in better days would have been pocket change.

It wasn't hard to see why Nelson was in financial quicksand. Dr. Mitchell and his wife Kay, who worked in his office, could see the reasons for all the problems. It was Sharon. Sharon. Sharon.

"She got him in over his head with the house, with the cars, with everything she wanted. Perry, for some reason, kept right on going along with her. Perry was the nicest, sweetest guy in the world. He never had a bad word for anyone. What he saw in that wife of his . . . poor old Perry,'' Terry Mitchell said later.

Trinidad was a town with more than its share of country bumpkins. Guys worked hard on the ranch or in the mines four days a week, getting so drunk on the fifth day they needed a long weekend to sleep it off. Their wives got together and talked about how many kids they had, how many more they wanted and what they could get from the shopper's catalog if their men had just worked a little harder. Sharon wasn't like that. She arrived on the scene with a different attitude; different interests. She came in and showed everything she had. She was the Vargas pinup for the rough-and-tumble *Hee Haw* set.

Terry Mitchell, for one, couldn't stand her tarted-up attire and sleazier-than-thou attitude. The chiropractor scratched his head as he figured out what it was that attracted a normal, nice guy like Perry to a woman like Sharon. That something had to be sex. It sure wasn't her personality. Her sparkling conversation. Her brains. Sharon showed everything she had to offer.

"She was the type of woman who would flash all the sexual stuff she had. She had the big boobs and round butt and she was swishing everything she had all over town."

In time, Dr. Mitchell's patients remarked about the woman they saw flitting about the adjoining office. All had a tale to tell. They had seen her putting the make on a buddy. One woman said they had gone to a dance out in the country and Sharon had practically forced herself on another woman's unsuspecting husband.

"Right on the dance floor rubbing that guy's dick!"

Another told of driving up to Sharon's house and catching her outside sunbathing in the nude. Dr. Mitchell heard a story of how Sharon had supposedly gone hitchhiking across country, picking up different guys, screwing them in the cabs of the semis before moving on.

If it had been any other woman, the chiropractor would have discounted the cruel remarks. With Sharon Nelson, however, it just seemed so plausible. It just seemed likely that she'd get into that kind of behavior. She had no limits.

Dr. Mitchell always saw his colleague's wife for what she was. In high-school days, she'd most certainly been called a tart, a slut. No doubt about it, the way the chiropractor saw her, Sharon had a mighty big problem: she believed sex was the cure.

Terry Mitchell often applied an old saying to Sharon Nelson: "If she had as many dicks sticking out of her as had been stuck in her, she'd look like a porcupine."

Whatever she wanted, she got. At least, it seemed so to the people on the fringes of Sharon Nelson's life. When she spotted a pretty ring in the local jeweler's case it was as good as already on her finger. Even when their bank account was starving, money was no object. Not for Sharon. One afternoon, she waltzed into the medical office brandishing a set of car keys for a brand new Jeep Eagle 4 x 4 from Hadad Motors.

"Look what I bought for me," she said.

Perry took a moment to say something, though the look on his face of utter amazement and disbelief was swift.

"Who's going to pay for it?" he asked.

Sharon spun around the office, letting the keys dangle against each other like a shiny charm bracelet.

The sound of a new car . . . the smell of a new car. All hers.

"You worry too much," she finally said with the smile of a woman who knew more than those looking at her. "It'll be paid for before too long."

Terry Mitchell was also surprised and a little pissed off when he got wind of the Nelsons' new car. Perry owed him back rent for the office and his wife kept spending money they simply didn't have.

After sex with Gary during one of their little rendezvous, Sharon insisted her only way out of her dismal life was to get rid of Perry. On one of those occasions, Sharon told Gary she and another of her Rocky Ford lovers had tried to kill Perry during the Nelsons' estrangement the previous year.

"They got Perry real drunk and pushed him in the pool,

and from what Sharon says, they thought Perry was drowning. They went in the house. They just left him floating in the water facedown. A few minutes later, Perry comes knocking on the door. He couldn't remember what happened. He thought he fell in,'' Gary remembered.

Sharon needed a man who would get it done—*right*.

"I want him out of my life," she said. "I want to be free."

A small group of eye doctors, all Seventh-Day Adventists with a bond of friendship forged over several decades, gathered together after a professional meeting in Denver. It was usually a group of jokers, all vying to top the other as they laughed about their lives and the absurdity of the world. One of the men wasn't laughing. It was Perry Nelson. He was talking about his troubles with Sharon.

Tears rolled down his face and his breath heaved, heavy with booze and remorse.

"I ruined my life," he said. "I have lost everything: my girls, my wife, I have lost my church. I have lost everything. Look what I did to Julie. Look at the mess I have made of my life."

The men tried to console their friend, telling him that, above all, he still could have the church. He could still come back to God.

Perry continued to cry and stare down at the floor.

"I wish I could," he said. "I really do."

When the friends finally calmed Perry, they were full of anguish themselves. None had seen a man break down as Dr. Nelson had. None had seen such sorrow.

Booze was his buddy. Before his marriage to Sharon, Perry Nelson seldom drank socially—and never in a bar. As an Adventist, alcohol was verboten, and if he dared slam down a beer with the boys, it was behind closed doors. Never where he could be judged so harshly. But once Sharon had her hooks in him, everything taboo was accepted. When it came to bar-hopping, it was surprising how quickly Perry adapted.

Or how unhappy the tall, salt-and-pepper-bearded man had become.

Friends from out of town came calling not long after Sharon

and Perry had fallen on hard financial times. The visitors could not believe how much the former churchgoing doctor had changed. He drank to get drunk. He partied to get drunk. He had forsaken everything he once considered important.

Sharon was another matter.

"She was in her element," said a friend who had accompanied the two of them out dancing at a Trinidad bar where Perry guzzled drinks and Sharon took to the dance floor. "She would twist and wiggle and hang on everyone she could. I just never felt comfortable going out with Perry and Sharon. I could never feel comfortable around her."

He was an eye doctor, for Heaven's sake. How come he didn't see so well? Kay Mitchell, the chiropractor's wife, felt sorry for Perry Nelson. He was being destroyed by hanging on to the woman that he had chosen as his wife. Sharon had done everything she could to ruin him. She had drained his business, trashed his reputation, embarrassed him at every turn. And no matter what Sharon did before or after she left Round House, he said he still couldn't get over her. He didn't want a divorce.

"You just have to get mad about this whole thing and get over it," Kay told Perry in the office one morning.

Perry said nothing. He just listened.

"If you can get mad at her, you can get over her. She's done some bad things, you have, too. But no one deserves to be treated like this. Get mad and get over her."

Perry promised to try.

Kay Mitchell doubted he'd be successful. There was something strange about Sharon's grip on her husband. No matter what she did, he still wanted her.

"Sharon was a typical gold digger," she said later. "She was out for whatever she could get. She had used Perry for all he had and then moved on. If I were him, I'd have wondered about what it was that he had that would make her come back. She was a complete user."

About that same time, Gary was working on a roofing job up in Denver and the two lovers had to keep in contact by telephone. He called Sharon on a Thursday just after she got the new Eagle. She was dying to show it off and suggested they meet at the Denny's in Pueblo.

"To make sure everything is all right," she said. "Don't want any mistakes."

While sipping iced tea at the Denny's, Sharon bragged that if everything went according to plan she would be a wealthy woman. She'd have the insurance money and the car paid off.

"Free and clear," she asserted. "And if it's done right, I won't even have to make a regular payment on it."

14

GARY ADAMS WAS NOT ALONE THAT BALMY
June night in 1983. He and another man, a friend from way
back, waited at the rest stop on I-25, just outside of Castle
Rock. The two smoked cigarettes down to their fibery filters
as they passed the time in the cab of Gary's Datsun pickup
talking about Sharon and how she had been beaten and abused
and ignored by her doctor husband.

Perry didn't love her.

Perry didn't treat her right.

Perry was a mean old bastard.

When a familiar little black VW putted by, Gary and his
buddy laid a patch of smoldering rubber to catch up. Perry
smiled and laughed out loud when Gary pulled his truck alongside and waved him to follow. They pulled over at a tavern
in Castle Rock for a few beers. Gary introduced his friend and
told Perry he was heading up to Denver, too.

"Sure was a coincidence that we'd meet on the way up,"
Gary said.

After downing a few rounds, the three men decided to go
to a strip club on the outskirts of Denver. By then, Gary's plan
had fully fermented. It was simple and sweet. While he and
Perry were in the bathroom, Gary instructed his pal to slip
some knockout drops in the doctor's beer. They'd walk the
doc out of the place and finish him off.

It was a simple, a good plan. It was a plan all for Sharon.

Back at the table, Perry put the glass to his lips and drank.

After a couple of gulps, he smacked the glass down. He looked disgusted.

"That doesn't taste good at all," he said. "Real flat tasting."

Gary said his beer tasted just fine, but Perry didn't want any more.

Perry Nelson held his liquor that night. He didn't get sloppy. He didn't make it easy for Gary to do what he had come there to do. The music blared and the mix of over-the-hill dancers with makeup-covered stretch marks and younger strippers who were working for enough money for implants slid across the stage. As the hours grew later, eyelids became heavy and it was time to go.

"Where do you want to stay?" Perry called out over the club's obnoxiously loud sound system.

Gary had no idea. He had no preference. Neither did his buddy.

"Why don't we just pull over to the side of the road?" he suggested.

With what they all had spent drinking, saving a few bucks on a motel seemed like a good idea. Neither Gary nor his friend knew the doctor had about as much money as they had. Sharon had been reupholstering the VW so he could sleep in it to save on a motel, anyway.

"Perry," Gary said, "don't tell Nancy you saw me up here. I don't want her to know I went to a strip joint."

Perry laughed.

"Don't you tell Sharon, either."

"Promise."

The water of Clear Creek ran through the chasm with the rushing sound that lulls weary travelers to sleep when nightfall comes and they cannot drive a mile further. It was after 2:00 A.M. and the sky was pockmarked with stars poking through pinholes in the blackness when the two vehicles pulled over along the highway in Jefferson County. They were just outside of Golden, west of Denver. Perry popped his seat back and stretched out in the VW, while Gary and his buddy tried to get comfortable in the cramped cab of the pickup.

Even though Perry had let him down by holding his booze

with impressive fortitude, Gary Adams still wanted to do the job. But he was tired. His friend was beat. The idea of hitting Perry Nelson over the head with a tire iron sounded like too much work.

"To hell with it, " he said to his co-conspirator. "Let's just let it go."

The next morning the three ate breakfast at a Golden cafe, chatted as if they were the best of friends, and waved good-bye.

Gary scratched his head years after, wondering why it was that the plan didn't work that night. It would have been just perfect.

Darn it anyway, he thought.

Hours later in the quiet solitude of Round House, Sharon got the shock of her life: Her husband came home. He was supposed to be dead. She was stunned and mad.

Gary Adams recalled what happened:

"Sharon was positive that Perry was not coming back. So when Perry came back she turned white as a ghost. She wasn't expecting it. She had it in her mind how she was going to tell the cops. How she was going to be the grieving widow. She said she was shaking, turned white as a sheet, you know, scared."

And very disappointed.

Thursday, a week after the fiasco with the dud knockout drops, Gary left Denver in his rearview mirror and returned to Wet Canyon. He had heard he could scrounge up some construction work in Trinidad, though that was not the real reason he came back. He had to see the woman he had disappointed. But before he made his way to Dr. Nelson's office on Country Club Drive, he ran into Sharon and a car salesman in downtown Trinidad.

"What happened?" She whispered her hot breath into his ear. *"What happened?"*

It was neither the right time nor the right place to talk. Sharon told Gary they'd have to meet another time.

"Perry's in town today," she said. *What she meant: Do not come to the office. Do not.*

"Maybe we could meet next week?" she said softly, out of earshot of the car salesman. "At the lake."

Trinidad Lake was still one of the lovers' special places. It always would be. Like an incredible sapphire, the lake shimmered across its surface from one side to the other. Conifers met the water like the jagged edge of a two-man saw. Eagles soared overhead searching for the fish that brought sportsmen from all over the region. Trinidad Lake was serene and lovely. Yet within the beauty of it all was a woman mad at the world. Mad at her lover.

Sharon had become increasingly upset in the days after Perry's miraculous return from the dead. She blamed Gary for botching the plan to murder the man who was the source of all her problems. Gary had no idea how hard it had been on her when Perry returned unscathed. Why hadn't he thought of how she would react? It scared her to death. Was he so selfish that could not have warned her that he had failed? Gary hadn't thought of her.

Gary held Sharon, trying to placate her and stop her tirade. He said he would do it again, but not right away. He suggested they might have to wait awhile, perhaps another year.

Sharon's face froze in disbelief. She wouldn't hear of it.

"Oh no, no," she said. "Perry's got another meeting up in Denver in July. It would be better to do it then."

Though Gary had hoped they'd have sex that afternoon, they didn't. Sharon said she was too upset.

A few days after the lake rendezvous, Sharon invited Gary and Nancy Adams to join her and Perry for dinner up at Round House. Though the timing was suspect, the invitation was not unusual. The Adamses and the Nelsons occasionally got together to play cards, share a dinner or drink coffee or beer. Despite what she had done with Nancy's husband, Sharon still considered the quiet, gentle woman her friend. After the meal, while the women stayed in the kitchen talking, Gary and Perry visited outside on the driveway. Gary told Perry he had heard he was heading back to Denver and he wondered if he could catch a ride.

"I'm going up there to buy some mini-14s," Gary said, piquing Perry's interest. The guns were stolen and selling for about $50, a bargain. Several men in the canyon had mini-14s and considered the combat-quality firearm perfect for shooting coyotes, even deer.

Perry definitely wanted one.

Gary's voice took on a conspiratorial tone. "Don't tell Nancy," he said. "She doesn't know I'm going to go up there for that. She thinks I'm going to go up there to make some money."

Perry laughed. He wouldn't tell her anything.

A week later, Gary Adams was working at a Trinidad construction site when he got word to Nancy that he wouldn't be coming home that Thursday night. He was going to stay in town to play poker with his buddies. He parked his Datsun at a repair center, telling the mechanics that his brakes needed work.

Next, he called the eye clinic on Country Club Drive.

Sharon, of course, answered.

"I'm planning on catching a ride with Perry," Gary said.

"Fine," she said as she handed the phone to her husband.

"On your way out," Gary said, "can you stop by and pick me up and we'll go up there and get the guns?"

Perry thought it was a fine idea.

Jim and Julie Whitley were the kind of outgoing people who always made a pack of friends wherever they went. They didn't know any social boundaries. Julie ran the Pinon Plaza truck stop, and her husband, a former Air Force man, was a mechanic. They were in their late thirties, raising four children in Trinidad, when they met Terry Mitchell and Perry Nelson. At first, they went to the offices on Country Club Drive for their eye and lumbar care. In time, Jim and Julie went just to say hello. Good friends in Trinidad were precious commodities.

One July afternoon when the Whitleys were over at Terry and Kay Mitchell's house going over details on a boat he had hired the couple to refurbish, Perry Nelson drove up in his VW. Perry showed up to show off what Sharon had done to the old car. She had redone the interior, made up an upholstered slant-board that he could pop in place of a seat so he could sleep in it when camping.

Julie said she was impressed and Perry beamed.

Despite how much Sharon had dragged him through the mud, Perry Nelson still could manage to be proud of her. Dr. Mitchell felt sorry for the guy. He just didn't see what everyone else did.

The drive from Trinidad to Denver is a long one. Four hours, six hours—depending on how fast one drives and how many pit stops are needed along the way. It is a beautiful drive up I-25 nonetheless: mountains rising to the west and the last edge of the Great Plains to the east. As the black VW sped along, Gary mostly listened as Perry chatted on about his life, his children and, of course, Sharon.

Sharon, he said, had purchased some emeralds from the back pages of a magazine.

"Some investment," Perry said shaking his head with a disgusted laugh. "Turns out when she went to sell them that they are worthless."

An animated Perry carried the bulk of the conversation as he pressed his foot against the floorboard and zipped down the highway. The doc was a genuinely nice guy, Gary thought. He didn't have a bad word for anyone. Gary was no expert on human behavior, but as far as he could tell it seemed out of character that Perry Nelson was an abuser of his wife and children. The bruises Sharon had pointed out on her body began to gnaw at the VW's passenger. Gary Adams wondered if he had been duped. While smacking Sharon wasn't out of the realm of possibilities, considering how she acted some of the time, Dr. Nelson didn't seem the type to do it.

"I don't think I'll ever see my older girls again," Perry said at one point on the drive. His words were full of resignation and Gary chose not to follow up on the comment. He didn't know if it was because of a wedge Sharon had driven between the girls and their father, though, he figured, that could have been the reason for it. Sharon had complained about the grown daughters.

Gary changed the subject. With what was on his mind, the comment bothered him.

When Sharon Lynn was a teenager in rural Maryland, she was seen as the dutiful daughter, prim and proper.

Top right: Sharon's mother drove the bus for the Seventh-Day Adventist academy and kept a spotless home for her family. She later wondered if she had "done enough for Sharon. Maybe she didn't know how much we loved her."

Bottom right: Sharon's older sister Judy was at once rebellious and very much concerned about her younger sister. It would take until the summer of 1997 for the two to reconcile. *(All courtesy Judy Farson)*

Even at the beginning of Sharon's wedding to preacher Mike Fuller, there were whispers among the congregation that she was spending too much time flirting with some of the elders.
(Courtesy Andrea Harrelson)

Perry Nelson and his daughter Lorri were especially close. When Sharon and Mike Fuller showed up in Rocky Ford, Colorado, Lorri saw her father's attention to the family take a dive. (*Courtesy Lorri Hustwaite*)

The Nelson family enjoyed family activities, including camping, until Sharon set her sights on Perry. After a scandalous split from their spouses, the pair married in July 1977. (*Courtesy Julie Nelson*)

It was in this Seventh-Day Adventist medical office in Rocky Ford that the first rumors were ignited that something might be going on between the preacher's pretty wife and the fun-loving eye doctor. (*Courtesy Blanche Wheeler*)

Top: It didn't matter that Perry's money was drying up, Sharon planned a fabulous home in the middle of the montains near Weston. She called it Round House for its semicircular living room.
Middle: Gary Adams and his wife lived at the bottom of Cougar Ridge—the closest neighbors to the Nelsons. The Adams' place was called The Dude Ranch.
(Both courtesy Rod Colvin)

Map © 1998 Mark Stein Studios

Downtown Weston.

Gary Starr Adams says he still loves Sharon . . . though there are times he'd like to killer. *(Adams County Police photo)*

Sharon Lynn Harrelson confessed to taking part in two of her husbands' deaths . . . but just how much did she do? *(Adams County Police photo)*

After a bitter estrangement caused by Sharon, Perry Nelson reconciled with daughter Lorri in time to walk her down the aisle in February 1982. *(Courtesy Lorri Hustwaite)*

Just before it all started to crumble, Sharon's sister Judy invited Sharon and Perry up to Colorado Springs for Thanksgiving. "We had some happy times, we did," Judy said later. *(Courtesy Judy Farson)*

Above: Andrea and Glen Harrelson remained close after their 22-year marriage ended in divorce. Andy was elated when her ex started dating again. "I wanted him to be happy," she said. *(Courtesy Andrea Harrelson)*

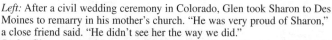

Left: After a civil wedding ceremony in Colorado, Glen took Sharon to Des Moines to remarry in his mother's church. "He was very proud of Sharon," a close friend said. "He didn't see her the way we did."
Right: Glen was an 18-year veteran of the Denver Fire Department when he became involved with the eye doctor's widow from Trinidad. *(All courtesy Andrea Harrelson)*

Above: Sharon is now in the women's prison in Canon City, Colorado. She has not changed her story and says that Gary Adams threatened her into keeping silent about his plans. *(Courtesy Judy Farson)*

Right: Clear Creek near Golden, Colorado . . . the river rages where Perry Nelson met his grisly fate in the darkness in July 1983. *(Courtesy Rod Colvin)*

It was close to 7:00 P.M. when the city of Pueblo came into view and they stopped for a bite at the Burger King. Perry had a chicken sandwich and Gary ate a hamburger. After eating, they zipped over to the mall so Perry could say hello to a friend who ran a Pearle Vision optical center there. When they pulled up it was obvious they were too late. The mall had closed.

Though Perry was disappointed, Gary felt relieved. He didn't want to see anyone; he didn't want anyone to see *him*.

Nothing really stops a Colorado highway. Mountains that get in the way are bored clear through. Ledges are blasted out of granite slopes and roads are laid in like Band-Aids. A mile above tunnel one on Highway 6, near Golden, is Clear Creek. In the summer it is a scenic spot for a picnic as water gently runs the rocky gauntlet. Boulders rise high enough from the water for kids to hopscotch across one side to another. But spring and fall bring a different picture. Water courses through a rocky canyon making Clear Creek neither clear nor a creek.

A diamond-shaped roadsign warned travelers who pulled over to rest or take photographs: CLIMB TO SAFETY IN CASE OF FLASH FLOOD.

Though it had been raining intermittently for hours, the clouds opened up and the freeway became the world's largest car wash. By the time the VW reached the creek, it was a full-fledged downpour. As they went through the tunnel, Gary asked Perry to pull over.

"Got to take a piss," the younger man said.

It was around 4:00 A.M. when he made it back to his place in the canyon. Gary Adams' blue jeans had dried by then, but his muscular body still hurt like hell. He winced vaguely as he pulled into the dusty driveway leading to the Dude Ranch. He was wired and agitated. He told himself Perry was dead, but he couldn't be sure of it. He hoped that he *was* dead, because if he wasn't there would be hell to pay. If Perry was alive, Gary knew he was going to jail for a long, long time. He watched the sun rise and paced the floor.

At 9:00 A.M., Gary could take just sitting around no more. He had to do something. He announced to his wife, Nancy, that he needed to take care of some business in Ratone, about an hour away. On the way out the door, he suggested a quick detour.

"Perry owes me some money," he said to Nancy as she got into the car. "Let's go by there and see if he's home."

Nancy agreed. Since it was early, she'd sit in the car while Gary ran inside to get the cash. It wasn't polite to go bother neighbors without a phone call or an invitation.

Sharon answered the door in her bathrobe, slit open to reveal most of her ample breasts.

"Everything is okay," he said. "Perry's not coming back." He didn't tell her he was not absolutely positive about it, because he worried that she'd get more skittish than he already was.

"You're sure?" she asked. "Everything's all right?"

"Everything's okay."

Sharon fished around for a hundred dollars and handed the money to her mountain man.

"You're sure he's not coming back?" she asked once more.

"No, he's not."

Gary and Nancy Adams spent the day and night in a Raton motel, a good hour from what Gary had assumed would be the heat of a crime investigation. Nancy, of course, had no idea why they needed to get away. She was just glad to be alone with her husband. When they made love, Nancy never noticed the scrapes and bruises on her husband's body. At least, she never said anything about it.

Nancy, Gary believed, suspected nothing. And why would she? Gary was certain his wife liked Sharon. Friends don't steal another friend's husband.

"Sharon and Nancy were best friends," he said later. "It might sound crazy, but I had everything covered."

15

SUMMER TEMPERATURES HAD SHORN THE mountains of much of their snow, but they were as magnificent as Bob and Donna Goodhead remembered from their visit in October, the year before. En route to a Denver optical convention, the Goodheads returned to Weston and Wet Canyon the afternoon of July 23, 1983. Of course, they came to see Perry, but they also wanted another look at the thirty-two-acre property they had purchased to bail him out of some serious financial problems. Bob Goodhead had it in his mind that he would build a cabin and retire in Wet Canyon. He and his optometry school buddy would shoot the breeze and pal around until they were old and gray.

Donna Goodhead wasn't so keen on the idea. She didn't like the idea of spending any time—especially not her final years—with Sharon Nelson. Bob pressed on with his dream. He frequently remarked to folks back in Oklahoma that his Colorado acreage was so darn beautiful that if it had been in Tulsa, it would have been a city park. Few would argue the point when they saw the pictures.

It was not a surprise visit. Bob called over the Fourth of July holiday and spoke with Perry. Both men were going to take courses offered by the Mountain States Congress of Optometry at the rambling Denver Tech Center. Perry was not going to attend the convention, per se. Instead, he signed up for a pharmacology course that would garner him the certification allowing him to prescribe medicine. Since the two eye docs would not be together in Denver, plans were made to visit before and after in Weston.

Going to see Sharon and Perry was not atop Donna Goodhead's Summertime Must-Do List. She understood her husband's friendship included Sharon by default. She'd have to put up with the woman. Donna didn't like going to Round House, either. She dreaded ending up in a place like that—Bob's retirement dream or not. Donna considered Round House too isolated. It scared her. It was like dropping off the face of the earth just to get up the Nelsons' godforsaken driveway.

Once Donna talked with Perry about that isolation.

"Perry, what if you need medical attention? What if something happens to you out here? You'll kill yourself getting out of here. What if you cut your arm chopping wood?"

"We don't think about that. We like the freedom of living in nature."

I'll bet, Donna thought. *More like au naturel, than nature.*

As they climbed the dusty, rocky driveway, the Goodheads noticed the topaz gleam of the new Jeep Eagle parked outside.

"I just can't fathom how they can afford a new car," Donna said. "Bob, they don't even have groceries half the time."

Bob didn't disagree with Donna's sentiments. As much as he liked the man, there was no mistaking Perry was mixed-up when it came to money. Maybe, he hoped, things were better now.

While the Goodheads continued to chew over the subject of the Nelson finances, Sharon appeared at the doorway. A neon sign of makeup flashed across her features. Her top dropped so low it looked more like an addition to her shorts than a separate garment. Even at 38, it was Sharon as she had always been: a hot tomato in sling-backs.

"Perry is really looking forward to seeing you guys," she said. Smoke curling from her lips, she smiled and waved Donna and Bob into her beautifully furnished livingroom. She exited to get some cold drinks.

"He'll be home in just a little while," she said.

So much had changed. The modest home in Rocky Ford. And the wife. The wife was so far from the first Mrs. Nelson they could not have been married to the same man. Bob Good-head pondered memories of Julie Nelson. She was a plain Jane, a matronly woman who focused her attentions on the children and the church. Sharon was the complete opposite. She was wild. She was a rebel. She was a sexual animal. She smoked. She ate meat. She dressed like a slut. When Sharon's kids ran amok, she paid them no mind. She was enjoying her own life.

And as usual, once Sharon began to blather, everything was fantastic.

"Perry and I had the best sex—the most wonderful sex— the night before he left," she said as she ushered them inside.

The comment was typical Sharon. So much of what she said was about sex and about how wonderful, how desirable she was.

While the kids ran around the house, the adults continued to make conversation in the living room. Sharon, of course, never needed any help in that regard. She could carry on a complete conversation by herself. Sometimes it seemed as though that was exactly what she did. As the clock swept away the time, it brought more worry and anxiety that Perry had not yet returned. Sharon started mixing more drinks and consumed one after another.

"Wonder what's keeping him?" Bob asked.

"He'll be home soon enough," Sharon said. She switched on the news and waited for the weather report.

Another hour elapsed.

When the TV weatherman reported Denver had experienced heavy rains, Sharon snapped up his words. She suggested her husband had been delayed by the storm, perhaps even in a car accident related to the nasty weather. Maybe he had car trouble and stopped at Sharon's sister's place in Colorado Springs?

As Sharon prattled on, she casually dropped a bomb.

"Bob, I don't believe you'll ever see your friend Perry again."

The statement brought the room to silence. The television was clicked on "Mute."

"What do you mean?" Bob asked.

Sharon played with her drink, and looked into the glass. Ice cubes clinked.

"It's just a feeling, I don't know," she said.

Donna continued to wish they'd never come to Weston. She had not wanted to visit in the first place. She wanted to go to Denver. Even in small doses, Sharon bugged her. Perry's wife seemed to be solely fixed on sex and men. Whenever they went to town, she'd sashay and wink at men in the grocery store or the gas station.

That evening, Sharon's conversation and actions bothered Donna more than usual. She was always irritating, but during one conversation in the master bedroom was particularly unsettling. Sharon sat on the edge of her bed.

"What would you do if your husband didn't come home one day?" Sharon asked her.

Donna shook her head. "Bob wouldn't leave."

"But what if he did?"

The reluctant guest stared hard at her hostess.

"That could never happen," she said firmly.

Sharon persisted and Donna finally sighed out an answer. "I'd go on and make a life for my children."

It was almost as if Sharon didn't hear the answer.

"Well, what would you do if Bob just disappeared?" she persisted.

Exasperated, Donna enunciated every word as clearly as possible. "I'd keep on living and make my life as good as I could for my children."

Donna nudged her husband when Sharon got up for another drink.

"Let's get the hell out of here," she said.

After 10 P.M., the Goodheads, still worried that Perry hadn't made it home, left for their motel room in Trinidad.

The next morning, the Goodheads returned to find Sharon assisting Harry Russell, a six-foot-six and 350-pound Peterbilt truck of a man, with the brake lines on his old truck. It was a job, Sharon explained to the Goodheads, that Perry had promised to do.

"Where's Perry?" Bob Goodhead asked.

"He hasn't made it home yet. He'll be home any minute."

"Something is wrong, Sharon," Bob said, shaking his head with worry. "Let's go call the Denver Tech Center."

The four of them went down to Al Robinson's mill to use the phone. No one they called knew anything of Perry Nelson's whereabouts in Denver. A doctor from Rocky Ford was certain that he hadn't seen Perry at all. No one had seen him. Perry, as far as that man knew, had never even made it to Denver.

Bob Goodhead put his hand on Sharon's shoulder.

"Call the highway patrol," he said.

When Sharon got off the phone she explained that the authorities had no record of a wreck involving a black VW bug.

The Goodheads gave Sharon their AT&T telephone credit card so she could continue to call from the pay phone. She seemed agitated, deeply concerned about her husband. She spoke in rapid-fire sentences, words strung together tighter than a pearl necklace. She was either crying or on the verge of it.

By dinnertime that evening, the Goodheads finally had to leave. Sharon was drunk and sputtering imbecilic statements about her husband's legion of enemies. There was nothing more they could do. They gave Sharon their telephone credit card and drove to Denver. All the way there, they studied the roadside for traces of Perry and his black VW.

When Bob Goodhead checked in for his class schedule, he inquired whether Perry Nelson had done so as well. The convention registrar indicated that, in fact, while Perry had signed up for the class on pharmaceuticals—he had not shown up. He had not confirmed that he was there.

Bob feared the worst: *Perry must have been in an auto accident.*

That same evening, they shared their concerns as they drove away.

"Something isn't right here," Bob told Donna. "Sharon knows something. I've got a funny feeling about this . . . she knows more than she's letting on."

Donna agreed, while her husband went on.

"I don't think a worried wife is going to throw a drunk," he said. "And what's all this talk about enemies? That's the biggest lie I've ever heard in my life. Everyone loves Perry. He's the kind of guy that if someone had a flat tire, he'd stop and fix it for them. People love that guy.''

Even in Colorado, joggers let nothing stand in the way of their great endeavor. In the snow, their feet become twin plows as they run in the ruts left by cars and trucks on the roadways. In the rain, they dodge droplets, but press on. On Sunday morning, 250 miles north of Weston, a man jogging along the raging waters of Jefferson County's picturesque Clear Creek stumbled across the mangled remains of a car. At least, it seemed that the hunk of metal had once been a car. There were no windows. No license plate. Nothing that could break off was still attached. It was four tires and a crushed and shattered hull.

The car was as battered as if it had been in a rock tumbler, which, of course, it had. It was a VW in such bad shape that the jogger might have assumed it was a junked auto that had been pushed into river.

People were always doing stuff like that, trashing the planet to save the junkyard fee.

Anyway, the jogger decided to report what he saw. He notified the nearest fire department.

The car was Perry Nelson's.

Later that morning, Sharon Lynn Nelson made her way to the Trinidad Police Department. She told friends she had been forced into going down in person. The police had told her they would be sending someone out to Round House to facilitate the filing of a missing persons report, but the deputy hadn't showed up. She dropped her son and daughter off at a babysitter and went inside.

''I've got people who have eye appointments at 8 A.M. I've got to get this done,'' she said, after an officer directed her to the missing persons section. While she was filling out the paperwork, the officer who had been told to respond to her house approached.

Sharon later recalled her visit with the police.

''I'm bananas by now. They are saying, calm down, calm down. We can call the doctor to give you something. I said,

'How can I calm down? You people don't even know what's going on here. You tell me someone is coming to my house, nobody comes to my house. I don't sleep all night. I know I've got patients coming in. I don't know where my husband is. Get my kids to the sitter . . . I've got an office full of people that's going to be sitting . . .' "

Something terrible had happened. Chiropractor Terry Mitchell was almost in tears as he stood at Julie Whitley's front door.

"It's Perry. His car went into Clear Creek Canyon up by Golden," he said.

"Oh no," she said. "He was just here last night."

"What do you mean?" Terry asked.

Julie Whitley had a vision, a dream. It was a message from that other place that a few people can tap into. Julie had been teased about being a witch or weirdo, but she didn't care. She could feel it in her bones. Perry Nelson was alive and he needed her help.

"He was at my door, asking for help . . . He's someplace and he needs help."

In the space of a few minutes, Sharon and her group of supporters and their children were gathered up and away they went in Dr. Mitchell's van to search for the doctor. Emotions ran high. Periods of silence followed bursts of speculation about what might have happened to Perry.

But halfway along the way, something strange happened between Sharon and Jim Whitley. He felt her rub his thigh.

Come again? he thought. *What's going on?*

For a minute, Jim Whitley passed it off as the innocent result of sitting in a van that was too crowded for comfort. When it happened once more, he felt very uncomfortable. Sharon kept touching his leg, stroking his inner thigh with her fingertips. It was very unsettling. After the second and third time, Jim could not discount his concern. The woman whose husband was missing was putting the moves on him. She was playing with his leg. Jim tried to scoot away from her, but there was nowhere to go.

Good God, what is this woman doing? My wife's sitting

right behind us! Her husband is missing in the creek! And she's groping me?

Sharon kept saying how upset she was, but her actions clearly didn't fit. There were no tears. There was no sobbing. Just a wandering hand and the unspoken communication that she was interested in the man sharing her seat in Terry Mitchell's van. Maybe her petting of his thigh was the way she sought comfort?

Jim Whitley didn't want to find out for sure. He did his best to stay away from Sharon.

God, she must be one mixed-up woman!

16

THE NEXT TWENTY-FOUR HOURS WERE A BLUR FOR the Trinidad gang. Sharon and the searchers stayed at a motel outside of Denver, heartsick that there had been no word on Dr. Nelson. Where could he be? Everyone wanted to know, though at times it seemed as though Sharon was the least interested among the group. She shed few tears. Instead, she was hungry. She was tired. She wanted to get some sleep.

And so they did. Sharon shared the motel room with Terry and Kay Mitchell and slept like a baby.

The next morning, the Trinidad search party visited the sheriff's department and the fire department. No one had heard of Perry Nelson's missing persons report. No one seemed to care. A visit to the wrecking yard was fruitless. When Dr. Mitchell asked if they had considered that the man could have been thrown from the car and was wandering the roadside in a dazed condition, they dismissed it. Beyond pulling the VW from the water, they hadn't done anything at all. Zero.

Sharon, who seemed very composed, stayed in the car while the searchers looked over the vehicle at the junkyard.

The VW had been flattened like a beer can under a worker's boot. Terry Mitchell barely could discern how that mangled object in the twisted heap had once been his friend's car.

"It looks like it's been through a damn meat grinder," he told his wife.

One of the emergency rescuers told the group that nothing was found in the car. The only thing that remained of its contents was a sleeping bag that had somehow hooked on to the passenger-side mirror and dangled in the water.

"Kind of weird-looking," the man said.

A patrol officer accompanied the searchers to the place where in all likelihood the little car and its driver had met their horrific fate. The guardrail was twisted and marred with the grinded-on striping of black paint. The officer explained that for the barrier to sustain that kind of damage, the car would have been traveling in excess of 80 mph.

Sharon informed the officer that the VW had been painted only two months before. The paint, she reasoned, hadn't had a chance to become "baked" on yet.

The search party went to the Coors plant in Golden to make sure that Perry hadn't been caught in the big screen the company employed to keep large debris from contaminating the water. From there, they backtracked, covering two miles along Clear Creek. Bits of the VW had washed ashore, bedding, maps. All were signs that Dr. Nelson's car had, in fact, taken the terrible ride down the raging creek. A stoic Sharon told the searchers not to give up.

"He's here," she said. "We've *got* to find him."

A former medic with the Air and Sea Rescue unit of the Air Force, Jim Whitley had brought along binoculars to aid in the search in a unique way. He used them look beneath the surface of the water. The rush of the surface is a curtain, but the submersed binoculars were used to create a window through it. Whitley was disappointed. The technique brought no results that day.

The group scanned the far side of the creek. Would anything catch their eyes? They looked for pieces of clothing. Blood. Limbs. Bits of Perry. Anything. But they found nothing.

Nothing at all.

When the Mitchells suggested it would be a good idea to bring photographs of Perry to the bus station, airport and various Denver cab companies, suddenly Sharon didn't want to be bothered.

"But maybe he's alive," Terry said.

"I don't think so," she answered with a measure of certainty. "I think he's gone for good."

The next day, the Trinidad *Chronicle-News* marked the sad story with the headline:

SEARCH FOR LOCAL OPTOMETRIST UNDERWAY NEAR CLEAR CREEK

Barb Ruscetti had locked her front door and was walking to her car when her neighbor yelled over to get her attention.

"Barb!" the woman called out from across Colorado Ave. "Did you know your old boss is missing?"

Barb hadn't heard a word. "What do you mean, he's missing?"

The neighbor recounted what she had read in the paper.

"Well, Sharon made a report that he had left their place Friday night and he hadn't shown up yet. She finally went to the police yesterday."

Barb felt dizzy. *What was going on here?*

"Why did she wait so long to report him missing?" she finally blurted out.

When the neighbor didn't have an answer, Barb spun around and went back into her house and called the Trinidad chief of police.

"Yeah, Barb, it's true," the chief responded when she related what her neighbor had said. "Sharon claims she waited so long because she thought he was going to come home."

"She killed him," Barb said flatly. "I know she did."

The Whitleys were not rich, but they had more than many in Trinidad. When Sharon asked if she could stay at their place on the corner of San Pedro and Goddard, Julie and Jim agreed. With what the woman had been through, it was the least the friendly couple could do. Sher said she wanted to be close to the police in case news about Perry came in, and, even more importantly, she had things to take care of with the optometry business.

"I don't want to drive back and forth," she explained.

Jim Whitley knew Sharon's reputation, as did just about everybody in town. He knew that she had slept with half the county and with the little move she made in the van, he was sure she was after him. He wanted no part of her and he did his best to keep her at arm's length.

"I need money," she announced one morning over coffee in the Whitleys' sunny kitchen. "We're behind on our bills and I've got to come up with some cash."

Jim understood. As they talked, Sharon said she was considering selling some of Perry's belongings—his guns, for example.

"I think I'll look for a buyer for the business, too."

Jim Whitley did a lot of listening. He thought it was a bit rushed—Perry could still turn up alive—but he didn't have her bank account or responsibilities.

The next day, Gary Adams, whom Sharon introduced as her neighbor and "Perry's good friend," showed up at the Whitley residence.

Sharon said Gary would help them gather up Perry's guns for sale. Jim was impressed by the guns the doctor owned. When Gary mentioned a 30-30 Winchester, Jim said he wished he could afford to buy it.

"You can pay me later," Sharon said.

Jim shook his head. Not only didn't he want to owe anybody money, he didn't think it was right to buy something that belonged to Perry.

"He could still be alive," he reminded her.

Sharon dismissed the possibility. She wasn't about to cool her heels waiting around for Perry Nelson to come to his senses and return home—if he could do so.

Over the week following the doctor's disappearance, Gary Adams became a regular visitor at the Whitleys. One time he came with the kids and picked up Sharon for an outing. Mostly, though, he came alone. Jim told his wife that he suspected Sharon and Gary had once been lovers, but he felt that part of their relationship was in the past. The way Sharon Nelson acted, it seemed she'd probably had a dozen men since Gary Adams.

"Something didn't feel right," Jim said later. "Something from the very start didn't seem right about those two. It wasn't

Gary. I liked Gary. He was decent. It was Sharon that gave me the creepy feeling.''

Jim didn't want to say anything to Sharon at the time, but he told wife Julie it was more than likely that Dr. Nelson was dead.

''There's no way he could have survived in that icy river after a crash like that. That car had been thrown down the creek and smashed up. Imagine what it would do to a man?''

Julie didn't agree.

''He wasn't in the car when it crashed,'' she said.

Jim didn't question Julie. He knew her well enough to trust her instincts—or whatever people wanted to call it.

''Hi, how are you?''

The voice on the telephone was her sister Sharon's, calling from a friend's house in Trinidad.

''Fine,'' Judy Douglas said.

''Have you talked to Mom?''

''No, I haven't. Is everything all right?''

''Haven't you talked with Mom?''

''Sharon, for Christ's sake, is Daddy dead?''

Sharon hesitated for a second. ''No, Perry is—at least he's missing.''

Though Sharon seemed oddly calm given the situation, Judy focused on her sister's words, not her demeanor.

Sharon proceeded to tell her how Perry had gone off to the convention in Denver and never returned. His car had been swept into a river near Golden during a flash flood.

''I'm on my way up,'' Sharon said. ''Please don't ask any questions about what happened. Misty and Danny have adjusted and we don't want to stir things up. No questions, Judy. None.''

Judy hung up the phone with a quiet and gentle touch. She blinked back tears as she gathered up her children to inform them Uncle Perry had been in a car accident and was most likely dead. The legacy of growing up in the Douglas clan was a lack of close family members. Perry was as much of an uncle figure as Judy's children had ever known.

''We've got to get our crying done now,'' she said. ''We

can't say anything about this to Aunt Sharon and the kids. We don't want to upset them.''

When Sharon and her children arrived in Colorado Springs, Judy kept her promise. No one uttered a word about Perry. There were no outbursts. It was a nice, pleasant visit. It was almost as if nothing had happened.

Back in Rocky Ford, everyone knew Dr. Nelson was missing, presumed dead—or, if he had a lick of sense left, had run away from his no-good second wife. When Sharon came to the Watkins Medical Arts Building to tell the tale of Perry's tragic disappearance, she gathered a group of women together in one of the back offices. She sobbed about being left alone, not knowing what happened or what her future held. She cried into a tissue as she professed her love for her missing husband.

Iona Hamilton was among those who saw Sharon that day. Iona, of course, had known Perry long before he got involved with the preacher's wife. She'd never thought much of the marriage in the first place. She remained cool to Sharon, and sensed Dr. Nelson's wife clearly understood that she'd get no sympathy from her.

After Sharon departed, Iona and Blanche Wheeler marveled over her grief-ridden performance.

"I doubt those tears were genuine," Iona said.

Blanche agreed with Iona's blunt assessment.

Sharon seldom returned to Rocky Ford after that particular visit.

If Perry Nelson were dead, he wasn't even cold by the time Sher put his Trinidad practice on the sale block. If Dr. Nelson were alive, she surely must have known he wasn't coming back. She had waited only a matter of a few days after his car was yanked from Clear Creek. As she had always done, Sher Nelson surprised everyone.

Later, she tried to explain her actions.

"The reason I put the practice up for sale so soon is—it took over two years to find a buyer for the RF [Rocky Ford] practice and I knew also that a practice without a doctor doesn't sell very well, and I want his practice to continue with a new doctor—and according to the president of the Colorado Optometric Association the sooner a practice is listed after death, the better chance a doctor will be willing to take it over. That's why."

Not long after Sharon put it up for sale, Jim Whitley talked with one doctor who had been mulling over buying Dr. Nelson's Trinidad practice.

"I'm looking into it," the other doctor said. "Sharon Nelson is going to continue on, keeping the books—"

Jim cut the man short.

"You don't want her. Buy the equipment. Buy the business. But leave her alone. Can't trust her for anything, especially bookkeeper."

Jim recalled an incident several months before when he needed a new pair of glasses and Sharon told him that she'd make him a deal if he'd pay her directly instead of through the regular billing procedure. She'd get the cash and he'd save a few bucks. Barb Ruscetti overheard the conversation and made a beeline for the back room to tell Dr. Nelson.

Sharon just grinned and rolled her eyes.

Ooops, caught again!

As she sold off assets, Sharon continued to keep office hours at Country Club Drive. She continued to fill prescriptions and order glasses for the few customers who straggled in. She continued to bewilder Dr. Mitchell. He knew that the Nelsons had no money and the business was a mere shell.

"How are you going to pay for this?" he asked one afternoon when Sharon placed another lens order.

"I'm not. I need the money and it's too bad for them. I've got kids to support. Perry's left a big mess behind."

She had no compunction about sticking the optical labs for more money. She seemed to be able to justify anything.

With Sharon so oddly calm, the Mitchells and the Whitleys began to wonder if the accident had been some kind of a setup. The Nelsons had been so desperate for money, they figured, Perry and Sharon might have cooked up the scheme to fake his death for insurance money. It wasn't an original idea. All had heard cases where the husband took off for a few years and his wife had him declared dead to collect a fat insurance settlement. Many recalled an episode of *Unsolved Mysteries* that could have been a blueprint for what Sharon and Perry might have carried out.

Terry Mitchell wouldn't put it past either of the Nelsons. Perry was in a world of financial hurt and was damn near suicidal. Sharon, he thought, had no conscience and would do whatever she could to get her hands on a wad of cash. He was sure that when it came to her questionable character, he had seen only the tip of the iceberg. Fraud and deception were a way of life for her.

Dr. Mitchell ran his suspicions past his wife.

"She didn't seem worried. She wasn't hysterical. She didn't even cry. When we wanted to go to the airport to hand out his picture, she said no. She didn't want to be bothered. She knows something."

Kay Mitchell agreed.

"And in the car there were no papers, no briefcase. He took everything out and just left his sleeping bag," she said.

"Yeah, because he wasn't in the car when it went into the river. Just watch, she's going to have him declared dead for the money."

Back in Oklahoma City, the Goodheads were still haunted by their visit to Round House the day after Perry disappeared from the face of the earth.

"I don't know what happened," Bob Goodhead told his wife Donna. "But one thing I'm positive about is that woman is a liar."

Donna thought the same thing. She decided to call AT&T and cancel their phone card.

"Bob," she said, reaching to dial the phone company, "I don't trust Sharon at all."

In rural areas like Wet Canyon, gossip is the number-one mode of communication. That had more to do with human nature than the fact there were few phone lines in the remote reaches of Colorado. When Gary Adams moved in with Sharon a few days after Perry disappeared, just about everyone knew it. Some even suspected the affair before the doc drove off to oblivion. Sharon had even complained her husband was cold to her.

"Most people discounted her complaints," one neighbor

said. "I never got the feeling Perry didn't love Sharon. I don't think he had a clue about what kind of woman she really was."

And yet, Gary Adams seemed to be taken in by the woman as well. How else could anyone explain how it was that he up and left his wife at the Dude Ranch and moved in with his lover?

And the question was asked: Where was the doctor? People pondered it in the coffee shop, at the mill and at the church. People who barely knew Perry Nelson were among the most mystified, while those closer to the Nelsons' situation understood he had tax problems. But to the casual optical customer or the neighbor down the road, he was just a nice fellow who up and disappeared.

Where was his body? People around Wet Canyon had their theories. Some thought he could be dead in the river, the battered victim of a car crash. Others thought he had met a more unseemly fate.

None of that crossed neighbor Ray Thornton's mind. He gave more credence to the possibility Dr. Nelson had fled the country to avoid the steep taxes that he had dodged.

"One of these days I'm going to give it all up and escape to the Cayman Islands," Perry had said. "A man can live there tax free. One day I'll be gone!"

Ray also recalled the signs Perry had posted on the perimeter of his property to ward off greedy emissaries of Uncle Sam:

NO TRESPASSING!
ESPECIALLY GOVERNMENT OFFICIALS!

The searches had turned up nothing. A plane with infrared equipment flew over the creek and its rocky shoreline, looking for the glowing blotch of red that would indicate the heat of a decomposing body.

Nothing was found.

But in Trinidad, some were beginning to wonder if the authorities ought to look closer to home. They wondered if the battered VW had been a ruse, a setup. Perhaps Perry Nelson had never left the mountain house in the first place. Perhaps his body was somewhere on Cougar Ridge.

One theory expressed by many suggested Perry had, in fact, been murdered. His corpse hadn't turned up because he had been buried somewhere on the acreage around Round House.

Sharon's fork hit her plate with a clatter loud enough to turn heads, though thankfully no one in the little restaurant in West-cliffe paid her any mind. Her hands shook so violently she set them in her lap to steady them. But she said nothing. Gary looked up from his breakfast and asked if she was all right.

It had been a month since Dr. Nelson's disappearance.

Sharon, now silently crying, said nothing. She raised her hand and pointed toward a man ten feet away.

Instantly, with no words uttered, Gary knew what she was thinking. The man, who had his back to them, was the same height and build as Perry. His thinning hair was longish and swirled in the technique many men—including Perry—employed to conceal the fact they were balding.

"Get me out of here," she coughed out. *"Now!"*

Gary felt his heart sink, and his stomach turn. *It couldn't be him. It couldn't be Perry.* He walked over and casually looked at the man's face. It wasn't Perry. He didn't look anything like him.

Perry was dead.

Sharon almost lost it as they sped away from the cafe. Her tears came in convulsions. Again and again. Gary reached over to comfort her, but she would have none of it. She was scared. Despite the fact the man in the cafe had not been Perry, Sharon had been shaken to the core. Gary checked them into a motel to give her some time to pull herself together. She needed it badly.

It wasn't Perry. Perry Nelson was dead.

Sharon wrote to Lorri a few weeks after Perry disappeared. It was the only letter she would send to Perry's youngest daughter by his first wife. Lorri wanted to come to Colorado to help in the search for her father's remains. Sharon wrote the letter to discourage her. And if the letter had meant to comfort Lorri, it only pointed out Sharon's own misery. It was, as always, about Sharon.

She wrote:

> *This is such unusual circumstances that even the friends in Rocky Ford have a difficult time knowing what to do or say . . . at the point where his body does surface, people will be able to see the reality of the nightmare I've experienced for the last month.*
>
> *Lorri, I want him found more than anyone, but I also know, I couldn't handle being the one to find him at this point. Your dad lives in my heart, wherever his body is another person will be the best one to find him, for no one who loves him would be able to emotionally handle the situation.*

Three weeks after the first search for the doc, more than a dozen of Perry's friends gathered along the banks of Clear Creek to look for the missing man. Leading the group was Sharon and her good pal and helpful neighbor, Gary Adams. All had come with the hope that they would make the grisly discovery. The searchers went with heavy hearts, saddened by the tragic circumstances which had brought them together. All knew Perry Nelson. Their hearts ached for Sharon and her children.

How terrible for them. How awful to go through this kind of tragedy.

Yet if anyone offered a contrast to the dark mood, it continued to be Sharon herself.

Her behavior and attitude was at odds with the seriousness of the exploration. She seemed a little *too* happy. No one expected her to bawl like a baby. No one needed to see handwringing. Everyone knew Sharon and Perry had a marriage rife with arguments and estrangements.

The search party studied the black paint left on the guard rail. Sharon echoed what the police had told her on the previous trip to the site. She considered it conclusive proof the little car had gone over the bank at that point.

"Maybe he lost control and spun out?" someone asked.

Of course, no one knew.

When the bulk of the group drove ahead to pick up the searchers as they walked downstream, Sharon and Gary remained behind, inseparable.

"It seemed like an outing. She was too buoyant. It struck me that something wasn't right. It was obvious something was going on between Gary and Sharon," said a man who participated in the search.

After they could look no more, the group ate at Pizza Hut and drove back to Trinidad. Gary and Sharon went up to Round House and went to bed.

By the time everyone knew Perry was missing, the rumors his widow was shacked up with a carpenter named Gary Adams made it as far as Barbara Ruscetti's ears in Trinidad. She was appalled, but not surprised. When Perry came back—if he did come back—there would be hell to pay. Sharon had messed around with Buzz Reynolds, but Barb, for one, didn't think her old boss would tolerate another.

This Gary Adams would be in big trouble, she thought.

Whenever Barb had the chance, she brought up Gary's name to see what others knew about him.

"Everybody said he was a real nice-looking man," she said later. "Very easygoing, but everybody said, too, there's a real scary part of him. That he makes you afraid of him right away. That you don't trust him."

As much as she professed her love for her "Mountain Man," Sharon wasted little time in making him over.

Gary Adams had never used hairspray in his entire life. He barely did more than wash and comb his brown hair into place. Yet Sharon had a manly beauty regimen for him. She actually blow-dried his hair and sprayed a style into place. There were bottles of lotions for his skin and a wardrobe of new clothes. She bought him skintight pants, she said, to show off every bulge to his advantage.

To *her* advantage, really. Sharon loved to look as much as she loved to touch.

Sharon, Gary once told a friend, tried to mold him into her

ideal. Into the image of the man she wanted above all others. It seemed she desired a man that would screw her like something out of a pornographic movie in the morning and take her out for a fancy dinner in the evening. She had imagined a life of lusty class. She had the money coming in and the appetite for both. Everything was the best that money could buy.

Gary was there for the ride.

Beyond the sex, Sharon and Gary had few moments of bliss in their relationship. In fact, the longer they stayed in bed, the better they got along. The kids were the largest bone of contention, though other things got in the way, too.

When Gary tried to hook up a VCR, Sharon jumped into the process.

"No," she said, in her know-it-all voice. "That's not the way you do it."

Ten minutes passed. More hopelessly confused than ever, Sharon gave up as if Gary had so screwed up the cables that no one outside of a factory-trained representative from Sony could fix it.

"Just do your cooking and let me hook up the VCR," Gary said bitterly, as Sharon left the room.

There were times when he wanted to smack her, too. If Perry ever hit Sharon, Gary could see why. In bed she was the best he'd ever had. But they could do that only so often. There were times when they actually had to talk or do other things. Those were the times when Sharon would make him mad.

And whenever it suited her, Sharon used sex to smooth things over with her lover.

"At times," Gary Adams said years later, "she would use it as a peacemaker. If she thought I was really mad, she'd really come on with the charm . . . turn it on and off just like a water faucet. And . . . other times, she could be as cold as ice toward me."

Sharon also put off what needed to be done. It seemed to Gary that she'd rather play (preferably in bed) than do anything. Sometimes that was just fine with him, but when hauling water or getting supplies in town was necessary, it was frustrating.

"You must think ahead," he kept telling her. "You can't play all the time. You got to work at times."

Sharon pooh-poohed his work-ethic. This was her turn to live a little. This was her time. Her dream. And if Gary didn't like it, he could lump it.

Within two months of shacking up, Gary Adams summoned the nerve to tell Sharon that he could not stand living with her. He told her that though he loved her, he loved his wife Nancy, too. He had called Nancy and she'd agreed to bring their son back to the Dude Ranch. She would give him a second chance.

Sharon didn't put up a fight. She didn't think it was working out with Gary, either. Besides, she had rekindled an old affair.

"I love you, too, but I'm moving in with Buzz," she said.

Buzz Reynolds—the man who had thrown Sharon out when she became pregnant—had always been the doctor's widow's backup lover during her affair with Gary. He was wealthy, kind and very much in love with her. And though Sharon had conceded a time or two that sex with Mr. Reynolds was not what it had been with Gary, he had plenty to offer.

Namely, he had money.

Perry's parents had done all they could to help Sharon and their grandchildren get through the difficult times after their beloved son's disappearance. When asked by their daughter-in-law, they sent money. When asked to take Danny and Misty for vacations they readily agreed. While they still had strong and loving relationships with Perry's three daughters from his marriage to Julie, the littlest grandson and granddaughter were their last link to their son.

When Mrs. Nelson wrote Sharon with the happy news that they were coming to Colorado for a visit, Sharon's response seemed peculiar. She phoned back, and acted as if she was glad they were coming, but told them she had other plans and could not break them. She reluctantly told her in-laws they could come, but only stay for a single night.

"Then you'll have to leave the next day," she said.

The Nelsons canceled the trip. What choice did they have? They weren't going to make the long drive from Michigan for a one-day visit. Their hearts ached for young Danny and Misty; they couldn't see the sense in it. Yet it nagged at them: Why didn't Sharon want them around?

A grief-stricken mind is a great and terrible trickster. The days, weeks, months after her father's disappearance was the most difficult time of Lorri Nelson Hustwaite's life. Crying jags lasted for days. Meals were skipped. Rumors coming from Colorado to Montana only added to her misery. It also added to her hope.

Whenever the phone would ring, Lorri would reach for it with the hope that it was her dad calling. She'd even imagine the words he would use:

"Sorry, Lorelco, for causing you so much worry, but I'm all right..."

When she'd pick up the receiver, Lorri could feel her heart stop for a second, only to start up again when it was instantly evident the caller was not her father. Sometimes her voice would catch just a little, perhaps signaling to the caller the young woman on the other end of the line was in some kind of trouble.

"I'm fine," she'd say.

At the grocery store, Lorri would see a man who resembled her father. Driving by a service station she'd crane her neck to watch a man as he pumped gas. *It was him!* She'd be certain, just for an instant, that her father was there. Then the disappointment would take over. And even though it was never Perry Nelson, even though no body had been found, she held out hope that he'd be alive.

"I wish my dad would send a postcard or call," she said to her husband for the umpteenth time. Darrell Hustwaite had grown weary of that particular broken record. It wasn't that the kind-hearted mechanic didn't respect his wife's terrible grief; it was that he saw the futility in it.

"Gee, Lorri! This is killing you. You've got to get over it."

But she couldn't. She seemed unable to set it aside. When word came from friends in Colorado that talk about her father had shifted to the idea that he had fled the country to Australia and was never coming back, Lorri was relieved.

At least he isn't dead, she thought.

Lorri confided to friends how she felt when she heard her dad might have left the country to escape Sharon and the IRS.

"If he's alive and safe, it's okay. Things must have been horrible at home. Maybe the only way he could get away from Sharon was to disappear?"

One afternoon a few weeks after Perry disappeared, neighbors and real estate agents Ann and Bernard Parsons drove up to go over some business matters Sharon had asked about. They noticed Danny Nelson playing in a sandbox in front of Round House.

As Ann walked to the front door, Bernard called out to the little boy.

"Is your mother home?"

"Mom's in the house. Dad's in the river!" the boy called out.

Bernard chuckled at the peculiar response.

"What did he say?" Ann asked as she walked up the steps to the front door.

"Tell you later."

When they got back in the car after talking with Sharon, Bernard repeated Danny's words.

"Mom's in the house! Dad's in the river!"

17

WHEN HE TOLD SHARON THE STORY OF HOW HE
killed her husband, Gary sometimes altered the tale. Sometimes he said he wasn't sure if it had worked. Other times he
embellished the saga. Sharon would later say she didn't know
what to believe. She didn't know what really happened. But
Gary, in fact, did know.

He told her about the drive up to Denver to get the guns,
how Perry had chatted along the way, not knowing what was
about to happen. . . .

Gary asked Perry to stop for a beer, though that wasn't the
real reason for the delay. As the two shared a beer in a tavern
in Castle Rock, Gary excused himself to use the bathroom.
With Perry sitting behind half-empty beer glasses, Gary Adams made his way to a pay phone and dialed the number of
a buddy with whom he had briefly lived near Denver.

"Pick me up at midnight at the first tunnel past Golden,"
he said.

The friend agreed.

The beer-buzzed doctor and the carpenter drank a while
longer, then left to get some shut-eye before driving back to
Wet Canyon in the morning.

It was around midnight. The road was slicker than still-
warm roadkill. The rain had been relentless, drumming the
windows of the old VW with pellets hard enough to make one
flinch. Perry hated driving in the rain. Any other kind of
weather condition was easier, even snow. Unless it was a

whiteout, at least the driver could see at night during a snowfall. Gary looked straight ahead at the roadway, his nervousness not overwhelming enough to stop him from what he had planned to do.

Perry pulled into a parking strip next to Clear Creek to get some sleep. Gary swung the door open and got out.

"Gotta take a leak," he said.

Perry nodded and went to work on reclining the car seats so the two could stretch out and snooze until morning light.

Gary didn't have a tire iron this time, so he went down to the water's edge to look for a rock that would do the job. It was dark and every stone seemed too large.

Finally, he found one he could lift. He memorized where it was and he returned to the VW.

"Perry," he said, "I lost my wallet down there. Can you give me a hand looking for it?"

Perry nodded before picking up a flashlight and following Gary down to the surging banks of Clear Creek. *Some creek*— the water from the storm had swollen it to a raging river. The beam of the flashlight stretched a white line through the night air as it slid across the wet boulders flanking the immediate creek side.

"Can't see anything," Perry said, his head bent low as he searched the area.

Gary hoisted a large rock of fifteen to twenty pounds and slammed it hard against Perry's slightly balding head. He would later admit he had used all his might to do so. He had no clue that the human skull was so resilient.

Perry fell to his hands and knees into the icy water. In a second, blood and water running down his face and into his beard, he jumped back up. Gary couldn't believe his eyes.

Why wasn't he knocked out? The icy water? The adrenaline pumping through his terrified body? Why wasn't he out cold?

Gary pushed Perry back down and tried to hold his head under the water. The two men thrashed, Gary trying his damnedest to keep the upper hand. Yet Perry was holding his own. He was much taller. He weighed more. And by then he must have known he was fighting for his life.

Gary put all his weight on top of his flailing friend and held him under the water. But again, just as he thought he'd completed what he set out to do, Gary was stunned by Perry Nelson's strength. He rose out of the water once more.

Like a freakin' horror movie.

At one point, Gary slipped under the frigid, waist-high water. The water's sudden depth scared him. The fighting had taken the two men further from the shore. And all of a sudden, as if it was meant to be, the current swept Perry Nelson away. Gary watched as the man he had called his friend, the man whose wife he had been screwing for months, floated down Clear Creek.

He was gone.

Gary, scraped and covered in sand, mud and blood, got behind the wheel of the VW and drove it a half mile away. When he hit about 20 mph, he swung the door open and rolled out. The car slipped into the creek, its headlights still on.

The goddamn thing's floating!

Volkswagens are watertight. Everyone knows that. Gary knew it. What was he thinking? Dr. Nelson's car had become a beacon. His heart raced as he watched the VW bob along the current of the creek. If a car came by the driver would surely see it. He held his heaving breath and waited. In a couple of minutes, relief came. The creek twisted and the car disappeared around a sharp bend.

It had not gone exactly according to plan.

"The plan was in my head: Knock Perry unconscious, hold him underwater so he'd drown, drag him up the bank, put him in the VW, then drive him in."

He couldn't be sure if he had done the job. There was the slim possibility Dr. Nelson had made it to shore and was still alive. Gary walked along the shore searching without the aid of a flashlight, hoping that he had killed his friend.

Hoping, above all, he would not disappoint Sharon.

With Sharon and Gary entwined like a vitrine of snakes, it didn't take long for people to wonder out loud. Wet Canyon neighbors Ray and Candis Thornton were among those who could not hold suspicions inside any longer. What was happening up in Round House wasn't right. A man disappears and his wife has a lover move in right away? Something was going on. Something ugly.

When the Thorntons ran into a couple friendly with Gary Adams, they finally said they thought Sharon and Gary had conspired to kill Perry.

"No," the friend said. "It couldn't be. Gary was in church the day after Perry was missing. He had his Bible with him and he was praying."

Kindergarten teacher Candis discounted the image. She didn't trust Gary Adams. Going to church was a ruse.

"He's like a wild man. He'd steal from you . . . and look you in the face and tell you how much he loved you. I've never seen anything like him. He has the most piercing blue eyes, so unbelievably evil."

Husband Ray agreed. "His eyes are like two blue ice cubes. They are coldest blue I have ever seen."

The eyes of a killer, he thought.

The woman in the sling-backs was also poison. Even Candis Thornton finally had to admit it. Yet she was torn. She still wanted to like Sharon Nelson. Candis was the kind of woman who wanted to see the good in people. There was enough ugly stuff in the world as it was.

If Sharon had kept her questionable escapades within the confines of Round House, that would be one thing. But over the course of her years in the Canyon, Sharon had proven she had no boundaries. A pattern had emerged. Dr. Nelson's wife was expert at befriending a couple, ingratiating herself and charming her new friends with stunning fluency.

Then, when the wife was sucked into a one-sided friendship, Sharon would have sex with the woman's husband.

"I know she's doing this beyond a shadow of a doubt," Candis Thornton told a friend, reliving the life and times of Sharon Nelson. "I saw it happen two times. I just can't believe how the woman is acting."

At least, Candis could count her blessings. Her husband, Ray, had despised Sharon from day one.

Barbara Ruscetti met Nancy Adams at a Weight Watchers meeting and liked her very much. When she heard about

Sharon and Gary messing around, Barbara felt a surge of sympathy for Nancy. Her husband was just another notch on Sharon Nelson's bedpost.

Barb would never forget a story she heard about the goings-on in Wet Canyon. It seemed Nancy wasn't as much of a pushover as her reputation had it.

"The mailman was a good friend of mine and he said Danny had taken the mail out of the Adams' box and put it into another mailbox and Mrs. Adams got very upset. So she went up to Sharon's house and told Sharon that if she didn't keep her goddamn brat away from her mailbox that they were going to have him arrested. So Sharon and Gary's wife had a great big fight. And I understand it was a knock-down-drag-out. And supposedly, Gary went up to Sharon and told her not to ever touch his wife again. They supposedly were sweethearts! He was supposed to be living with her! But then the first move she made on Gary's wife, Gary was defending the wife, *not* Sharon."

Another time there were more fireworks between Gary's women. Bolstered by her husband's promises, Nancy felt it was she that would stay Mrs. Adams.

Sharon was sure she was the one.

Nancy Adams fixed her eyes with the kind of steely stare the Other Woman dreads. Without a single word uttered, there would be no mistaking that she was about to tell Sharon to back off and keep away from her man.

The man is mine. He shares my bed, not yours. Keep your mitts to yourself, you bitch. You home-wrecking whore.

It was that kind of look.

"Stay away from Gary," she said. "Don't drop notes in the mailbox. Don't do anything."

Sharon didn't say a word. She simply turned and walked away.

Living a life between two women had become routine for Gary Adams. Whenever he had the chance, he'd make up an excuse to leave the Dude Ranch and head up the ridge to Sharon's place. Nancy knew what was going on, but she couldn't stop her husband. And while the draw had been the sex, Gary knew in time there would be money. Lots of it. As the days went on and her husband went out to visit or go to town, Nancy Adams was left alone to smolder. She was fed up.

When Gary told Nancy it was best for her to take their son and get a job in Denver, she gladly complied.

Though he had sought the separation, Gary, however, remained agitated. His nerves were shot like a rural roadsign. He was falling apart and he knew it. It wasn't that he didn't love his wife and son; he needed Sharon more. Sharon was everything.

Nancy packed up, drove away from Wet Canyon and moved in with her mother. She was justifiably heartbroken over her husband's relationship with Sharon, but she didn't want to give up so easily. The small woman with the big eyes had a history with Gary that went back to her teenage years. He was her one and only. She lost her virginity to the man, and there had been no others. In love as she was, Nancy was not a complete dummy. A few weeks after she left for Denver, Nancy decided to return to the Dude Ranch. She found out her husband and Sharon Nelson were living together, carrying on like lovesick teenagers. Everyone in town knew it, too.

This time Nancy stood up for herself. Damn the ties. Damn the years they had spent, the family they had been once. She told her blue-eyed honey that she was leaving him. She was filing for divorce in Denver. She wasn't going to play the fool to Sharon Lynn Nelson.

Not anymore.

If the men were receptive to her charms, women were decidedly anti-Sharon. It only took a couple of encounters with the brassy beauty to see what she was up to. Some Weston women saw a conniving woman who turned her back on the wives as she played up to their husbands. When Perry was gone and Gary Adams was not around, Sharon would ask for help for jobs which were too tough for her to do.

One neighbor told her husband not to go up to Round House.

"If you do, better not bother coming back," she said.

When men went up to help Sharon, the standard line batted

about was "better watch out, she'll put some insurance on you and look out!"

When sawmill owner Al Robinson told his wife, Melanie, that he was thinking of going to Sharon's after she said she needed lumber, she had a knee-jerk retort.

"Better not catch you going up there," Melanie said.

It was only a half-joke, but Al convinced her not to worry.

"This is all business. No hanky-panky," he said. "I can't stand the woman."

Melanie could relax. Al Robinson said it like he meant it.

It figured. As ridiculous and horrendous as it was, it didn't seem too far off base for Trinidad. Sharon Nelson had probably pulled off the perfect crime. As mechanic Jim Whitley figured it, she had probably eluded arrest by doing what she reportedly did best.

"You had two ways of paying for things in Trinidad: cash or sex. They've got their own justice system like nowhere else in the world. I wouldn't put it past her to have slept with lawyers, judges, whoever down there. She'd use her body any way she needed to. She was just one of those people. She'd be the type to sleep with some guy, then blackmail him about it to get what she really wanted."

18

GOOD GOD. IT WAS NOT ASPEN. IT WAS Trinidad. The fetching woman standing in the checkout line at the Safeway was dressed more appropriately for the glitz of the ski Mecca than tourist destination wanna-be Trinidad. Her makeup was flawless, her hair fluffed like a Persian cat combed out with baby powder. And despite her cloud of furs and heels that could trim fat off a roast, Barb Ruscetti knew the woman was Sharon Nelson.

Barb, working at a new job and firmly on her feet again, left her cart and made her way toward her nemesis. She wanted to take the opportunity to inform Sharon that another office assistant from Rocky Ford also had been denied unemployment benefits.

"You didn't pay *her* unemployment insurance, either," Barb said, after barely saying hello.

Sharon shook her head emphatically. With an annoyed look, she pulled her fur coat up on her shoulders.

"That's not true. I paid it. I know I did."

"I don't think so," Barb snapped. The office worker was not a liar, but Sharon was an expert one. While Barb continued to clutch her coupons and grit her teeth, Sharon smiled sweetly and waved good-bye. She said she hoped they'd be able to get together soon.

"I've been so busy," she called out.

Barb Ruscetti had been dismissed. The Queen of the Mountain would have nothing to do with her and, in every way, that was just fine with Barb. Barb couldn't stand her. The Bitch on Wheels disappeared into the parking lot, leaving a lasting impression that time would never erase.

"She was dressed up to the whattie. I mean she was all spiffy in her fur coat and high heels and her hair was done and the whole bit," Barb later told a friend.

What was it about women like Sharon? Barb Ruscetti could never quite figure it out. Women like Sharon had everything going for them, youth, beauty and smarts. Yet whatever it was they possessed, it was never enough. The more God and their husbands gave them, the more they wanted. If their perfect nose could be made shorter, it would be done. If they could find a lover with more money or a bigger penis—or whatever it was they wanted—they would search for him. Whatever they desired was whatever they could get their hands on. Barb had lost her husband when she was a young wife. Yet she'd raised her kids on her own, never looking for the man who would sweep her off her feet and end her financial worries. Barb Ruscetti was content with her lot in life, convinced by her own life experiences that the grass was not always greener. She was everything Sharon was not. Moreover, Sharon could never aspire to achieve what Barb had done so successfully on her own.

Whatever Sharon was searching for, Dr. Nelson's former secretary doubted the younger widow would ever find it. Not in North Carolina, not in Colorado. Not anywhere.

Up and down the wobbly little mountain roads to houses clinging like toadstools on hillsides, gas man Louis Volturo was a welcome sight for everyone in Wet Canyon. Everyone, it seemed, but Gary Adams and Sharon Nelson. Holed up once again in their mountaintop love nest, they didn't seem to take kindly to visitors. In fact, they were downright hostile.

Volturo felt a sharp poke in his ribs as he was filling the Nelsons' butane tank. It was Gary Adams with a revolver.

"What the hell are your doing up here?"

"Just putting gas in for Mrs. Nelson," Volturo said, nervously.

"You put in the gas and get the hell out of this place right now. I don't want you looking around or anything. Get the hell out of here!''

Later, Louis told his friend Barb Ruscetti about his encounter with the widow Nelson's omni-present boyfriend.

"I was scared," he said. "I told my boss that if you want to deliver gas up there, you take it yourself. I won't take it."

Barb agreed.

"I wouldn't go up there, either," she said.

Sharon's sister Judy had been through the mill when it came to men. She had her abusive marriage and no-good boyfriends. Over time, her sense of smell became acute when it came to men: Judy could smell a rat.

There was something about Gary Adams that gnawed at her sensibilities. He had a kind of innocuous handsome country-boy look, but underneath the aw-shucks facade was something unsettling. She could never put her finger on it. Instead of forcing the issue and analyzing the man, she tried to back off a bit. Gary Adams was a little scary.

One weekend visit at Round House ended abruptly for Judy and her children. Gary was fussing at one of Sharon's children, and Judy jokingly flipped him the bird. In an instant, Gary turned his ire from the child to her.

"This is my house!" he raged. "I'll do anything and treat anyone any damn way I please. This is my place and no one is going to tell me what to do!"

Judy became frightened. Sharon tried to intervene, albeit halfheartedly. Judy didn't care what Sharon said. She knew Gary meant every word he was saying. Yet this wasn't his house. It was Sharon and Perry's house. Judy decided to leave. She was not going to spend one more minute, let alone another night, there. It was the last time she ever visited Sharon at her home in Wet Canyon.

In a way, Judy Douglas needn't have worried too much about her sister. Sharon's old ways kept her from forging permanent relationships with any man, good or bad. Sharon's backup boyfriend Buzz stayed in the picture whenever Gary Adams was shoved aside. Every couple of weeks, it seemed Sharon would tire of Buzz and return to the mountain house. Back there, she'd summon Gary to her bedroom. Over and over. Back and forth. Sharon was the one holding all the cards; she ruled the world.

Barbara Ruscetti knew the address the instant she pulled the envelope from her thick stack of holiday mail. She knew the handwriting on the envelope belonged to Sharon. It was a greeting card sent by the woman she was certain was behind a terrible murder five months earlier.

Under the cheery holiday salutation was a note: *Barb, I miss you very much . . . could we still be friends? Could I come by and see you?*

Even though there were times when she despised Sharon, Barb couldn't help but be moved by the pathetic little note. She addressed a little card for Sharon and indicated that she would be happy to see her.

Forty-eight hours later, Sharon was in Barb's holiday-decorated and Christmas tree-scented living room, drinking fresh-perked coffee and eating fruitcake. As the buxom widow with the new winter outfit and the cinnamon-twist headed former secretary sat across from each other, there was no denying the tension. Even the muted strains of Christmas carols could do little to mitigate the awkwardness and antagonism.

If Sharon had wanted to be friends, if Barb had thought by inviting her over she was doing the right thing, both were wrong.

Barb had a question that she had wanted to lay on Sharon since that Monday morning when her neighbor had called across the street with the news Dr. Nelson was missing.

"I have something to ask you," Barb began, her chest heaving slightly with stifled consternation.

Sharon smiled sweetly and looked up from her steaming cup.

"What?" she asked.

Barb let out her breath and blurted the question.

"Did you kill Perry?" she asked.

Sharon set her cup on the table. She turned pale and shook her head with great vehemence. Her fingers brushed her lips.

"No," she said, "but I sure wish I had."

Though Sharon punctuated her response with a nervous little laugh, Barb didn't think it was a joke. Uneasiness hung in the air. Though Sharon chatted a bit more before making up a hasty excuse that she had to leave, the conversation over coffee fruitcake was over.

"She never came back to my house. She knew I knew. When she left, she said, 'I'll be seeing you.' But she never came back anymore. She'd see me on the street and cross over to the other side. She knew. She was a rotten baby. You can't believe the things she did."

The school Christmas play had been a community tradition for as long as many could remember. Everyone in Weston halfway connected with the school attended the event that kicked off the holiday season with the joyous song of Weston's youngest children.

Sharon Nelson entered the school auditorium wrapped in fur and dressed to the nines. Audience members stopped talking and turned to watch her. And watch, they did. She wore heels and a short dress. Her makeup was done to movie-star perfection. For a minute, many stopped breathing.

All knew she had wrangled a portion of some life insurance money before there had been conclusive proof that Perry Nelson was dead. Everyone knew it was blood money that had paid for the sumptuous coat. Everyone knew she was shacked up with Gary Adams. The big question was still bantered about, however: What really happened to Perry?

While most of the women had little regard for Sharon, either because they were jealous or they felt she was a world-class husband hunter, men continued to be divided.

And yet as one local explained to an outsider, when it came to Sharon Nelson it seemed men fell into two camps.

"Those who would fall for her and those who were disgusted by her. It was as if their eyes were looking at two different women. A man who could read Sherry was a lucky man. Many were not."

If Perry was dead, at least Sharon was left with some money. Julie Whitley's memory turned back to three weeks before Perry's car went in to the black water of Clear Creek.

Julie had stopped in to the eye clinic to pay for some glasses and made a remark to the effect that if it isn't one thing, it is another. Money just didn't seem to go far enough.

"I know what you mean," Sharon said.

As they talked—Julie couldn't recall how it came up—but the subject of life insurance was broached.

Sharon confided that she had purchased three policies on her husband's life. It was her way of ensuring her survival in the event that the unthinkable happened.

"If anything happens, I can't make it alone. I had to forge his name," she said.

Sharon was such a talker, such a relentless braggart, Julie Whitley wasn't sure if she had in fact forged her husband's name, or if she was just thinking out loud.

"I wish I could get away with that," Julie shot back. "If I could, I would. Dying is the only thing that you can count on. Might as well have someone profit from it."

Sharon nodded.

As Julie Whitley saw her, Sharon was a woman with ambitions far beyond Trinidad. She wanted to be ensconced in the country-club set in a place where the cachet actually meant something. Trinidad wasn't big enough, fast enough, good enough.

"In Trinidad they are either on welfare or they are wanting out. I didn't think anything of Sharon's desire for more. I wanted out of Trinidad, too," Julie later said.

When the rumor mill churned with the persistent gossip that Perry had fled to Mexico and was awaiting Sharon to break away to come to his side, those closest to the Nelsons almost laughed. Why would sleeping with Gary Adams be part of such a plan? Why would Perry renew his pilot's license just days before his disappearance? Why get the VW all fixed up for camping when you'll never have a chance to use it?

Sharon continued to be a figure who invited opinions, a woman who courted rumor. Innuendo was her shadow. As her true character became more evident, the talk increased. She was a slut. A whore. Probably a killer. Even though they were the closest neighbors to the Nelson place, the Thorntons tried to stay out of the fray and kept their opinions to themselves. When

Nester Baca, a Las Animas County Sheriff's deputy, visited with Ray one afternoon at their ranch house, he started the ball rolling. His gut told him that Sharon had killed her husband.

"I know it," he said. "I just can't prove it."

Sharon wasn't completely out of the loop. She heard the occasional comments about her character after Perry disappeared. She knew people could be nasty with their comments. Gossip was an Olympic event in rural Colorado. But what did they know of her life? What did they know of what she had gone through before Perry died?

"I can easily understand why people would say I was greedy," she told a friend sometime later. "I can understand that. Things, status, meant a great deal to me. They were my shell, I guess you could say. *I wasn't white trash.* I loved the things Perry bought me. I loved the freedom to buy whatever I wanted without having to account for a dime. It was almost like everything Sharon wants, Sharon can have. She doesn't have to account for it. I'd had to account for change from a quarter if I bought a dime pack of gum with Mike."

Terry and Kay Mitchell couldn't wait to get out of Trinidad. The chiropractor and his wife considered the town a pit. When they relocated Dr. Mitchell's practice to the Denver area in December 1983, they assumed most of what had bothered them about the place would be left behind.

Sharon Nelson had other plans. She wanted to keep in touch.

Over the course of 1984, Sharon made several visits to the Mitchell home. Despite the fact her husband was still missing, Sharon seemed happy.

Very happy.

"You haven't let things get you down," Kay commented during one of the visits.

Sharon nodded affirmatively. "Things have worked themselves out," she said.

Kay was uncomfortable with the happy-go-lucky attitude. Perry didn't even come up in conversation.

It hasn't been a year since his disappearance and she's not even thinking of him anymore, she thought.

Kay said, "It's amazing how quickly you've gotten through this."

"Everything's just falling into place," Sharon answered. "Everything is working out so well for me."

Over the next few weeks and months, it became clear the reason she was doing so much better than most would have expected was on-and-off-again Gary Adams. Sharon brought her new man up to Dr. Mitchell's office in Parker, Colorado, for treatments. Gary had suffered some hearing loss and was treated with acupuncture.

Dr. Mitchell had no doubts—even at the first visit—that Sharon was sleeping with her helpful neighbor. Sharon, as far as he knew, didn't hang around with a man unless she was having sex with him.

One time in 1984, Sharon arrived alone at the Mitchells' residence. Her hair was done, makeup perfect. She never looked happier. She was also busting with some news.

"Gary and I got married," she announced.

Kay acted surprised that she and Terry hadn't been invited. *As if we would have wanted to go.*

"Oh, it wasn't that kind of a wedding," Sharon said as the two women sat down to talk. "Gary and I went together to the mountains and said our vows in a field of wildflowers."

"Oh, I see," Kay said, thinking it was about the dumbest thing she'd ever heard.

Some wedding . . . another of Sharon's useless little lies.

Sharon Nelson had her own way of doing things. She was not shy. She didn't care one bit what anyone thought of her, especially when she was in love. Not too many months after her husband disappeared, Sharon and Gary paid a visit to the single-wide mobile home of Ann and Bernard Parsons. The Parsons were in the midst of building a new home, and for the time being had to make do with the tiny quarters. When Sharon and Gary arrived, they were invited inside. Ann Parsons was the kind of woman who peppered her speech with "hon." Bernard was a man who never knew a stranger. They were glad for the company.

Visits in the country were few and far between and, consequently, almost always welcome. Yet this visit was unsettling to the hosts. Sharon was holding Gary's hand, very much in love. She snuggled up next to him on the couch. In doing so, the glint of gold was unmistakable and overt. If the sun had been shining on the diamond-studded pendant around Gary Adams' neck, it could have blinded someone.

Sharon noticed Ann's eyes linger on her boyfriend's pendant.

"I had a jeweler make it especially for Gary," Sharon said. She recounted how she had come up with the design. That was like Sharon, she was always the one with the best, the most unique ideas. She was always proud of her creations. But as she talked, it was the source of the gold that made the Parsons a bit uneasy.

"I had the jeweler melt down Perry's wedding ring. I couldn't see any sense in keeping it anymore."

Ann and Bernard exchanged fleeting glances. Neither wanted to call attention to what they were thinking, but neither wanted to miss the opportunity to ensure they were on the same wavelength.

When the visit was over and Gary and Sharon had gone, Ann Parsons immediately turned to her husband.

"What do you think about that necklace?" she asked.

Bernard Parsons shook his head.

"I know what you mean."

Ann was appalled. "Have you ever heard of such a bloodthirsty thing in all your life? Imagine melting down your husband's wedding ring for jewelry for your boyfriend."

Bernard was nearly dumbfounded.

"Pretty cold, I'd say," he finally muttered.

As they talked a bit more, a chill passed between them.

"You're not going to tell me that Perry's not dead? Those two know something," Ann said. "I've got a gut feeling that he's dead and they know it."

It was on May 29, 1984. As Perry Nelson's youngest daughter by Julie, Lorri, marked her twenty-first birthday, she came to the realization her father was gone forever.

"My dad would never miss my birthday, not *this* birthday.

No matter what kind of trouble he was in, my dad would have called me,'' she said.

She could barely let the idea pass through her mind: Her father must be dead.

19

THE MAKESHIFT FAMILY—ANOTHER MAN'S WIFE, a part-time lover and a missing or dead doctor's two young children—drove the brown Jeep Eagle toward Trinidad, nearly to the lake that had been the place of so many trysts. In the Jeep was Gary Adams, Sharon Nelson, and her children Misty and Danny. It was a happy time, so needed when happy times had been in short supply. Sharon scooted next to Gary, in the manner in which teenage girls often do, while her boyfriend drove. Windows were cracked to suck out the silver smoke from Sharon's ever-present cigarette. The kids sat quietly in the backseat.

It was August 14, 1984, almost thirteen months after Perry Nelson vanished.

A sheriff's car coming from the opposite direction stopped and did a U-turn, sirens blaring. Gary skidded to the side of the road and got out, ready to tell the deputy that he wasn't going all that fast.

"I want to talk with Sharon," the deputy said. "Away from the kids."

Gary nodded and told Sharon to come out. In an instant, and as gently as the man in uniform could, he told her about a discovery made up north. A few minutes went by and Sharon returned to the car. Tears filled her eyes, though she did not let any fall.

"They found Perry's body in the creek," Sharon said. "Along a sandbar up near Golden."

Without talking about it much more, Gary drove the car to town, where they did their laundry and shopped.

Remarkably, for more than a year of exposure in the brittle freeze and griddle heat of Colorado wilderness, the body found along the waters of Clear Creek was quite preserved. It was wearing the same clothing as Sharon had described when her husband left for the optical convention in Denver thirteen months before.

Terry Mitchell got word that Friday that the corpse found in Jefferson County was purportedly his friend. Yet the description didn't ring true. News accounts indicated that the man found on the sandbar was in his thirties.

Perry was fifty when he disappeared.

The body was still clad in socks, trousers and a shirt.

"This doesn't sound like it could be Perry," he told Kay. "I'm going to go see the body."

Kay thought an inspection was a good idea, too. She had been bothered by the details.

"How could they mistake a thirty-year-old for a fifty-year-old?" she asked.

Since the Jefferson County coroner's office was not far from their home, it was not a problem for Dr. Mitchell to get over there right away. He got a woman on the line and told her who he was.

"I'd like to come and view the body of the man pulled from Clear Creek. He's supposedly a friend of mine."

"Oh, you can't see him," the woman montoned.

"I'll be fine. I'm a doctor."

"He's in a bag and I can't open it."

"I can open it. I'm a doctor. I can handle it."

"You can't, I'm sorry." She droned on about proper procedure and told Dr. Mitchell he would have to call back on Monday when the coroner was in the office.

Disappointed, Terry Mitchell agreed and hung up.

First thing Monday morning, he telephoned the coroner. A clerk answered.

"This is Dr. Mitchell calling. You have a Dr. Nelson there, I want to come in and view the body."

"Sorry, Doctor," the clerk said. "Dr. Nelson's remains

were sent to the crematorium this morning. His wife is having the remains sent to Michigan for burial.''

Terry Mitchell couldn't believe it. What was the hurry? The clerk said the body had been identified through dental records. Why had they moved so quickly? Why had they cremated him when they knew another physician wanted to make a visual identification?

The timing of everything seemed so odd. Just days before, an insurance adjuster who thought Perry, Sharon and Gary could be in cahoots had called Dr. Mitchell to set up an interview appointment. Sharon had not been paid all of her life insurance proceeds because there had been no body to prove a death had, in fact, transpired.

The insurance man called back a few days later and told the chiropractor the body had been found. The case was closed. *Why so fast?* Terry wondered. Then the answer came: Sharon was getting her money. Every last dime of it.

Dr. Mitchell continued to doubt the body extracted from the creek had been there for more than a year.

"I saw what the river did to that Volkswagen. It had been crushed to barely two feet tall. It had been beat up so bad that you could barely tell it had been a car. What would a year in that river do to a human body? There would be nothing left. Not socks on a man's feet? A shirt? That water rushed through there at forty-five miles an hour. It would rip the arms off a man. If it was Perry, I don't think he was in there that long,'' he said later.

It didn't take long for Dr. Mitchell to alter his theories on what had happened to his friend, Perry Edson Nelson, II. When he first came to doubt Sharon Nelson's story, he thought she and her husband had plotted the disappearance in an elaborate insurance fraud scheme. When Gary Adams became part of the picture, the Colorado chiropractor thought the carpenter with eyes for the widow was a part of the plot.

"All three of them are in on this,'' Terry told his wife.

But when he thought of the condition of the corpse and the quick disposal of it, he wondered if Perry had been the victim of a double-cross.

"Perry came back to get the money and Sharon and Gary

Adams didn't want to split the pie three ways. They hit him on the head and threw his ass in the river. That's what I think."

When Barb Ruscetti heard another doctor's description of a mostly intact corpse, she was dumbfounded, too.

"Why didn't that body disintegrate? Why didn't animals eat it?" she asked.

The man, an MD from Rocky Ford, didn't have an answer for that. No one did.

But Barb kept pushing. "There's coyotes up there," she said. "There's bears up there, there's mountain lions. They would come down and eat him. Why didn't this body disintegrate? Why didn't this body blow up?"

When Barb ran into Sharon after she returned from making the identification of her husband's body, the former secretary asked if she was sure it was Perry.

Sharon held no doubts.

"Yes, Barb, I am. I'd know that long-legged bastard anywhere."

When she had composed herself after the terrible news, Lorri Nelson Hustwaite sat down and wrote a letter to her father, a tribute to the man she loved. And even though she held his picture close, it was hard for her to focus on his life and not the unseemly facts surrounding his death.

> "... your body laying in the river, neglected and at times, forgotten, for the past year. You were left to the mercy of nature, slowly rotting away, with the rest of us were caught up with rumors and stories that you were still alive ..."

She wrote how she wanted her father to know that she hoped in time she could claim the traits that had made him such a wonderful man. She wished for his friendliness, his generosity, his sense of humor.

> "... most of all, your ability to make a child feel so special and loved ..."

Word came from Sharon that there would be no memorial service for her late husband.

"I just can't deal with the trauma of losing him all over again."

Three days after Perry Nelson was found, his widow and her lover brought him home to Round House—in a box from the crematorium.

She shook it carefully, like a curious child does to a Christmas present when someone has just exited the room. The box was so small it hardly seemed possible a man's remains could be compressed inside. The glint of her painted fingernail caught Gary Adams's eye as she pierced through the tape that kept the ashes from leaving a trail from the door to the kitchen counter. Sharon told her lover that she was curious . . . she had gone so long without the certainty she had wanted . . . she had to see what was left of her dead husband.

Sharon's curiosity turned to sobs as she peeled back a corner of the lid. Inside, the fine, granular ashes of Perry Nelson shifted in the box.

"There's no doubt," Gary said, trying to console her with a dose of reality. "Perry's dead, all right."

A body meant more money. A body meant the end of financial worry. A body meant Sharon could have whatever she wanted. With the discovery of Dr. Nelson's remains, the insurance companies holding out more than $200,000 had to pay up. Sharon dropped her legal maneuvering with her attorney in Trinidad. She didn't have to sue anyone and she didn't have to have her husband declared dead, because he *was* dead.

Sharon and Gary had talked about what the bucks would mean and how they'd divide it all up. It was Gary who came up with the first proposal. He was back in bed with Sharon, while wife Nancy had left for errands in town.

"I'll take a third, you take a third," he said. "And you take a third of it for the kids."

Splitting the insurance proceeds had not been an issue before Perry's disappearance, because it was assumed by both Gary and Sharon that they would live together happily ever after. Wrong. It was clear almost right away the two were great as lovers, lousy as a couple.

The money, they asserted, would be as great a bond as their love.

While there was celebration in Round House, hundreds of miles away in Michigan there were more tears. Perry's distraught parents tried to understand their daughter-in-law's strange grieving process. Good Lord, they tried. When they learned there would be no memorial service for their beloved son in Colorado, they planned one in Michigan.

The little box of gritty remains that Sharon had displayed on the kitchen table was laid to rest in the Cedar Lake Cemetery.

He sleeps awaiting the call of the Life-Giver.

Gary Adams was glad he found the note in the mailbox, and not Nancy. He was once more at the Dude Ranch with Nancy giving him another chance, and he didn't want to blow it. Some wondered if he was with Nancy for the sake of their son. Others figured he was whipped by both women and couldn't make up his mind. Yet, when Sharon's note came, her siren song drew him away from Nancy.

"Come up and see me," it read.

He made an excuse and left his family. He wondered how they could believe him about anything, he had lied so often. One lie, he knew, was always used to cover another. The lies would stack up until they tumbled and fell, taking him with them.

He went to the outside door off Round House's master bedroom and let himself inside.

"Here's ten thousand," Sharon said with a smile as she handed over a fat-with-money envelope. The two made love, the money an unnecessary aphrodisiac.

Over the weeks and months that followed, more insurance money rolled in. Sharon didn't have to prove Perry was dead. She didn't have to put up with the cruel remarks that her husband had fled the country for Mexico. She didn't have to sue to get what was hers. When the checks arrived, she planned on paying off Round House, splurging on some goodies and putting the rest into investments that would keep her secure for the rest of her life. She also had to pay off Gary.

Checks in her purse, Sharon and Gary drove up to Colorado Springs to take care of a little banking. Gary wanted his name put on the six-month, $55,000 certificate of deposit that Sharon had purchased with proceeds from the insurance windfall. While the interest from the CD was coming directly to Gary, he wanted to make sure when it matured, he'd get the full amount.

The bank refused to eliminate her name. Instead, they wrote in a co-owner of the amount: Gary Starr Adams.

Sharon told the teller that when the CD matured, she wanted the funds released to Gary.

So happy, so agreeable. Things were so good.

While it was true that she liked to spend the dough on herself, Sharon was anything but tightfisted with her money when it came to others. She bought new clothes and toys for her children. When Gary wanted a new motorcycle, Sharon plunked down the cash. For herself, she bought a blue fox and a mink coat on a trip to Pueblo. She could afford it. When all the death benefits rolled in, Sharon had added more than $250,000 to her bank account.

Gary appreciated what Sharon gave him, but he told her to slow down. It was the old grasshopper and the ant scenario. She was playing and spending all day and night, while she should be saving, planning and preparing for the future. Gary grappled with her extravagance and mixed-up priorities.

"I tried to tell Sharon she needed to spend the money wisely, but she'd go and have her fingernails done, have little gold things put on them . . . it cost fifty dollars. I'd try to explain to her that fifty dollars maybe doesn't seem like much when you've got all this money. But years down the road, it could buy a lot of food."

His suggestions for cooling it down only brought spasms of anger from Sharon. Mike had tried to control her, Perry had, but not Gary. She wasn't going to cave in to anyone.

Others noticed Sharon's penchant for waving her money all around town and beyond.

Barb Ruscetti, still bitter over Sharon's failure to pay for her unemployment insurance, was one. It stung whenever she heard of Sharon's latest purchase with the blood money from Dr. Nelson's death.

The former optical assistant never let a chance to berate Sharon slip by.

"Let me tell you all the stuff she bought," she told a friend. "She bought a new Bronco, she bought her a fur, she bought a mink coat. But you add up all the other things she bought for other people."

Barb let out a heavy sigh.

"She spent it all! She spent it."

And though she had all the money she had ever dreamed about, Sharon still wanted one more thing. She wanted Gary to divorce Nancy and marry her. She wanted it so bad. She couldn't understand why Gary kept putting her off. Why didn't he just dump that mousy little woman and get on with living the high life? Sharon wanted to marry Gary and she said so many times. She assumed that with his divorce from Nancy final, they'd set a date. Even with the on-and-off foundation of their relationship, she still wanted the ring that told the world he was all hers.

For some reason, perhaps unclear even to the man himself, Gary stalled her.

"If we get married, Sher," he told her a time or two, "you'll lose your Social Security. That's four hundred dollars a month you'll lose! It's not worth it. We can live together. Why don't we just keep pretending we're married?"

20

EVEN WITH A BANK ACCOUNT FATTER THAN A SIDE
of Nebraska beef, Sharon still liked to sneak into the movies
or away from restaurants without paying. She did it two or
three times at Pizza Hut, until an employee confronted her in
the parking lot.

"You didn't pay your bill," the young employee said.

Sharon feigned shock. "Oh, didn't I? I'm sorry, I forgot."

When Sharon and Gary enjoyed a little getaway in Las Vegas, Sharon cajoled Gary into skipping out on a $30 dinner
bill at an Italian restaurant.

"Sharon liked the rush. She liked the adventure," Gary
once told a friend, though he didn't think much of his lover's
choices when it came to adventure. "If you're going to do
something, do something big," Gary advised. "The rest of it—
always be straight. If you're going to be a criminal, hit a bank,
don't rob 7-Eleven."

Teenager Rochelle Fuller was the spitting image of her
mother. She had thick, dark hair and full, pouty lips. She even
sounded like Sharon when she spoke. To those who knew
them both, the resemblance was almost eerie. Yet, Rochelle
wasn't Sharon. She had spent her whole young life wondering
about a mother she didn't really know and at the same time
wishing she wouldn't make the same mess out of her life.
Distance had been a blessing. She and her younger sister, Denise, were raised by their father, preacher Mike Fuller, in Ohio.

When Rochelle's world had been rocked one last terrible time by her mother, the young woman would tell a confidant that as far as she was concerned, the woman who had given birth to her had never been a real mother to her.

"She made my life hell; every time I reached out to her and all the time knowing that she didn't have anything to give. The whole time I've known her, it has been one big charade."

And even though there was a deep bitterness between the two, a mix of abandonment, jealousy and distrust, there was also an undeniable connection. When Rochelle, at 15, pleaded with her mother to let her live in Colorado—away from her minister father and the tedium of the Midwest—Sharon agreed.

Sharon, however, could no more be a mother to Rochelle than she had been to Lorri Nelson. Sharon had to be her daughter's friend. She wanted to drink with, dance with, carouse around Trinidad with Rochelle.

Sharon was an equal—until, of course she needed to exert her considerable power to get her way.

And so they tried to be mother and daughter. Sometimes it worked. Sometimes it didn't.

The two enjoyed watching videos in front of the television with a bag of chips or bowl of butter-sopped popcorn. One movie in particular absorbed Sharon's attention: the Debra Winger/Theresa Russell thriller, *Black Widow*.

"She mates and kills," had been the film's tagline.

"It was like she was so fascinated with the movie you wouldn't believe it," Rochelle told a friend later. "She was so drawn to it that I couldn't talk to her or anything."

Rochelle, like everyone else, tried to sort out her mother's boyfriends, lovers, whatever she called them. Gary Adams was so off and on, that Sharon's daughter didn't know for certain where he fit in. Sharon would live with him, get dumped by him, rebound over and over. She would pick up a new guy. She would go back to another. Buzz Reynolds, the man who had been the source of the greatest hurt in Perry Nelson's messy marriage to Sharon, was one of those on the yo-yo string. Sharon told her family, her parents and sister, that she was going to walk down the aisle again. This time, she was going to marry Buzz Reynolds. Sharon's parents said they'd make the trip from Maryland to attend the wedding.

Maybe she was going to settle down, once and for all?

It was as if their daughter stayed up nights thinking of the most inappropriate acts, the most hurtful things that she could do. The checklist was long. The affairs had never been discussed, but Morris and Josephine Douglas were not completely blind. They knew more than Sharon ever gave them credit for. And before their visit to Round House on the eve of Sharon's supposed marriage to Buzz Reynolds, they might have thought the very fact that their daughter took up with another man while wed to a preacher would likely be the topper for most good girls gone bad. Not for their Sharon Lynn.

When the Douglases arrived for Sharon's wedding they were shocked to find their daughter shacked up with a man—and not even the groom. Gary Adams was sharing Sharon's bed as the ceremony with Buzz loomed. Even as she cut out the pattern for the wedding dress she was sewing, Gary was sprawled out waiting for her in the master bedroom.

It was too much. Once more, their middle daughter's behavior was over-the-line and unbelievably offensive.

The Douglases could not stay another second in Round House. They gathered their things and left with barely a goodbye. They would not come to the wedding. They would not come to the reception. The future Mrs. Reynolds had, once more, gone too far.

Sister Judy remembered an indignant Sharon talking about it later.

"Sharon has always been mad that Mom and Dad made such a big deal out of it and left before the wedding. What did she expect?" she asked.

Judy went to the wedding, which actually amounted to little more than a big poolside party at the Reynolds' sprawling ranch. A fairly decent band played and dozens, maybe a hundred, locals showed up. Judy considered Buzz a nice fellow and she hoped her sister would be happy.

When Judy left, however, she doubted things would work out between Sharon and Buzz. Sharon had been so vague about the legal aspect of the ceremony, Judy questioned if her sister was really married this time. Of course, just as she hadn't really married Gary Adams in the mountain meadow, she hadn't legally married Buzz.

Judy considered the whole thing another of her sister's strange charades.

"I doubt this wedding is real," she confided to a friend. "I hope Sharon knows what she's doing."

And while she was "married" to Buzz, Sharon, in fact, did have plans. She did have other things in mind. She still had her mountain man in her life.

How was it that Sharon could make the most outrageous requests seem as garden-variety, as benign, as asking someone to take out the garbage? Gary Adams stared at Sharon, focusing first on her eyes, then the gloss of her lips. Her lips had a life of their own; they drew him closer. Wet and luscious. Maybe whatever came from the lips was too powerful for him to dismiss.

He fought for reason to take control.

"Buzz needs to have an accident," she said.

"Accident?" Gary asked, though he knew Sharon's idea of an accident meant *causing* the accident.

"Yes. I think he could have an accident real soon."

Gary shook his head.

"Sharon, it's too soon."

Why didn't he say, "Sharon, you're crazy?" Or, "Sharon, you are out of your fucking mind?"

"Too soon, baby," he told her. "It's only been a couple of years since Perry."

Sharon nuzzled her face in Gary's muscular chest and took a deep breath. She didn't seem to care about how something might look. Coincidences happened all the time. One mother gave birth to three sets of twins. One man won the Lotto twice. Surely other women have lost two husbands. She didn't want to give up. Water had worked before. It covered all mistakes. Gary himself had said so many, many times: Fire and water were the ways to cover a crime.

"It'd be real easy," she cooed once more. "All you have to do is hit him on the head and have him fall in the lake."

Gary wasn't buying. It was a stupid and greedy idea.

"Think, Sharon. Here you are 'married' to two people . . . they're dead and water is connected."

Sharon backpedaled for a moment. She ditched the idea of the drowning. She suggested when Buzz was out making business deliveries might be a better time to get rid of him.

"He drives around out in the Canyon, you could drive by and shoot him and make it look like a robbery," she said.

Gary changed the subject, telling his brazen beauty that no matter what was done, it was too soon.

"Besides, you two aren't even legally married," he concluded.

Bart Mason had never met a woman like Mrs. Nelson. What Bart didn't know was that in the course of most lives very few people had. Bart was a good-looking guy whose interests were in perfect sync with his surroundings. He liked to hunt elk and deer. Several of the mounted deer heads that eternally gazed from the wall of his parents' restaurant were his trophies. Bart was raised in a farm community a dozen miles from Trinidad; he graduated from Trinidad State Junior College with certificates in diesel mechanics and welding.

If his friends described him as a hell-raiser, that spoke more to his personality after a beer or two than his everyday demeanor.

When Harry Russell, a friend of the Mason family, asked Bart to come up to help put up sheetrock in the basement of Sharon Nelson's house in Wet Canyon, the young man agreed. Though Bart didn't know it at the time, Harry had been involved on and off with the widow whenever Gary was out of the picture or when Buzz no longer satisfied her. In fact, it was Harry—not Gary Adams—that Oklahoma optometrist Bob Goodhead and his wife, Donna, observed in the driveway the day Perry was first deemed missing.

Years later, Bart would wish that he never laid eyes on mother or daughter.

Bart's first glimpse of Rochelle Fuller was one morning when he saw her still wearing her nightgown as she went outside to haul water. Bart offered to help and she didn't even look up as she declined.

You snotty little bitch, he thought.

The next day, Bart returned to help out with the Sheetrock. And though he thought Rochelle was a pretty girl, she was undeniably and dangerously young.

"Are you going to spend the night?" Sharon asked not long after he first started coming around to do the basement finish work.

"It don't matter," he said. While the drive back to Trinidad was a bitch after a long day, it wasn't so far he couldn't commute.

Sharon took his ambivalence as interest.

"You can sleep downstairs with Rochelle," she said.

Startled, Bart didn't know what to make of the offer. He couldn't imagine a girl's mother—a *normal* mother—making that kind of a statement to a young man. If she was asking for trouble, Bart Mason made up his mind, he certainly was not going to give it to her. That night Bart slept with Rochelle, but he kept his pants on and fully zipped.

"I never touched her," he said of that first night. "I just respected her." But in time, Bart succumbed to his attraction for the pretty, young girl. The two, in fact, began to date.

Sharon continued to court the role of best friend when it came to Rochelle. She told Bart that Rochelle had been under Preacher Mike's thumb for too long and she needed to spread her wings. It was Rochelle's turn to have fun. Consequently, Sharon asked nothing of her oldest daughter. And beyond hauling water now and then, Rochelle did little to help out around Round House.

Two weeks after Bart started seeing Rochelle, a father was talking to Sharon about his worries about his youngest son. He hoped his boy had enough sense not to mess around and get some girl pregnant.

"I don't have to worry about my daughter," Sharon said, indicating Rochelle. "She's on the Pill."

Bart felt his face grow hot with embarrassment, then a surge of anger. It didn't seem right that a mother would broadcast that about her own daughter.

Sharon doesn't have any self-respect, any respect for anyone, he thought.

About four months after Bart and Rochelle started dating, Sharon asked a question that almost knocked him over.

"Is Rochelle good in bed?" she asked.

Bart shot her a harsh stare and turned away. This woman was unbelievable.

On an outing to a Wal-Mart in Pueblo, Rochelle whined that she wanted a set of hot curlers. Bart, who had just started a new job, said there wasn't enough money to go around for that kind of item. Not then. When the paychecks rolled in, he'd buy it for her.

"But I want it now," she whined.

Bart stuck to his guns. "Can't have it."

During the young couple's discourse, Sharon stepped forward with a smile. As always, she had an answer.

"If you want it bad enough, there are ways to get things," she said.

The next thing he knew, Sharon and Rochelle had gone through the checkout line and were headed for the car. They had hidden bulky boxes containing a blow-dryer and some hot curlers in the folds of their clothing.

When Bart found out, he blew his top.

"I don't appreciate this," he said. "It isn't right. I could lose my job over something like this."

"Bart," Sharon said with a laugh, "sometimes you gotta do what you gotta do to get what you want in life."

And then what became her mantra: "If it ain't illegal, it ain't fun."

One day, Bart and Sharon's retread lover Harry got into a heated argument over Rochelle. Sharon had invited Harry to move in when she returned from another fight with Buzz Reynolds. No one knew if the break from Buzz was permanent or transitory or if Gary would be back. Nevertheless, while Sharon stayed with Buzz at his ranch, Bart and Rochelle had the run of the house. When Harry Russell moved into the master bedroom of Round House, things changed. He acted like he owned the place. The argument between Harry and Bart started out small and snowballed, the way arguments often do when alcohol is poured into the mix of misunderstanding and control. Bart wanted Rochelle to come to town to watch him play in a Saturday softball tournament. Harry didn't want Rochelle going anywhere. Harry Russell was in charge—all 350 pounds of him.

"This is my house!" Harry bellowed.

A stunned and angry Rochelle and Bart went outside and Harry followed.

"I'll do what I want and so will Rochelle!" Bart called over his shoulder.

"I'll kick your ass!" the older man yelled.

"I doubt it," said Bart as he and Sharon's teenaged daughter got in to his truck and drove off.

A couple of days afterward, Harry stormed into the little restaurant operated by Bart's parents. He was still hopping mad. Bart, in the midst of getting ready for work at a supermarket construction site, didn't have time for Harry Russell. Harry, however, was in a talking mood.

"I'm leaving here," he said.

Bart could care less. If anything, he was glad the guy was getting out of town.

"It don't matter to me," the young man fired back.

Instead of getting angrier and stomping all over the place, Harry Russell dropped the bomb.

"Last night in bed," Harry said, "Sharon said that she had Perry killed for fifty thousand dollars and if I didn't move out she'd have me killed, too."

Bart didn't think so. *Harry Russell was such a liar.*

"Yeah, you big piece of shit," Bart said.

Not long after the scene at the restaurant, Harry departed from the Trinidad area. Scuttlebutt had it that Sharon gave him $5,000 and a pickup to disappear from Wet Canyon.

As far as Sharon was concerned, everything, it seemed, had its price.

Try as she might, Judy Douglas was unable to feel a fondness for Sharon's mountain man boyfriend. There was something about the man that kept a bizarre foothold in her sister's life. She figured some might romanticize it as macho and tough. She saw it as controlling and mean-spirited. Sharon had a hard edge to her at times, too. The two of them were all wrong for each other.

She watched from a window as Sharon and Gary exchanged heated words in her Colorado Springs backyard one afternoon after Sharon ditched Harry and Buzz and went back to her true love from the ramshackle house at the bottom of Cougar Ridge.

They'll never make it, those two, she thought as she turned away. *Never in a million years, not unless they give up the power game they keep playing with each other.*

Sharon was no quitter when it came to games. But in the end, Judy figured, the two would simply tire of each other and call it quits. It was all she could hope for. And with Sharon's practice of moving from man to man, it seemed like a good bet.

Few could understand Lorri's obsession with her former step-mother. It was motivated by hate, not devotion. Sharon was always on her mind. In her dreams. Lorri could never forgive the former preacher's wife for all that she had done to her family. As far as Lorri could see, her parents might still be together if Sharon had stayed in Durham where she belonged. Though Lorri didn't know it at the time, she needed closure. She needed confrontation with her stepmother. Though her faith told her to forgive, her heart was still broken over the time she had lost with her father. At the very least, she blamed Sharon.

On a visit from Montana to Rocky Ford, Lorri convinced childhood friend Kerry Wheeler that the two of them ought to drive out to Buzz Reynolds' place to confront Sharon. When the two young women arrived, they immediately spotted Sharon's Mustang in the driveway. A dejected Buzz stood outside, apparently having heard them drive up.

"Sher's not here," he said, when Lorri made inquiry.

"Then how come her car's here?"

"She's not here. Moving up to Denver. She's sending Rochelle back for her car later."

Lorri didn't believe him. She looked over Buzz's shoulder

toward the house, straining to see a shadowy figure lurking behind the curtains.

And though Lorri would have liked to have it out with Buzz, too, she softened a bit. Though he wasn't about to cry, the man with the dark, weathered complexion of a rancher was clearly upset. His heart had been busted.

"I love Sharon," he said, sadly. "I wanted to be with her and raise those kids as my own. I would have done anything for her."

They talked for a few minutes, about Sharon, about Misty and Danny, and the young women left.

"Maybe she's here, but she just doesn't want to see you?" Kerry suggested.

Lorri shrugged. "I don't know. I guess with Sharon, I'll never know."

Kerry Wheeler grinned. Trying to catch up with Sharon Nelson was a bit like acting out in a television show.

"Did you see the curtain move?" she asked.

Both laughed as Buzz's ranch disappeared from view.

Gary and Sharon had been talking about their impending marriage for months, probably for as long as they had been together. Throughout the ups and downs, the Harrys, the Buzzs, the others, they had always come back to each other. No one who knew them could make any sense of it. For all Bart Mason knew, it was a marriage made in lust. Gary and Sharon were moving to Denver to get away from all the bullshit of the Canyon. To escape the stares and the whispers. To start over.

Bart and Rochelle were planning on staying in Round House while Sharon and Gary rented a house outside of Denver.

One day while Bart worked outside in the frosty chill of a December day, Sharon and Rochelle approached him.

"Rochelle wants a commitment," Sharon said.

Rochelle stood there, saying nothing.

Bart was caught off guard. "Yeah?"

"Well," Sharon said, "will you marry Rochelle?"

Bart was unprepared. He never expected his girlfriend's

mother to make a marriage proposal on behalf of her daughter. Rochelle wasn't pregnant. She hadn't even pressed the issue of marriage.

"Yeah," he found himself saying.

Sharon was ecstatic, maybe more so than her teenage daughter bride and the bewildered groom-to-be.

"We can make it a double wedding," Sharon gushed. "You and Rochelle and me and Gary."

The plans had been made. Mother and daughter, estranged for years by miles, misunderstandings, and buckets of lies, were going to share something very special. Bart and Rochelle, Sharon and Gary, would be united in a double-wedding ceremony. Sharon was thrilled.

Rochelle and Bart slept on the floor in the living room, the kids in their bedrooms, Sharon and Gary in the master bedroom. Gary stayed up there three nights in a row. When they woke, the morning they were to leave, Gary was gone. He had done it again. He went back to Nancy.

Sharon dragged herself from the bedroom in tears. She was devastated by her abandonment. Who would not have felt sorry for her? After all she had been through, wasn't she entitled to some happiness?

"I'm going anyway," she said.

Rochelle and Bart exchanged wedding vows in the county clerk's office while Sharon and her youngest two children looked on. It was supposed to be her day, too. But Gary had left her high and dry.

Gary was free, but aimless. He had skipped out on Sharon before their wedding, but he still didn't know where he was going or what he would do when he got there. He just had to get away. He drove up to Denver to stay with some friends, but no one was home. He went to his grown daughter's house near Denver and visited with her all day. At one point, as he tried to figure out what to do, he slipped away and called the landlord of the rental home that he and Sharon had planned to lease, and asked if the place was still available.

"No," the landlord said, "the people are moving in right now."

Gary thanked him. He let out a deep sigh of relief. Sharon

was moving in. She was not going to be cooling her heels waiting for him in Trinidad. He really was free.

Gary drove south. And just like Sharon, he planned to start over.

"I wanted Sharon out of Wet Canyon . . . out, away from me, away from Nancy, away from my son. Maybe it was a rotten thing to do, but I just couldn't think of any other way. She had a power over me and I knew I had to break it. The best thing was to get her up to Denver. She'd have a job up there. She'd still have the money. Just away from me."

Back in the Canyon, folks had become used to the phantom neighbor. Sharon was home. She was gone. She moved to Denver. She moved to the Springs. She never stayed in any place very long. Some wondered if her coming and going had more to do with how *they* had treated her, than how she viewed her home.

"She wanted to be a part of the community, I think," said one of her neighbors. "A lot of people kind of ostracized her. It was always out of sight, out of mind."

Bart Mason had just left Robinson's sawmill when he saw Gary Adams' familiar pickup truck. *The nerve of that little guy showing up in the Canyon!* Rochelle's husband was still bitter over how Gary had dumped Sharon, jilting her nearly at the altar. Bart positioned his truck across the roadway in a fashion that blocked both lanes. The two men got out of their trucks.

"You fucking pussy!" Bart yelled at his former beer buddy, his former defacto in-law.

Gary shrugged sheepishly.

The response only brought forth more ire from the hot-headed younger man.

"You're a fucking coward!" Bart yelled.

"I know, Bart," Gary said, clearly taken aback. He was obviously sorry that he'd run into Bart. He was also sorry that he had left Sharon in such a bad way. He just didn't want to divorce the mother of his son.

"I'm sorry. I just couldn't leave Nancy."

BOOK III:
Fireman's Wife

"I've known half a dozen guys who have helped her get wood or done ditch work, but everybody would hold her at arm's length because of the opinion of what had gone on."
—Bob Robinson, Weston resident

"It seemed like all of a sudden she got real greedy. It was buy, buy, buy."
—Rochelle Fuller, Sharon's daughter

"Mommy, why do all our daddies have to die?"
—Danny Nelson, nine years old

21

THE FAMILIAR HIGH-PITCHED, RED METAL ROOF rose in front of the windshield as Glen Trainor turned off the highway in little Walsenberg, Colorado. Next to McDonald's famed golden arches, few restaurants were so recognizable as the Pizza Hut. Sharon Nelson Harrelson knew the restaurant well. She and Gary Adams had been there before, as had her children. One time when she was sneaking out for the thrill of "dining and dashing," the former preacher's wife was caught by some pimply faced kid and hauled back inside to pay her meal bill.

It was a place full of memories. It had been such a place for Perry Nelson, too. Once when Perry and Julie were going through the motions of holding their tattered marriage together after Sharon had left for Texas, Perry started crying uncontrollably at the Pizza Hut.

"This is where Sharon and I used to go . . . I can't stand to be here anymore," he said to his heartsick wife. "This is where she told me good-bye."

The Walsenberg Pizza Hut was the place where Sharon Nelson took her pointy heels and stomped on his heart like a Mexican hat dance.

The Thornton detective, along with his partner Elaine Tygart, still didn't know what Sharon was going to confide when she asked them to drive there. Though they had no time to talk about it, both cops had the feeling the woman with the bunched-up Kleenex and smeared lipstick was going to inform them who had killed her husband, fireman Glen Harrelson. *She knew something.* Tygart and Trainor were sure of that. Somehow Sharon was up to her pretty eyeballs in it.

"I'm tired of living a lie," she had said back in Trinidad before they drove the forty miles to Walsenberg.

Even though Sharon indicated she knew the truth would set her free, she was still quite frightened. At least, she had said so many times. She cried and gasped for air. She was so scared.

Of what? The police? A boyfriend? Who, Sharon? *Who?*

Det. Glen Trainor made a brief phone call to his captain in Thornton.

"She's going to talk," Trainor said. "Send some people down here."

Done. In a few minutes a posse would be sent for Sharon. The captain told Trainer to arrest her.

Advised of her rights and the little waiver signed, Sharon slid into the dark folds of a Naugahyde booth, while Danny and Misty were given a fistful of quarters to play arcade games in front of the restaurant. Neither child appeared to be aware their world was changing forever. Sharon knew she was in trouble. The silence she had maintained in front of her children en route to Walsenberg was about to end.

She knew she could go to jail.

"It all started a long time ago," she began as if she were about to launch into a bedtime story. She started slowly, carefully. Words were chosen one at a time, giving her sentences a cadence that suggested worry and uncertainty. She told the detectives how she and her husband Perry had tax and financial obligations that were consuming their marriage. No marriage is easy, she said, but one with money problems can be doomed from the start.

Sharon stopped herself for a moment to ask a question.

"First of all, tell me why you—why do you suspect Gary Adams? What do you know?"

Det. Tygart did not want to reveal any more than necessary to keep the conversation going. She wanted Sharon to tell *her* story. And as she had at the interview at the sheriff's office in Trinidad, Sharon fixed her gaze on the female half of the pair of detectives.

"Well, his name came up amongst the townspeople," Tygart said.

Trainor jumped in, adding it appeared Gary and Sharon had been involved in a love affair.

Sharon slowly nodded and continued. She referred once more to her financial worries. The lien the IRS had placed on her Round House in the Wet Canyon was a whopping $265,000.

Trainor tried to focus her on the issue at hand: the death of her husband, firefighter Glen Harrelson.

"Okay," he said. "What happened after . . . what does that have to do with—"

Sharon complied. She continued recounting her see-saw marriage to Perry and her unhappiness. Though she clearly had an agenda that she hoped would ease her complicity in whatever crime had been committed, she still was going to tell the truth.

Yes, she knew, the truth would set her free.

"Okay. During our marriage, I fell in love with Gary. I don't know why, but I did. I got to the point that I didn't know what to do. Gary said he could arrange for Perry not to be around anymore."

"Did he say how?" asked Tygart.

"Yes."

"What did he say?"

Sharon wept into a tissue. "He said he'd do it," she said.

Sharon Nelson spilled her guts in the sticky booth of a pizza restaurant. She was spinning a tale so strange that if there hadn't been a recorder preserving every word, the detectives might have asked her to slow down so that they could log down every peculiar utterance.

"He rode with Perry from Trinidad to Denver—and I don't know—I still don't know whether he killed Perry first and then pushed the car in the river—or what happened. I really don't know."

She indicated there had been insurance money after Perry's

death, and she figured the police could consider the money part of the motive.

Glen Trainor pressed the widow for further details. He wanted her to cough it up. He wanted it all. He wanted The Big Confession.

"Now, people make mistakes, Sharon, and sometimes we make some really big ones, but when you're a good person like you know you are, it always comes to light and you always do what you can to make it better. Okay? And this is the first step toward starting a new life, doing what you can do to just make things right. Did Gary ever report back to you, tell you what he did?"

Sharon nodded through her sobs.

"He said it was . . . 'it's done'."

"And never brought up the subject again?"

"I went through all the investigation of Perry's death. Gary said the only things that really covered tracks was fire and water."

The investigators let the woman talk. She had things on her mind, and it seemed that she was going to follow her own instincts when it came to what she would or wouldn't talk about. She told them Gary wouldn't let go of her. Their on-and-off relationship had torn up her life. Even when she married Glen, she could not shake Gary Adams' attentions. He was jealous. He hated seeing the two of them together.

He killed for love and money.

Elaine Tygart turned off the recorder at 3:52 P.M.

What to do next? The Pizza Hut was filling up with hungry diners and with quarters exhausted, Sharon's children were bored. Though she was not handcuffed, Sharon was reminded she had been arrested and was in custody of the Thornton Police Department. Rather than sit in the car and wait it out for the Thornton contingent to arrive, the two detectives decided to rent a room at the Best Western Motel next door.

Glen Trainor made arrangements for Danny and Misty, telling Sharon he'd drive them back to Rochelle's house in Trinidad.

The little boy and girl started crying. They didn't want to

leave their mother. They didn't know what was happening. No one told them to what their mother had confessed while they were eating pizza and playing video games. No one told them that their mother had set up their father and stepfather. Sharon held her son and daughter and tearfully instructed them that the nice policeman would drive them back to big sister Rochelle's house in Trinidad. Sharon said she had some business to take care of and she wouldn't be coming home that night.

Det. Trainor did his best to console the kids; and once on the road, away from their mother, their tears, in fact, did stop.

In the confines of the modest motel room, Sharon chatted about her fate, about her crimes.

"What is it going to be like in prison?" she asked.

Elaine Tygart was surprised at the question. In her mind, Sharon had moved herself from victim of a twisted lover to convicted killer ready to serve out a life sentence.

"You'll probably go to Pueblo," she answered. "It's newer. You'll get fed and taken care of. It's clean and warm."

Sharon nodded and made more small talk.

"We've got some time to kill," the detective said. "It will be a few hours before the troops from Thornton get down here. If you want to rest or take a nap, be my guest."

Sharon said she would.

Tygart had a hard time connecting the woman with the crimes. Sharon seemed so very ordinary. She was the next-door neighbor. She was the Avon lady. She was not particularly glamorous, nor was she rough.

Over the next few hours, as the police came from up north and discussions were held with a deputy district attorney from Adams County, plans were made to arrest Gary Adams. By that time, Sharon had told the police where they could find the wedding ring Gary took from Glen as proof of his deed. It was in the house back in Weston. She also told her captors that the note he wrote indicating when he left town after killing Glen was still in her mailbox.

She said Gary had several guns, a supply of ammunition and perhaps some explosives. Outside of a gun he kept in his truck, she did not know where he stored any of his arsenal.

Sharon explained how Gary had come to see her in the early

morning hours after killing Glen. She said they had tried to make love, but he had been too tired and couldn't do anything.

"She made it sound as though it was a seal of duty," the detective later said.

Elaine Tygart knew it was true. She held no doubts about the underlying reason for the murders of Glen and Perry. Sharon Lynn Fuller Nelson Harrelson was in love with Gary Adams. It was an obsessive and a dangerous love. When she talked about him, it was clear that their hold on each other was deep.

He was everything she had dreamed about in her teenage years. He was the lover that she had wanted.

When Sharon ran down the list, it was lengthy.

"Ruggedness . . . a wild side. Totally outside of every boundary I'd ever known. Not religious. Black hair . . . blue eyes . . . ice blue eyes. Survivalist. Protector, I thought. Military. Macho. Guns . . . I'd never experienced this side of life before. I'd never been around anyone like this before. I didn't know people like this existed. I thought, I wonder what this side of life is like?"

Elaine Tygart could see where Gary Adams fit into the whole crazy scenario. He was the bad boy to Sharon's good-girl image. Gary was the biker-greaser a preacher's daughter runs away with in her senior year. The Thornton detective could see that Perry Nelson was the bridge to another life, one of money and power. But what of Glen? Sharon insisted there were no insurance polices, no great wealth for her to make claim to in the event of his death. Elaine was left to wonder: Maybe Sharon liked Glen, she might even have loved the fire-fighter.

To hear the woman sacked out on the Best Western Motel bed, her love for her most recently murdered husband was deep and mutual.

"What's wrong? Don't I make you happy?" Sharon claimed to have asked Glen one night, when it was evident something was eating at him. The conversation took place early in their living-together arrangement.

"No," he said, "it's not you. Sharon, I couldn't ask for anybody who was better suited for me. It's just that I'm having a hard time with your kids. It's my problem, not yours."

Sharon asked Glen if he wanted her to pack up and get out.

"No," he answered. "I want you and the kids to stay here. This is my problem and I should be the one to go."

No woman knew a more chivalrous man. Even for a woman used to getting her way, Sharon was nonplussed. Glen Harrelson was some kind of nice guy; perfect for what Sharon had in mind.

There was something familiar about Sharon Nelson Harrelson. Elaine sensed it, but couldn't come up with any reason why she might know the woman who had confessed to setting up two husbands to die. What was it about her? In time, a memory came back. First foggy, then clear and indisputable. Frighteningly so. And though some might wonder how it could have eluded her, Elaine Tygart's brush with Sharon had been months before in the most unlikely of places.

Sharon Lynn Harrelson had been to the detective's home in Thornton that summer . . . so had her second victim, her husband Glen.

Elaine Tygart's motorcycle had to go. It wasn't that she didn't love the exhilarating feeling she got when she rode with her husband; she loved the thrill of the speed, the air rushing by, the sense of freedom all riders enjoy. Elaine simply loved her husband much more. He had been injured in a motorcycle accident and Elaine had decided that she could no longer enjoy her Yamaha 750. Her riding days were over.

So Elaine Tygart ran an advertisement in the local paper in July 1988.

Todd Harrelson answered the ad. He was a nice kid, a senior at Thornton High. He told the detective he would bring his father over to take a look at it. It was to be a graduation present.

Todd introduced Glen and Sharon to the detective a week later. Sharon burbled about how proud she was of her son, and how excited she was that he might be getting the motorcycle.

"It's cheaper than a car," she said.

Elaine invited Sharon inside while father and son talked

about the merits of the Yamaha. She talked about her husband's job as a fireman and how her son worked at Checker Auto. She was friendly and pleasant. When a beaming Todd came back, it was definite: The motorcycle was going to be his.

Sharon got out her purse and wrote out a check. They'd go to the credit union for the rest of the money.

When the recollection of that earlier encounter came flooding back, Elaine worried Sharon might remember her, too. She wondered what the odds were for a murderer, the victim, and the arresting police detective to have met *before* the crime.

"It made me think how ordinary a killer can be. A person responsible for killing two people . . . can kill your neighbor, your husband. A murderer was in my home."

Everything had been where the Black Widow said it would be: the wedding ring in the bedroom, the note in the mailbox. Sharon Lynn Nelson had been an investigator's dream come true. She had laid it all out and had the evidence to back up what happened.

The only thing missing was the key to the burned-out house on Columbine Court. Sharon had put it back on the key ring that held her car keys; that set of keys had been given to Rochelle when the kids went to stay with her after the first interrogation at Trinidad's police station.

It was left to Det. Tygart to tell Rochelle Mason her mother was never coming back to Trinidad to take care of Danny and Misty. It was more than likely she would never be coming back, period.

"You'll need to make arrangements," the detective said to the unblinking nineteen-year-old. "Your mom told us she had a part in Glen and Perry's deaths."

Rochelle nodded. The grown daughter of the minister and the murderer did not cry. She seemed to take it all in stride.

The detective said Sharon was on her way to Pueblo for booking and would be formally charged in Adams County. She also told Rochelle she could not go up to Round House. Detectives were conducting a search there.

"Can I see my mother?" the young woman asked.

The detective shook her head.
"Not now, but soon."

Gary Adams' dogs wouldn't stop barking. It was around 1:30 P.M., Monday. Gary wondered if a coyote had come down from a mountainside den to tease the dogs and rustle a chicken. At times like that, he often reached for his mini-14 and fired at the coyotes from his back deck. But that morning, he didn't reach for his gun. If he had, things might have turned out differently.

What in the world were the cops doing at the Dude Ranch? Gary Adams didn't poke a gun in the direction of the lawmen driving up to his place. He wondered if they had come to question him about poaching a deer.

Glen Harrelson's murder was the furthest thing from his mind. He was certain no one had seen him or his truck in Thornton. He didn't know what had happened with Sharon at the Pizza Hut.

"Gary Adams?"
"Yeah, how you doing?"
"We have a warrant for your arrest."
"What for? What's going on?"
"First-degree murder. Don't move."

22

THOUGH IT WAS ALMOST SPRING 1987, WITH winter's leftover chill, it certainly didn't feel like the warmer season was imminent. Sharon Lynn Nelson braced herself against the cold to retrieve a local freebie paper that had been stuffed into the mailbox of her Denver, Colorado, rental home. It was a Saturday morning and she didn't have anything to do but sit back and relax. She lit a cigarette and drank coffee as she flipped through the pages before stopping on a personal ad section.

What had once been burn-in-hell taboo was now second nature for the woman starting over without the love of her life, her Mountain Man, Gary Starr Adams.

Sharon had seen other such dating forums before—little rags promising lasting love if the respondent submits an attractive photograph along with a romanticized resume. But this one captured her full attention. It seemed fun. No photo was needed. No games in the mail. Simply by dialing the number and giving the operator her vitals, she would be patched over to voice messages from the men who were desperately seeking Sharon—or women just like her.

Only one of the lonely guys' bios caught her interest. It was written by a firefighter named Glen Harrelson.

She dialed the number.

Like many of his generation, when Glen Paul Harrelson did his tour of duty in Vietnam and returned to the United States, he wanted to make changes in his life. The handsome young man with the receding hairline had seen too much. He had *done* so much. Life could be so short. The son of William and Ruby Harrelson, Glen knew that if he was going to do something with whatever time God gave him, he'd do so somewhere else. Somewhere away from home.

Glen was raised in the northeast suburbs of Des Moines, Iowa, and he longed for a change after the war. In short order, on September 20, 1963, he married Andrea, the girl of his dreams. When the two vacationed in Colorado the first year of their marriage something clicked. Glen wanted to live near the mountains; away from the flatlands of the Midwest. Away from his family, but not because he didn't love them. He just needed a little space.

Settling near Denver, Glen and Andy, as she preferred to be called, eventually had two children. A son, Todd, was born in 1969; a daughter, Tara, two years later. Between the births of what would be his only children, Glen Harrelson found his niche and his life's work when he became a Denver firefighter. It was a perfect fit of man and vocation.

Personalities magnify in the frequently stress-prone confines of a firehouse. Glen's easy nature was always a welcome addition. He played the guitar, sang beautifully and pitched in whenever anyone needed help. He also put up with the good-natured humor of the practical jokers that invariably end up among the eight men who work the long shifts together.

During the middle of one night, a fellow firefighter filled Glen's boots with cold spaghetti. When a false alarm was sounded by the firehouse trickster, Glen jumped up and slid his feet into slimy, wet pasta. Like the good sport that he was, Glen laughed harder than anyone. But when it was payback time, it was Glen who came up with the scheme to put lipstick on the earpiece of the telephone. Red-smeared ears dominated that particular day.

Again, Glen laughed the loudest.

No one would argue that during his tenure at Denver Stations 9 and 26, Glen was one of the most respected and liked of his peers.

During that period his best friend was Jim Schindler. Jim and his wife, Jayne, grew close to the Harrelson family, sharing meals and holidays as time allowed. Jim and Glen also joined forces as business partners on a carpet and decorating sideline, and a few years later, a car wash. Whether it was in the confines of the firehouse or off the job counting change at their car wash, the two men never knew a better friendship. Not in their entire lives. Both figured they'd be best buddies forever, wives included. All four of them, always.

They were wrong. In time, signs were evident and could not be ignored. The Harrelson marriage was ebbing toward failure.

Twenty-two years and the gentle fireman's marriage went up in smoke. For Glen and Andy Harrelson, the split didn't take place overnight. It wasn't the jarring and inevitable result of an affair or an infidelity, as often is the case in marriages that fall apart when couples reach the sneaky desperation that can overtake their forties. Glen and Andy had two children and a fabulous new home on eight acres. They had new cars. Nice manners. But they also had different agendas for their lives. Andy Harrelson was taking Communications classes at the local college, and Glen was following his wanderlust for new ventures and new investments. Glen had the heart of an entrepreneur. The car washes and the carpet and decorating business were absolute testament to that.

So sadly, more than anything, it was the financial matters that broke up the Harrelsons. Glen liked to take financial risks and Andy was more security-conscious. She could no longer get by on her husband's promises. Andy didn't want to worry. She loved Glen, and she knew her complaints—no matter how gently offered—were wearing him down. She was keeping him from doing what he wanted to do.

When the Harrelsons arrived at the Schindler home for a pre-Christmas get-together in December 1984, Jim and Jayne saw firsthand how strained things had become. Things were bad; though they prayed their friends would work it out. Their prayers, it seemed, went unanswered. A few days later, on Christmas Day, a distraught Glen called Jim to tell him Andy had asked him to move out.

"He was at the absolute bottom of the world," Jim later recalled. "He felt it was coming. He was very much in love with Andy. He didn't know what to do to put his marriage back together."

Glen was crying.

"I don't want my family to break up, I really don't," the soft-spoken man muttered over and over.

Not long after the separation, Glen saw a counselor. With help, he hoped he would be able to put his life back together. He was lonely. He missed Andy. As Jayne Schindler later said, "he seemed like a lost puppy."

It was around that time he decided his lonesomeness could not be slaked by his same old friends. Glen wanted to date again. As his divorce became final, Glen joined a singles group at Northglenn Christian Church. He also bought a toupee.

Starting over in middle age is always tough. It was especially hard for Glen, who had not wanted to start over in the first place. The bar scene was intimidating, and he'd never been the type to strike up a conversation with a woman in the produce aisle at the supermarket, as some of the fellows in the firehouse had said had worked for them. Glen was not overly shy—his music was proof that performing for others was a joy, not a dread. But in his forties, he was awkward and alone.

When Glen talked to Jim Schindler about entering the dating scene again, it was with a sense of worry, not excitement. Glen was lost. He did not know what to do. The singles group at the church was a start, but he felt he was too old for most of the women there. Twenty-year-old Mikki Watson, for one, at half his age, would never be more than a friend.

One night Jim and Glen talked until the sun came up. Glen rambled on about his fears and regrets and Jim, who was worried about his friend's mental state, shirked off much-needed sleep to keep his buddy talking.

Glen Harrelson was not a loner and he was very lonely.

When he told Jim and Jayne Schindler that he was advertising in a singles magazine, they were skeptical. They wondered what type of woman he could meet that way.

Glen told them he had already responded to a woman's ad.

"She told me to bring two six-packs and come over to her place."

"What did you do?" Jayne prodded.

Glen flashed a smile. "I went," he said.

The Schindlers burst out laughing. Glen's sense of humor was evident for the first time in months.

"What happened?" Jayne asked.

He let a wry smile cross his face. "I'll tell you this, I didn't stay that long. She wasn't my type."

A few weeks after the woman with the six-pack, he met a new woman. A fun-loving, classy beauty.

"Her name is Sharon, but she likes to be called Sher," he said.

Rick Philippi, 38, was glad for the invitation to join Glen Harrelson and Sher Nelson for lunch, even if they were only eating at the Burger King off 104th Avenue and Federal Boulevard, a few blocks west of Thornton. Rick, who knew Glen through a church bowling team and his friendship with Jim and Jayne Schindler, had heard so much about the new woman in his friend's life that he was pleased he'd finally be able to put a face with the name. He had been seeing less and less of his friend around church and around the events that promoted their mutual interest in classic cars. It was high time to meet the woman behind it.

Glen and Sher were already at Burger King when Rick, a good looking fellow with blue eyes and a blond moustache accenting the northern Spanish features of his ancestors, arrived from the nearby Ford dealership where he was a lot manager. It was one of those moments that begged for a Kodak to prove the description later, the gal made such an unforgettable first impression. Sher sat like a homecoming queen gone bad in tight slacks with a cigarette lodged in the corner of her mouth, moving like a metronome when she spoke. She was neither warm nor particularly friendly.

The lunch, not surprisingly, went downhill from there. It seemed that Sharon didn't really want anyone around other than her beau. She sat between the two bowling buddies, intentionally leaning forward to block Rick's view of his pal. It was obvious as could be. She didn't want Rick involved in the conversation she was having with her new boyfriend.

Once or twice when Rick tried to wedge his way into the discussion, Sharon turned and glared at him. It was subtle and out of Glen's view.

Annoyed, Rick studied his watch as though he was concerned about the time.

"Oh, I have to get back. You guys probably have a lot to talk about," he said, swallowing hard. He had lied to one of his closest friends. He didn't have to get back to the car dealership for any reason at all. His lunch hour was far from over. He just couldn't stand sitting there with Sharon for one more minute.

"She didn't even have to talk, I just didn't like her. I tried to be nice. I tried not to show my feelings. The way she looked, the glare, the stare. The way she carried herself like she was cocky," he recalled later.

As the days passed into weeks of the spring and summer, Glen's circle of friends shrunk until it barely included anyone but Sharon. Old friends were set aside as the friendly fireman and his love took long drives together, went out to dinner, to the movies. Everything seemed to happen so fast.

Sharon complained she didn't like her rental house. She didn't like the neighbor's skinny mutt barking all hours of the night. It wasn't a good place for Danny and Misty to live.

Glen offered Sharon and the kids a place to stay. They could move into his house on Columbine Court. The ranch-style home had a nice yard for the kids, was close to Sharon's job at the eye doctor's and would give everyone a chance to see if they could work things out. When Sharon agreed, Glen told friends he was the happiest man in the world. The haste of their living arrangement surprised many, but no one said a word to Glen about it.

No one wanted to ruin what happiness he had finally found.

Tara Harrelson was a typical teenager of divorce. Though she lived with her mother, she felt a special closeness for her father. The split of the Harrelson family had been hard on the teen. She harbored resentment and a little bitterness, and she rebelled. And even though the stirred-up feelings from her parents' divorce had settled, she was still hurt that they could not be a family as they had once been. When it came to women and their interest in her father, Tara was fiercely protective. She wanted the best for her dad.

When she met her father's live-in, Sharon, for the first time,

Tara Harrelson had a feeling that this former preacher's and doctor's wife was different from the others he had dated. She was nice, but a little pushy. It seemed to take no time at all for Sharon to force herself into their lives. In almost the blink of an eye, Sharon took over her dad's house. She posted religious verses throughout the house. She arranged the furniture the way she wanted it. She did a little magazine-inspired decorating makeover on a couple of the rooms. She allowed Danny and Misty to have the run of the place.

Soon after Sharon and the kids moved in, Tara found business cards from an optical company. The surname astonished her: SHER HARRELSON.

What is this? The teenager had not heard any talk of marriage. Not a peep. Her father and Sharon had just started going out. It was true that Sharon had moved into the house in surprisingly short order, but that didn't mean the two were getting married. What Tara saw on the little card bothered her. Using another man's last name seemed inappropriate even to a sixteen-year-old who might doodle *Mrs. So-and-So* on the back of a Pee-Chee school folder.

"I think she just kind of pushed her way into his life. He just wanted to be loved," she said later.

At first, at least on the surface, it seemed Sharon also wanted to be liked.

When Tara whined about wanting to drive her father's prized 1967 Camaro her pleas fell on deaf ears. It was Glen's pride and joy; he had lovingly restored the car with buckets of money and gallons of sweat. No way was he going to let a sixteen-year-old drive it.

It was Sharon who pressured Glen to give in.

Give the girl a thrill.

She'll be good.

I'll be good, too.

"I think that she did it just to get me out of her hair because I was bugging her so much," Tara commented later. "She didn't care about the Camaro, not as much as my father did."

Sharon, of course, had been down that route before with Perry's daughter, Lorri. How it was that she would find men with teenage daughters was beyond her. She had buddied up, cajoled, sucked up and lied to her lovers' and husbands' kids to get them out of the way. She had done so with the kind of finesse that's born of practice.

23

DIVORCE HADN'T NULLIFIED THE RESIDUAL feelings of closeness and affection Glen and Andy Harrelson had shared during their two-plus decades of marriage. When Glen told his former wife that he was out of his personal funk and involved with a wonderful woman named Sharon Nelson, Andy was delighted. And as time went on, it quickly became obvious this Sharon was more than a fling. Glen wasn't the type to engage in serial dating. He wanted to settle down. He was in search of his second chance.

"There's one problem," he told his ex-wife over the phone during one of their almost daily conversations. "She doesn't know if she wants to get married again."

He explained how his new love's first marriage to a preacher had ended in divorce and her second husband had died in a terrible auto accident.

"She feels like it's bad luck to be married to her," Glen said. "Like there's a black cloud hanging over her."

Andy Harrelson didn't say anything, but the words bothered her. She felt like the woman's comments were a manipulation of a lonely hearted man. She was pulling back, to make Glen want her more.

Andy concluded Glen's new sweetheart was an operator.

It was very peculiar. Whenever Andy Harrelson showed up to pick up the kids or return something she had borrowed, Sharon would disappear into the back bedroom before introductions were made. And she stayed there.

Glen would make some excuse, but the fact of the matter was clear to Andy. Sharon simply did not want to meet her face-to-face. Andy wondered if Sharon was embarrassed about sleeping with her ex-husband. Maybe she was just plain ashamed. She had been a Seventh-Day Adventist minister's wife, after all. "Living in sin" was definitely not Adventist-approved.

The odd aspect of her back bedroom disappearing act was that Sharon was always very pleasant on the telephone whenever Andy called. She was warm, chatty and very accommodating. It was so strange that Glen's new love was able to talk to on the phone without any apprehensions, but could not face her in person.

Maybe Sharon is shy, Andy thought.

It was late at night when the bedside phone woke her from slumber. Andy Harrelson's heart thumped, as most are prone to do, when the startling ring comes in the dark hours. The voice was familiar, though somehow different. It was Glen, but he sounded very weak.

"Could you get me and take me to the hospital?" he asked in a near whisper.

Andy knew Glen had mononucleosis and had been languishing with the debilitating illness for several days. Andy got up and dressed in record time to go after him. All the while, she worried about her former husband and wondered about his girlfriend.

Where was this new love of his life, Sharon?

Her answer came mid-morning when Sharon finally showed up at the Denver hospital where Glen was on medication and bedrest.

"I met an old friend," Sharon announced to her boyfriend while he lay within the stainless steel rails of a hospital bed as IV tubes provided precious liquid to his depleted system.

"It's okay if we go out with other people, isn't it?" she asked.

Glen's dry lips barely moved. And really, what could he say? When Andy Harrelson thought about it later, she considered Sher's comment to her laid-up boyfriend very strange. *Very cruel.*

"Of course, Glen wanted the relationship exclusive . . . I guess it was a manipulation to make him hold on tighter," Andy told a friend.

Outside of Rick Philippi and Mikki Rector—soon-to-be *Baker*, having fallen in love with Porter Memorial Hospital orderly Steve Baker—none of Glen's friends met Sharon Nelson. Glen talked about Sharon effusively. She was the most wonderful woman that had ever landed in Colorado. She was a great cook. She was a sharp lady. And while he never went into the details—he was too much of a gentleman for that—he told a few buddies Sharon was a fantastic lover. Even though just two had met the mystery woman, most of Glen's other pals saw her influence.

None more so than fire department dispatcher Dean Hastings.

Dean had known Glen for almost ten years, having worked alongside him both in dispatch and at the firehouse. Not long after Glen told him of his new girlfriend—whom he said he met through church—he came into work one day without wearing his toupee.

The transformation startled Dean.

"How come you're not wearing your hair?" Dean asked.

Glen flashed a sheepish smile. "Well, Sher wanted to see me without it and she likes me better without it."

Later, when they talked about his new love, Glen told Dean how happy he was. How nice her children were. How Sharon owned a beautiful place down in southeast Colorado, a mountain house near Trinidad.

"How could she afford that?" Dean wondered out loud.

Glen was quick with the answer.

"Insurance money after her husband died in a car wreck. She has the money now, but it was quite a wait for her to get it."

The friendship had frayed like the hems of someone's weekend blue jeans. Rick had stood firm in his resolve to be a true friend, a friend who wouldn't lie. He hated Sharon from the onset and blamed her for the dissolving relationship between the two friends. Whenever the group was getting together, Glen would make an excuse for Sharon's absence. In time, Glen stopped coming around, as well.

"I don't trust her," Rick said, his blue eyes boring a hole through his friend. "She's trying to keep you from your friends."

Glen didn't get it. He disagreed. He said he was stuck in the middle.

"I'm trying to keep the peace," he said.

"But we've been friends longer than you and Sharon."

None of that mattered to Glen, at least not enough to pull away from Sharon.

"She was always the controller, always wanting to control," Rick said later. "I kept telling him she's no good, but he wouldn't listen. He just wouldn't stay away from her."

Sharon Lynn Nelson was not the type of woman the now-newlywed Mikki Baker would have picked for Glen, either. She was not the type of woman he had picked in the past for himself when he expressed interest in a woman. Andy Harrelson was a natural beauty, with fine features and little need for makeup. While Mikki, who had battled a few extra pounds, thought Sharon was pretty and had a good body, she considered her sense of style to be somewhat tawdry.

Thank goodness she has a nice figure, because her pants are so form fitting.

"They were so tight you couldn't believe it," she told Rick Philippi. "She probably had to lay down to put them on. She had camel toes."

When Sher wore shorts her attire left nothing to the imagination: it recalled the fashion of the 1960s.

"She doesn't dress like a woman of her age . . . or like a mother," Mikki said.

Rick concurred.

"The girls we know just don't wear that type of stuff."

As far as Glen's closest friends were concerned, Sher Nelson was a hot divorcée on the make and Glen was a lonesome guy looking for love. It was that loneliness and desperation for love and companionship that must have made him go with the woman from Weston.

Rick shook his head at the improbable.

Glen was not that type of person that would have a woman like her, he thought.

"I wonder what he sees in Sher?" he asked Mikki. "I can't get him to see what I see. She has something that blinds him."

Mikki didn't have an answer. She didn't really need one. Not long after it seemed that Glen and Sharon were inseparable, reports came through other friends that the relationship was over.

The day Tara Harrelson learned Sharon had left her father and returned to Trinidad was both happy and sad. When she saw her father, her heart broke as he cried about the woman who had left him. Tara felt an awkward surge of happiness for herself. She had not felt that close to her father since Sharon had taken over his life.

"I thought we were back on the right track," she told a friend later.

Reality had set in. Hooray for reality. Rick Philippi would have jumped for joy if he was sure Glen Harrelson wouldn't sense it on the other end of the line. He could not have been happier with his friend's disclosure.

"Sher's out of my life," he said.

"Why?" Rick asked, though the *why* didn't really matter.

Ding dong the witch is dead!

"She's got another boyfriend."

Glen's voice was wracked with grief, but Rick didn't want to rub it in. Now wasn't the time for that; there probably never was a time for that. Sher Nelson had done what she was bound to do. Rick hadn't liked her since their lunch at Burger King.

"She's got another boyfriend and she's been dating you at the same time?"

"Yeah," Glen said.

"How long has this been going on?"

"On and off for a few years."

They talked for awhile longer and made plans to get together in a day or so. When Rick hung up he had a smile on his face. His old friend was back. Glen was back.

It wasn't that everyone was jealous of Sharon and her all-consuming relationship with the mild-mannered firefighter. It wasn't that no one wanted Glen to be happy. Far from it. It was simply as clear as a Colorado summer sky to those closest to Glen that Sher was not the right woman for him.

Maybe for anyone.

And yet Glen still told friends that he wouldn't give up. He was going to marry her.

Some never thought the marriage would take place—the relationship between Glen and Sharon had been so erratic. In fact, most of them also had opinions about whether it *should* take place. The couple couldn't even manage to live together for any extended amount of time at the house in Thornton before Sharon hightailed it back to Trinidad. If she loved him so much, why did she leave him? She said she needed her space. She needed to clear her head. Why in the world, friends said, would Glen think a gold band on her finger would make a difference? Get real, man. It was a wedding band, not a leash.

Not long after Glen admitted Sharon had a backup lover in her life, the lovelorn firefighter visited at Rick Philippi's. The news was not good. He and Sharon were talking of getting back together. When the two men went outside to talk, Rick couldn't bite his tongue, couldn't hold back any longer.

"Glen, don't you think it's a good idea to push her out of your life?"

"I can't. I really love her," he said. "And she loves me."

"Well, she doesn't love you as much as you think she does," Rick continued, walking that high-wire act that friends often do when it comes to another's failed relationship. Most people know when a relationship is on the rocks, there is always a chance the estranged couple will reunite. Most know disparaging the other person can often bite back later.

Rick couldn't stop himself.

"From the day I met her, I didn't like her. There's something about her."

"Rick, I understand, but when you're in love you just don't throw it away."

The two men were at an impasse and both knew it.

Rick grabbed the last word.

"I'm sorry, Glen, I think you better find someone else."

For Glen Harrelson, it seemed there would be no other. Sher Nelson with her flashy, fun-loving ways, was the ideal woman for a lonely man looking for love. With Sharon by his side, he felt alive.

Glen Harrelson's smile went from ear to ear. He was as happy as pal Mikki had ever seen him when he ambled into the Thornton offices of the American Family Insurance Co. at the same time she was getting quotes on renter's insurance.

He was beaming. "Sher and I are getting married," he said.

Mikki wasn't surprised. She had seen it coming. She was happy for Glen. At least, she wanted to allow herself to be. She only wished him the best and if Sharon made him happy, then that was all she cared about. The eternal optimist, Mikki hoped it would work out.

After announcing his engagement, Glen told Mikki why he was at the insurance office. He came in to put Sharon down as his beneficiary.

24

SHARON LYNN WAS IN GLEN'S BLOOD LIKE A
virus. The woman was in every thought passing through his
mind, day or night. She was everything he had ever wanted.
He didn't want to lose her. Glen recorded an audio tape and
mailed it to the P.O. box Sharon kept in Weston. He knew
from a previous conversation that her children Danny and
Misty would be flying out to see their grandparents in Clear
Lake, Michigan. Sharon had to come to Denver to put them
on an airplane.

"Stay with me that night," he pleaded on the tape.

Glen had ulterior motives that went beyond making love for
old times' sake. He wanted marriage. And while Sharon had
balked at the proposal in the past, she never said it was an
utter impossibility. She said she didn't know if she could love
him enough. She said she felt she was oil and marriage was
water. She had two disappointments and didn't want to end
up married as often as a Gabor sister.

Rick Philippi, naturally, was one whose stomach turned
somersaults at the prospect of a wedding in the event that
Sharon would agree to marry Glen. Glen was such a fool. He
was making a big mistake. When Glen asked Rick to attend
the wedding, Rick lied, and said, of course, he would stand
up for him. Deep down, he knew he could not be there. He
could never stand by while that woman married his friend.

Not if she was the last woman on earth.

In answer to Glen's audio missive, Sharon agreed to stop

by the house on Columbine Court. She brought along Denise, her second-oldest daughter. She said she couldn't stay, but as the hours flew by, she made no effort to leave. The three shared some laughs and a meal and made plans to go out for breakfast the next morning.

But there was more. Sometime between the lovemaking they shared and the early morning, Sharon gave in to Glen's determined persistence. She would pick up the relationship where they left off. He told her that he had taken vacation time from work and would drive her back to the Midwest to pick up the kids.

"I love you," he said. "And I want to get married. I don't want to stay in motels with you without being your husband. My mother raised me to be a gentleman."

Sharon would later say she was unprepared to get married in the chambers of an Adams County judge. It was a spur of the moment affair.

On June 2, 1988, Mrs. Glen Harrelson—wearing shorts, sandals and a tank top—walked down the steps of the courthouse.

No one ever seemed happier than the man at her side.

Glen Harrelson's present and former wives finally met face-to-face at Todd Harrelson's high school graduation a few days after the wedding. For Andy, Sharon was no longer the voice on the phone, the phantom who disappeared down the hallway.

Glen had never seemed happier, nor more proud.

"Better not smoke in front of Andy," he said as Sharon lit up another of her mile-long cigarettes.

A fleeting look of resentment washed over Sharon's face, but she caught herself and laughed it off.

Upbeat and buoyant, Sharon chatted away. She said she was so glad to finally meet Andy; so glad to be there to celebrate Todd's big day. She even said she would never presume to take Andy's place as the children's mother. Instead, she would be their best friend.

After the ceremony, Sharon and Glen packed up and headed east to visit Glen's family in Iowa. Glen's mother, Ruby, wanted her son to get married in a church and he agreed to her request. Sharon didn't put up a fight. She loved to be the center of attention.

Sharon made a lovely bride once more. No one could deny it. No one could take their eyes off her. Sharon stood before the minister at her mother-in-law's Des Moines church, wearing a carnation pink dress with a fitted waist. If the dress was a bit tight, it didn't matter. Sharon Harrelson had the figure for it.

As Rick Philippi faded into the background, Glen continued to invite Mikki and Steve Baker over to Columbine Court. Sharon wanted to play hostess, and Glen was happy to have his friends over to share in his new life with his new wife.

"Don't talk about her late husband, Perry. She's very touchy about it. Don't bring it up. Drop it," Glen warned before the Bakers' first visit.

Mikki considered the request a bit on the strange side. After all, there were several pictures of Perry Nelson hanging in the house. If she was so touchy about it, why did she invite remarks by having the photos displayed? It bothered Mikki that no pictures of Glen hung on the walls.

And it was *his* house!

From the beginning, if there were any problems between Glen and Sher, it was only that she continually took credit for everyone's accomplishments. It was she who worked for hours in the yard, weeding, edging, pruning. It was she who had toiled in a hot kitchen cooking and cleaning all day.

"I stained the porch," she said when Mikki and her husband were over for one afternoon. "It took all day long, but it looks great. I'm very happy with it. Tired, but happy."

Later, Glen complained to Mikki about the comment. It was he, he said, who had been the one to do the work on the porch.

"I wouldn't mind if she said *we* did it, but, damn, I get real tired of her taking all the credit for the work *I* do."

Within a very short time, it became clear that the relationship was going to be a commuter one—forever. Sharon stood her ground when it came to her ties to the mountains. She flatly refused to give up her beloved Round House for Glen or anyone.

"I will not raise my kids in a city," she announced. "They will be raised in a small town."

Glen tried to persuade Sharon, but she refused to listen to reason. When he suggested finding a house in Castle Rock, so that he'd be closer to work and she'd still have a rural atmosphere for Danny and Misty, Sharon alternated between considering the idea and outright pooh-poohing it.

"I don't want to leave," she said. "If you have a problem with that, mister, then look for someone new. I'm staying put."

Wet Canyon was every bit as rugged and beautiful as Glen had told friend Mikki Baker. She could see instantly why he was willing to make the long commute from Weston to Denver for the sake of a woman; it was an outdoorsman's paradise. Glen invited Mikki and Steve Baker to come for the Fourth of July. Though Sharon had taken over every aspect of Glen's life, it was enlightening to see her in her own environs. Sharon was a bit of a know-it-all. There was only one way to do things: her way.

When Mikki let the kitchen tap run too long, Sharon chided her for being wasteful. When Glen failed to get the barbecue hot enough, quickly enough to suit Sharon's schedule, she was the first one to show him just how to do it. Sharon was the expert. She knew better than anyone.

Saturday afternoon as Sharon and Mikki baked in the sun while their husbands were off target shooting, Sharon said she knew ways around the unemployment benefits program. Mikki had just lost her job. Though Mikki had been fired over a misunderstanding, Sharon insisted the young woman could still collect on unemployment benefits.

"Just lie," she said. "It's easy."

Mikki didn't think she could do that, but she appreciated Sharon's brashness. Sharon didn't seem to be afraid of anything.

Sher also boasted how her house was paid off.

"Look what I have," she said, as she rubbed coconut oil all over her beautifully bronzing skin. She motioned to her surroundings. "My house, my acres, everything paid off. I don't have to work a day in my life, because of my Social Security benefits.''

Take advantage. Take what's yours. It was a motto telegraphed all weekend long.

The night of the Fourth, the adults and children gathered to watch a fireworks display Glen set up on the driveway. With each fountain of sparks and spray of fire, everyone *oooohed* and *ahhhhed*. Mikki snapped a roll of film with the point-and-shoot camera Steve's mother had given the young couple as a Christmas gift. Later, she would be heartbroken that none of the images had turned out. There were no photos of Glen.

Glen Harrelson was known by only a few of the locals in Wet Canyon. Sharon talked about her fireman husband; sometimes glowingly, sometimes skeptically that they'd be able to make a go of their long-distance marriage. One who met Glen in person and had a firsthand assessment was schoolteacher Candis Thornton.

She was out walking when Glen stopped her one day. They chatted a few minutes, small talk about nothing much, when the subject of his concern for Sharon's isolation came up.

"You know, Candis," the soft-spoken man said, "I've been wanting to talk with you about your telephone. I know you don't have regular phone service here."

Candis shook her head. "No, Glen," she said, "we have telephone service from C and C Communications out of Clayton, New Mexico."

But it wasn't readily available to Sharon's location.

"I know some folks up in Denver who have cellular phones," he said, "and I'm really worried about Sharon, up there by herself all the time—with no way to communicate."

Candis listened and encouraged him to talk with C and C to see if Sharon could get the same service she and husband Ray used.

He promised he was going to do it right away.

"He was the nicest man . . . almost as nice as Perry Nelson," she said later of Glen Harrelson. She couldn't help but wonder what it was that Sharon possessed that could attract such a nice fellow as Glen. He was loving, caring and concerned. And, it seemed to many in the Canyon, here was Sharon with Gary Adams whenever her husband left for Denver.

As sure as the sky was blue, Sharon would always have a man on her arm. That was so true, it could easily have been written in stone. When she showed up at the Parsons home in Wet Canyon one afternoon with her new husband, Glen Harrelson, Ann was at once resigned and delighted to make his acquaintance.

Sharon held Glen's hand. She said how they had met through a "love column" in a newspaper. They were so happy. They couldn't stand being apart. She said she was thinking of selling Round House and moving up to Thornton full time.

"What's the place worth?" she asked.

Ann told her she'd get back to her on the house. Real estate was soft, and some market research would have to be done. After Sharon and Glen left, the neighbor wondered what it was men saw in the woman.

She had Gary Adams on the string and this guy in Thornton. What the hell, talk about a two-timer!

Sawmill owner Al Robinson also met Glen Harrelson during one of his visits to the Canyon. Al immediately liked the Denver fireman. He wondered why a nice man like Harrelson would get involved with a woman like Sherry.

My God he thought, *is there some way that I can warn this guy? Something's telling me that he'd better watch this woman.*

Al wrestled with his worries, but kept out of it. He didn't know what the man would think of such a warning. He decided to mind his own business.

Newlyweds not living together? It seemed very odd to Andy Harrelson when she heard that Sharon had packed up her children and moved back to Weston for good.

She called Glen and asked him about it.

"She thinks her kids should be in a smaller school system,"

he said, his voice seemingly unconvinced, though he didn't say so.

"I think it's strange," Andy said, probing for more details.

Glen became closemouthed. He didn't want to get into it.

He made only one remark that clued Andy in to what he was feeling.

"Maybe I made a mistake," he said.

Glen did not say so, but it did cross Andy's mind that there was more than just schooling issues that had caused a rift in the house on Columbine Court. Maybe Sharon's old lover was back in the picture?

"He knew that there was a man back in her hometown who bothered her. She made it sound as though his attentions were unwelcome. Kind of interested in Sharon back home. Glen knew about it," Andy said later.

Sharon was a climber. She used her claws to scale her way out of the mundane life that had been ordained by her parents and her religion. She had gone after what she thought would make her complete. She was no dummy. She had seen the TV shows, read the books. Sharon understood—though everyone denied it—that money can buy happiness.

With Mike Fuller, she was bored, bitter and broke. With Perry Nelson she was only broke.

Over Cokes and potato chips with a friend, Sharon once tried to put it all in perspective.

"With a minister for a husband, you don't have to grab on to any kind of resources, all you have to be is this little china doll on display. For the doctor's wife you have to be a little classy if you're in the right society. You have to be smart enough to pick up the lingo of his profession, to keep the books, to do the ordering, fashion-conscious enough to help people with frames that they are really happy with. That's not who I am inside. I think I always did what everybody else wanted me to do."

Maybe, some would ask later, Glen Harrelson was merely a stop on her way to get what she wanted?

25

IN SHARON'S WORLD SOME THINGS WOULD never change. She would never really be a blonde, no matter how often she bleached her hair. She would never have a reputation as a woman of class and dignity. She would never look as lovely as she had envisioned herself to be. She would never be younger.

But she would always have Gary Adams.

Their love should have been a tattoo, so indelible had it become. Their love was the song on the radio that stayed in the listener's mind all day long. Their love was undying.

Their love was a prison.

Sharon had married Glen, but she had not forgotten Gary. She never got over the sex. Never got over the fact that Gary somehow preferred Nancy to her. How could that be? Why wouldn't he leave that mousy little wife for her? Didn't he love her? Didn't she please him in bed? In the woods? On the shores of the lake?

He was the Mountain Man and she was his Lady.

Things were stable at the Dude Ranch below Cougar Ridge, so when Gary Adams had heard Sharon had moved back, he didn't go see her right away. It wasn't that he didn't want to or that he wasn't curious. He just knew that like an alcoholic on the wagon, one sip of Sharon and he'd be gone again. To taste her "secret sauce" was to consume a drug.

A chance encounter along the country road where Sharon and Danny and Misty waited for the school bus brought the lovers back together. In an instant, the two were kissing while Sharon's son and daughter looked on.

Sharon told Gary two things. She missed him and she was married.

Gary told himself to stay away. Special sauce or not, the relationship with Sharon was nothing but trouble.

But he couldn't stay away. As the air threatened to drop to freezing and the wind howled from down the canyon, Gary Adams made his way up Cougar Ridge to Round House. He knew Sharon was grading the driveway, and he told himself he was going up there to see if he could lend a little help. There she was. Sharon was driving the four-wheel drive with a makeshift I-beam grader pulled behind to make the road less than the bumpy stretch it had been since she and Perry first had it cut.

Sharon was, as he always contended, the most desirable woman in the world. She was a wildcat in bed; a vision of beauty in the light of day. Gary couldn't shake her from his memory. No matter what they had done.

"How's married life treating you?" he asked.

Sharon made a disgusted face. "Terrible," she said. "It isn't what I thought it would be."

"What's the problem?"

Sharon complained that Glen was too demanding. He was always telling her what to do. He wasn't nice to Misty and Danny. He didn't treat her like Gary had. Gary, she said, knew how to please a woman.

"Let's go in the house and talk," she said.

It was against his better judgment to go up to the house. He knew once inside, they'd be back in bed.

He was right.

Sharon tugged her Mountain Man to the bed and wrapped her legs around him, pushing her tongue into his mouth. Gary could not resist. He tore at her clothes; the breasts that he admired as the most beautiful he had ever seen were released from her bra. Though Sharon begged for him, something was wrong.

Gary Adams couldn't maintain an erection. Just as had been the case the first time the two tried to make love, he couldn't get it up.

Sharon did everything she could to get him to stand at attention, but to no avail. Two hours later, she gave up and rolled over.

On the bedroom wall was a picture of Glen and the children. Another framed photograph was the image of Perry.

"Get that off the wall!" Gary said, pulling his jeans back on. "I don't want to come up here and see Perry's face."

Sharon refused. Perry was Danny's and Misty's father. It would be wrong to remove his image from the house. The children should be able to remember their dad.

And though Gary stormed out of there over the pictures, it was a foregone conclusion that Sharon had not seen the last of him. Gary Adams would be back. He'd always come back to her.

Of those who had met Glen in Trinidad and Weston, most considered him to be several cuts above Sharon. Though most felt Glen Harrelson could have done better, everyone knew love was never logical.

Sharon brought Glen over to her son-in-law Bart Mason's parents' Trinidad home for a visit one afternoon late in the fall. During the course of the brief visit, Glen casually mentioned he thought someone had been breaking into his Thornton residence whenever he was down in the Canyon with Sharon.

"You should call the police," Bart's mother urged. "You really should report it."

Though he had to be somewhat concerned to mention it, he tried to downplay his worries.

"Nothing's gone," he said. "Must have a key to get in, too."

Mrs. Mason suggested it could be Glen's son and daughter or friends of theirs. Kids were always looking for a place to party when their folks were out of town. An empty house was a perfect target for that.

Glen didn't think so. He had asked them already. The two had convinced him that they had not done any such thing. Glen was satisfied that Todd and Tara weren't the type to lie.

Someone else had to be spending time at Columbine Court.

26

THE FRONT DOOR ON ROUND HOUSE WAS NEVER locked. Wet Canyon, after all, was seldom the scene of a crime. People familiar with the Nelson place knew the home was big enough that patience was in order whenever a knock didn't bring an immediate answer. They knew it would take Sharon awhile to make her way from one end of the residence to the other. Those who knew her best never waited. They simply knocked and went inside.

Sharon must not have heard the pair of visitors let themselves in one afternoon.

Or she didn't care.

In the middle of the kitchen floor, a hot and sweaty Sharon was in the throes of reckless abandon, engaged in sexual intercourse with a man. His face was not one that the visitors to Round House recognized.

He was not Gary Adams, Sharon's steady lover.

Not Glen Harrelson, Sharon's new husband.

"Oh, hi," she said, as she came down from the moon and collected herself. Her tone was typical Sharon. She appeared neither ashamed nor embarrassed. It was as if she had been caught doing nothing more than picking her nose.

"Just a minute," she said sweetly.

The visitors had seen enough. They didn't see a reason to stay any longer. As quickly as they could they got out of there. This was too much even for Sharon Fuller Nelson Harrelson.

In Sharon's eyes, Gary Adams was the last of a breed. He was a Louis L'Amour invention: a mountain man, a cattle rustler, a renegade. And he was the greatest, most tender lover she'd ever known. He was the type to steal a neighbor's beef cattle, butcher it with a chain saw and throw a couple of steaks on the grill for a romantic dinner for two. She had been married to a preacher, a doctor, a fireman, but her heart belonged to the outlaw in the shack down the mountain. She deserved to feel the way he made her feel. She had a right to the excitement and the danger that he brought in to her life.

Later, though the facts would never really be in dispute, Sharon would deny she meant for any harm to come to the men in her life. She only wanted freedom. Freedom to be a woman with the man she loved.

It was at Round House, Monday, November 15, 1988, when Sharon made her move.

While she cuddled in bed with Gary, she told him that the time was right to get rid of Glen.

"I want it done before Thanksgiving," she said. "Glen's mother is coming from Des Moines and I don't want to spend the holiday with her. I can't stand her."

She drew out a Thornton area map on a small slip of paper, indicating that Gary park in the King Soopers parking lot or at the adjacent Safeway. She noted another possibility: an area of new construction not far from Columbine Court. The map directed Gary to drive up I-25 to 120th to Claude Court.

Then she made a bizarre request, not unlike asking Dorothy to bring back the broomstick of the Wicked Witch of the West as proof that she had killed her: Sharon wanted Glen's wedding ring.

She alerted Gary to the fact that Glen didn't wear the gold band often.

"The last time I saw it was on top of the dresser in the bedroom," she said. If it wasn't there, she told Gary to check the watch pocket of Glen's jeans.

It had worked so well with Perry Nelson's murder, that the idea of another supposed accident had been frequently discussed between Sharon and Gary's incessant cigarettes and screaming-at-the-Rockies orgasms. Though she seemed to want the deed done more than Gary, Sharon was somewhat leery of a murder taking place too close to home. A murder at Round House would raise too many red flags. Too suspicious. Too attention-getting.

Gary considered the best approach would be to murder Glen at the Thornton house, put his body in the trunk of his car and drive it to some remote place in the Canyon where some kind of skull-crushing, bone-busting car accident could be faked.

"See if you can get Glen to bring the Camaro down here," he said.

Sharon didn't understand. She looked blank.

"Glen's truck is too visible with that snowplow unit on the front. Everybody in the Canyon knows the truck," Gary explained.

Sharon shook her head.

"I don't think he'd ever bring the Camaro."

"Why not?"

"Well, I just don't think he would," she said, explaining how the car was Glen's pride and joy and he didn't want to risk his paint job on unnecessary drives. He seldom drove it, not even around Denver. Hell, he didn't even like anyone brushing against the car when they passed by it in the garage on the way into the house.

"Well, if you can get him to bring the Camaro, leave a note in the mailbox."

She left a note the next day: "No, bringing truck."

After a particularly nice visit with his wife and stepkids, Glen Harrelson left for Denver on Wednesday night. By Thursday, Gary Adams was back in Sharon's bed.

"Why wouldn't Glen bring the Camaro?" Gary asked once more.

"I asked him to bring the Camaro and maybe we'd take off and get a sitter for the kids and go to Taos for the weekend, but he just didn't want to bring the car down."

Sharon insisted the murder couldn't take place in Weston, anyway. It was too close.

Even so, Gary persisted.

"Well, is there a way that Glen might go out through the Canyon, you know, the back way?" he asked.

Sharon dismissed the idea. "I don't think so," she said.

Mikki Baker felt uneasy. Her best friend was in trouble. Glen Harrelson was not himself. He seemed very worried, and though he tried to hide it, it still showed. For awhile, Mikki considered that it was the stress and strain of the long commute from Weston to Denver, coupled with the long hours of his extended shift at the fire station. But it was none of that. It appeared to go deeper. It was his relationship with Sharon that was troubling Glen.

"She seems so distant," he told the young woman over coffee one day. "Then the next day, she's all lovey-dovey. Sometimes she says she needs her space, other times she can't get enough of me."

Mikki tried to reassure him. Perhaps Sharon was wrapped up in being a mother. Anyone with half a brain could realize that motherhood was more than a full-time job.

But the issues went deeper, and in time, Glen confided his suspicions. Gary Adams, Sharon's old lover, was back in her life.

"I know Gary's around," he said, his face showing the strain of worry. "She thinks I'm an idiot, but I'm not stupid."

"How do you know?" Mikki asked.

"I found some cigarette butts around the mountain house. Sher smokes Bel-Air, I smoke Marlboro and these aren't either one. The ones I found are Gary's brand."

Mikki comforted him, but her words fell flat. She simply didn't know what to say. She tolerated Sharon, maybe even liked her a little, but she didn't put it past her to cheat on Glen. She tried to cheat unemployment. She was always working a deal. She was the type of woman who would go after what she wanted, damn the rest of the world.

But Glen and Sharon had been married only a few months. A marriage shouldn't fall apart so fast, she thought.

"This isn't the marriage I thought it would be," he said. "I've made a mistake. I don't think I should have married Sher."

Glen fumbled for an explanation, staring into his empty coffee cup.

"I don't trust her," he said.

Mikki didn't know what to say. She wasn't sure if Glen wanted a divorce or needed a marriage counselor. She just listened. She didn't know if the subject of divorce should be broached so soon—after all, Glen and Sharon were newlyweds.

Either there was nothing going on or all hell was breaking loose. At nearly every fire station across the country, that was pretty much the scenario. One November morning in 1988, there was just enough activity building at the station where Jim Schindler worked that left the veteran firefighter with complete certainty it was going to be a busy day.

Amid the jumping beans of activity was the watch desk, the hub of any firehouse. The desk was a magnet for calls and firemen. Emergencies came in and help was dispatched. When the Centrex Line—or main line—buzzed with a phone call it was surprising that the man on the end of the line was Glen Harrelson. As a fireman, Glen should have known better.

Jim Schindler was called to the telephone.

"I need to talk with you," Glen said.

Jim could barely hear his friend and former business partner, though he did make out an urgency in his voice. He asked if he was all right and Glen said he was, but he did need to talk.

"It's important."

"Give me five minutes and call me on the other phone."

Glen promised he would. Yes, he knew the number.

Jim Schindler pried his way out of the fray of the watch desk and stood by a silent telephone in the back room. Five minutes passed, then ten.

The phone never rang. Glen never called back.

Jim wondered if the call had been about Sharon. Rick Philippi had been filling him in about his concerns over their friend's new wife.

"When Glen is there, Sharon is as sweet as pie . . . but the minute Glen's back is turned, look out. I told Glen she's two-faced. He said, 'No, she's not, she's really sweet.' He's trapped in something and he doesn't know how to get out.''

Though Jim Schindler didn't know it then, the call from his friend on the Centrex Line was the last time they'd speak.

She did not know Glen Harrelson well, but on the occasions they shared together, Sharon's sister, Judy, found him to be a caring, gentle soul. He was always doing what he could to show that he wanted to belong with his new extended family. Judy was especially touched by his concern over her well-being when her husband died in late spring of 1988. In a family so divided, so distant, the call from Sharon's third husband was unexpected and wholly appreciated.

Over the course of the summer months and into the bone-chilling nights of late fall, Glen called Judy several times to say hello and to see how things were going.

The last time he telephoned it was not about how Judy was coping, however; it was about Sharon and Gary. Glen confided that he was worried that the affair between his wife and her mountain man lover had heated up once more. Though he hoped he was wrong, he asked Judy if Sharon had said anything that would bolster his concerns.

"No," Judy said with great assurance. "She's finished with Gary. She's told me how happy she is with you. I'm sure that Gary Adams is no longer a part of her life."

As far as Judy knew it was the truth. Sharon had been telling her for months that her long-distance marriage to Glen Harrelson was working better than she could have ever dreamed. They had renewed their search for a place to rent or buy in Castle Rock to ease the commute for Glen.

"We couldn't be more in love," Sharon told her sister.

The dust never settles on murder, and blood never really dries. When the deed is done and two are involved, finger-pointing is as inevitable as the lies told to cover the crime. Sharon Nelson had a different take on her encounter with Gary Adams that Monday when the plan for Glen Harrelson's murder was broached. She had never wanted anyone dead.

Gary had been pressuring her. He was in her face, she would

later say, demanding that they do what they had done before.

Fire and water.

He wanted the key to the door at Columbine Court. He wanted a map. He wanted to know if Sharon knew if there was a gas can in the garage.

"Give me a key and I'll get it done," he said.

He harangued her. He pushed every button he could think of. She deserved better. She could use the money. She could be with her Mountain Man for good.

"Sher, give me the key!"

In a second, the line was crossed again. Sharon's voice began to rise from deep within.

"Here's the goddamn key! Get out of my face!" she screamed.

She didn't know with any certainty if it was a game or reality. She didn't know if he was playing the macho man to her damsel in distress. Later, she would insist that if she had thought for one minute that Gary would really kill Glen, she would have driven down the mountain and called for help. She would have warned him.

She would later say she wasn't sure if Gary Adams was a killer or a big talker.

Long after it barely mattered to anyone, she told a sympathetic ear where her doubt came from.

"You haven't seen the tender side of him," she said. "You haven't been in bed with him. I can't imagine being in bed with a killer. The tender man that he could be could not be a killer."

Diann Browning was glad Friday had arrived, payday had come and she was able to get to Trinidad and do the week's grocery shopping. For the mother of four, it seemed like payday never came fast enough. Her arms brimming with bags and boxes, Diann unloaded her groceries in front of her little house at the Robinson sawmill where her husband, Mike, worked. She wanted to put things away and relax. She even had a couple of videos for Friday-night entertainment, *Pippi Longstocking* and *E.T.*

It was 4 P.M., November 18, 1988, and the sky was starting to spit snowflakes.

When Sharon and her two children pulled up, Diann had not yet unloaded everything from her shopping trip. She smiled warmly at her three visitors. She knew the family was alone that weekend; Diann had waved to Glen Harrelson on the road near the tiny town of Segundo. He was heading toward Denver, back to work, away from the mountains.

By the way she invited herself in, it was clear to Diann that Sharon wanted to stay for awhile. Sharon was in good spirits, happy with her marriage. She was wearing a Denver Fire Department T-shirt.

"Glen gave it to me this week," she said.

Diann said she thought the shirt was nice as she went about the business of making hot dogs and heating up a can of pork and beans.

Sharon and her kids had invited themselves for dinner.

When the snow started dredging the roadway in white, Diann figured her visitor would leave. Sharon hated driving up to Round House when the roads got slick. Without exception, whenever Sharon had been around and it started to snow, she would hurry home.

Except that night. That night, the snow didn't bother her. She planted herself on the couch, munched popcorn and watched the videos.

And she talked about how wonderful her marriage was to Glen. She was so much in love with him. Everything was wonderful. She complained about how she and Glen just couldn't get enough of each other.

"Glen and I had the best sex last night," she said.

Around 9 P.M., the last tape ended and Sharon stood to leave. It was nearly as abrupt as had been her surprise visit. She packed up Danny and Misty and drove off to Round House.

27

HOURS LATER, MILES NORTH OF SHARON'S Round House, the wetness she had left on Gary had dried to a noticeable itch. It was a sweet annoyance, a niggling reminder of the hours Sharon and he had spent together under sheets dampened by their careless passion. Of course, no reminder was really necessary. The world spun on an axis created by the two from Wet Canyon and the promises they had made to each other. The smell of her still lingered on him. It aroused him when he smelled her. *When he thought of Sharon.* He shook his head as if the abrupt action would sift her image from his consciousness. There was no chance of that.

Gary Adams tried to re-focus his weary eyes. Once again, he was a man on a mission, a soldier for love.

Gary parked about a mile away at a bar, and walked the rest of the way to the house. He followed the map made out by Sharon, her handwriting curving in schoolgirl loops and swirls. Seductive, sweet. She had also passed on the key. Gary was glad she had made things so easy. He didn't want to be found out. He didn't want to attract attention. He had a job to do, a promise to keep.

It was 8:30 P.M. The Colorado night air was black and cold; as still as a frozen lake.

His mind was racing by the time he stood outside Glen Harrelson's tidy blond brick-faced ranch home at 12370 Columbine Court in Thornton. Though he shouldn't have, he had a hell of a time finding the place, and had nearly panicked when he passed a fire department only a few minutes from the house.

The same fire department where Glen worked as a firefighter and dispatcher.

With sweat spreading from his armpits down his sides, Gary knew he'd have to get away quickly once he struck the match. After—of course—he had done what he had promised to do.

Gary patted his jacket pocket, confirming the pistol was still there. An eighteen-inch lead pipe he'd stuck into his dusty Levis passed his belt-line and pressed hard and cold against the middle of his rib cage. The .22-caliber handgun had been brought along merely as a backup. It was the pipe he intended to use. A pipe, Sharon reasoned during one of their trysts, would make what was about to happen appear as if a botched burglary had taken place.

A fire would lay a black veil over what had happened. No one would ever know the truth—as they had not known the time before.

Gary glanced over his shoulder as he stood in the doorway. So quiet, so still. Though he was short of breath from his hurried walk, his heart picked up a beat as he slid the key into the lock and turned the knob.

Light from street lamps cut through the expansive glass of a picture window in the front room. The room was barren, save for a pair of recliners and a television set. It was the home of a man who had just moved in, or whose wife had left him with the remnants of a broken marriage.

Deep in the shadows, Gary made his way down the hallway. He wanted to know the layout of the house, though it had been described in detail by Sharon. The first bedroom was empty. At the end of the hall, he found the master bedroom. A dark mahogany bed was neatly made up. On the dresser, he saw the glimmer of gold: a man's wedding band. It was just where Sharon had said it would be. He put the ring in his pocket.

"Bring it to me! Bring it when you are done!"

The numerals on the digital bedside clock glowed in the darkness. It was 8:45 P.M.

"He is home no later than nine! He is so predictable you could set your watch by him!"

Gary padded softly through the living room to the kitchen, where he checked the back door's security lock. There would be no escape from the rear of the house. Nor would there be a way out through the windows—all were shielded by decorative wrought-iron grates. His only way out would be the way he came in—through the front door.

He could feel his heart thump as he checked his watch. Returning to the living room, he drew the lead pipe from his pants before settling into a recliner to wait.

"Do this right and we'll make love all night. Every night. You and me. Forever."

Minutes passed and the conversations, the promises of sex and money, filled Gary's head, nearly distracting him from the plan at hand. Over and over, he re-focused on the reason he was there. And as it played in his head, Gary became increasingly jittery. He was nervous. He was unsure. He could not do it.

Not again. Not for her.

Acting on impulse, he bolted from the recliner just as headlights swung wide across the driveway and pierced the darkness through the picture window. It was too late. The wheels that had been set in motion so long ago were moving with a speed he could not halt. There was no turning back.

God, he loved Sharon.

As he listened to Glen get out of his car and walk toward the door, Gary Adams crept to wait by the door. If he still had wanted to turn back, it was too late. He had to do what Sharon had begged him to do.

Gary raised the lead pipe and swung at Glen Harrelson's head. Glen went down, but just as Perry Nelson had done, he tried to stand to fight. He was not out cold. And this time there wasn't the icy water of a raging creek to revive him. It was fear and the instinct to survive that gave him the burst of strength to fight his attacker.

Gary hit him once more with the bloody pipe.

It didn't put him out. Thought he'd be out like a light.

Glen Harrelson grabbed Gary Adams's arm and forced him to the floor, flipping him onto his back.

With the light streaming in from the garage door, they could see each other. Two men brought together by the same woman. Their eyes met. Glen Harrelson had the look of a man who was fighting for his life. It was the same wild-eyed look Perry Nelson had that night along the edges of Clear Creek five years before. Glen kicked Gary's leg and knee. Hard, with a force of a man that was going to kill the killer.

The pipe was not going to work and Gary knew it.

He reached for the gun, which he had set off to the side as his insurance policy for such a moment as what was taking place in Glen Harrelson's house. The gun fired two times.

It was over. It had gone all awry. Murder is like that. Gary Adams knew that there was no way he could make it look like an accidental death. It was going to have to resemble a botched burglary. He heaped a pile of clothing about the room to make it look as though the place had been ransacked.

Sharon had told him that the grates over the basement windows could be removed. Glen went downstairs and confirmed that one, in fact, was loose. He moved a chair to the window, got up and pulled the grate off, quietly setting it to the side. There had been enough noise coming from the house. Gary went back upstairs and took a jar of coins from the closet and scattered its contents. He went into the garage where Sharon had said Glen kept a supply of gasoline. When he returned he stepped over Glen's body and doused the area with the liquid.

Before he struck a match, Gary decided he needed a delayed fuse. He lit a cigarette and placed it inside a book of matches. That, he thought, would give him the five minutes he'd need to get away.

And he was gone. In a few minutes, Gary was sitting in his truck waiting for the sirens to signal that a neighbor had seen the fire. But five minutes, then ten more, passed. Nothing.

He wondered what went wrong. Did the cigarette go out? Why hadn't anyone called?

Gary Adams walked back to Columbine Court. He went into the open garage and cracked the door open. Like yardage of black plastic, a curtain of black smoke ripped out of the opening. Gary slammed the door and ran like hell.

Eighteen-inch-deep footprints ran up the ridge from the Dude Ranch to Round House. It was frigid outside, colder than a witch's tit in a brass bra, as the locals liked to say. Sharon had left the yellow light on the deck, casting a warm glow over the snowy hillside. The tracks were left by Gary Adams as he trudged up from his place to tell Sharon that he had taken care of everything back in Thornton.

It was a little after 4 A.M. when Sharon let him into her bedroom.

"It's done," he said, taking off his coat to let the air of the house warm him.

"Are you sure he's dead?" she asked.

"Everything didn't go according to plan."

Sharon smiled. "You look like you're in one piece," she said.

Gary shrugged, his attitude remarkably casual for a man who'd just killed another. "I got some bumps and bruises."

He reached deep into his pocket and brought out a circle of gold. It was Glen's wedding ring, taken off the bedroom bureau as proof that he had been in the house and done as he had promised.

Sharon took the ring and regarded her lover with mock skepticism.

"Are you sure he was dead before you started the fire?"

"Yes. There was smoke coming from the windows, I didn't see any flame, but I wasn't going back in."

He also returned the key and the map. Sharon put the key back on her key ring and threw the map into the fireplace, a small flash of light illuminating their faces as the slip of paper burned to ash.

Gary said that he made it look like a burglary by scattering some coins around her dead husband.

He even remarked that he had to change a tire on the way up to Thornton.

Sharon wanted to make love. She said she wanted to hold her mountain man, the Adonis of the Rockies, the sipper of her special sauce. She pulled Gary closer and ran her tongue over the salty areas of his muscular body. But nothing happened. Nothing stirred. Nothing stood to attention. Gary couldn't get it up. Their passion had been extinguished like a birthday candle attacked by a fire hose.

Gary muttered how tired he was. He kissed Sharon and put on his Levis and shirt. They'd make love tomorrow.

And every night after that.

When Gary went back down to the Dude Ranch, he told his son he'd been out with friends. He was tired and he went to bed, the images of what he had done for love haunting him as he drifted off to sleep.

Jayne Schindler reached over to stifle the ringing of the telephone. She and her husband were still in bed when Ron Motley, a firefighter from Station 26, phoned to speak with her husband. The time of day and the brusque seriousness of his voice made it clear that his call was business-related.

Jayne sat up while she watched Jim's face.

"It can't be," he said. "Glen died in a fire . . . at his house?"

He repeated the words so that his wife could hear, but also so that they could sink into his no-longer-slumbering consciousness. His mind flashed to his last conversation with a troubled Glen. What had he wanted to say?

In a minute he got off the phone and faced his concerned wife.

"Suicide," they both said. "Glen must have killed himself."

A few minutes passed, and their dual first reaction went by the wayside as reason began to set in.

"No," Jim said, "Glen wouldn't do that. Something is wrong."

Jayne agreed.

Both knew that the odds of someone trained in fighting fires actually dying in one had to be extremely remote. Motley had said that Glen had been found in the crawl space.

Perhaps he had changed his mind and had tried to get out?

"A seasoned firefighter doesn't die in a fire in his own

home," Jim told his wife as he began to dial Chief Bob Snyder. "You crawl your way out. It's your house, you know where you are."

Chief Snyder, who had been in on the early stage of the investigation, agreed with Jim Schindler's growing skepticism. The two conferred by telephone that morning.

"This doesn't ring true," Jim persisted. "Something is wrong. Investigate this thing."

The chief assured him it was already being done. The arson squad was at Columbine and a meticulous examination of every inch of the charred house was underway.

Jim made another phone call to the police department; they agreed that something was up. In fact, they did not want it released that Glen's body had been discovered. Information that might lead to an arrest would be kept close to their vests.

His last call would be to Glen's first wife; the mother of his son and daughter.

It was the last person Andy Harrelson expected to connect with, but it was a nice surprise. When Jim Schindler phoned out of the blue that morning, Andy thought he was calling to catch up. She took a seat at the kitchen table and prepared for a leisurely chat. The couples had drifted apart after the divorce and Andy had missed the Schindlers.

"Have you heard about Glen?" Jim asked abruptly. His tone was soft, suggesting something had happened.

Andy felt a jolt. She braced herself. "What?" she asked, her heart sinking to a place lower than she thought possible. Something terrible had happened. She knew it, even before he said it.

"There was a fire in his house . . ."

The rest of the words would escape Andy Harrelson, but their meaning was clear. She gripped the phone and asked what hospital Glen was taken to.

"He didn't make it, Andy," Jim said. "I'm so sorry."

"I'm going to the house," she said.

"No. You stay there. I'm coming over."

Todd Harrelson overheard his mother's end of the conversation and joined her at the kitchen table. As they held each other, the teen and his mother cried before going upstairs to tell Tara. The sixteen-year-old girl fell apart. She and her father had been close, despite Sharon's frequent meddling. Tara loved her dad. She was, in her eyes and his, Daddy's Girl.

Andy Harrelson still loved Glen. She loved the good parts of their marriage and the children they had made together. By the time she had her wits about her, her home was filled with people from the fire department, the police, even a witness assistance professional from the county.

Shock was displaced by sorrow and worry. She asked if Sharon had been notified. An officer said they had not yet made that call. In fact, they couldn't call. Sharon Harrelson had no phone in her remote house in southeastern Colorado.

"This is going to be so hard on Sharon," Andy told the victims assistance woman. "She just lost another husband not too long ago."

The victims assistance person excused herself to make a call.

Todd and Andy went upstairs, away from the activity that was enveloping their home. A mob of uniforms had taken over. Tara had gone to be with a girlfriend. Andy caught her son's anguished face in the dressing-room mirror.

Clarity had begun to set in as the initial shock turned from upheaval to numbness.

Andy's own words echoed in her consciousness: *"She just lost another husband not too long ago."*

"Sharon did it," she said.

Todd looked hard at his mother, prompting her to say more.

"Oh my God," she said quickly, as if she could censor what she had blurted out. "I'm sorry I said that."

But she wasn't sorry, not really. From what she had seen, Sharon was the type of woman who'd be behind something like her husband's murder.

Anxiously, Mikki Baker took another look at the clock. What was keeping Glen? He was supposed to get in touch with her before they met for coffee that Saturday morning at Village Inn off 84th Ave and I-25. She reran what he had said, and she became worried.

"I have something to talk to you about. I can't tell you, now. I just need to see you."

Mikki told her husband, Steve, about her concerns. It wasn't like Glen to not call when he said he would. She got dressed and planned on going to the coffee shop to see if Glen had forgotten and showed up.

Instead, from her bedroom telephone, she dialed his number on the off chance that he had returned to Columbine Court.

A man identifying himself as a police officer answered her call.

For a minute, Mikki thought she had misdialed. But she knew Glen's number by heart. She hung up.

"Call the number again," Steve told her.

The same man answered. "Who are you?" he asked.

"Mikki Baker. I'm trying to reach Glen Harrelson and his number is ringing you."

"Why are you calling?"

"He's a friend of mine. We're getting together for coffee this morning."

Steve watched his wife's face grow white. Later, when Mikki Baker recounted what the man said, she would not be able to come up with the exact words. Something about an accident. Something about a dead man. The line had been patched over from the burned-out house to the Thornton police station.

"Glen's dead," she said, tears already flowing.

Steve Baker reached out for his wife and held her.

"What's Sharon going to do?" Mikki sobbed. "This is the second husband she's lost to death."

Steve shook his head.

"Mikki," he finally said, "don't be too hasty. I told you there's something about her. I don't like her."

Mikki stopped listening to her husband for a moment. Her thoughts slipped to Glen and the reason they were going to have coffee that morning.

"He never got to tell me what he so desperately wanted to say," she said.

* * *

A hot shower was all he wanted. Rick Philippi returned from pheasant hunting in Kit Carson, on the Kansas state line and was on his way to the shower when his wife, Theresa, stopped him with the grim news.

"Glen's dead. He's been killed in his house! His body, Rick, was set on fire."

Rick was shocked into silence as grief took hold. How could that have happened?

Something wasn't right, he thought.

Finally it hit him. "Where's his wife?" he asked.

Theresa Philippi knew what her husband was thinking.

"They're looking for her," she said.

"She did it. I know she did it. I just *feel* it."

When Sharon's son-in-law, Bart Mason, picked up the phone in his rambling old Trinidad house, it was Glen Harrelson's mother, Ruby, calling all the way from Des Moines, Iowa. The kindly old woman had some bad news and needed to reach Sharon right away.

With a worried look on his face, Bart pressed the receiver into wife Rochelle's outstretched palm.

Mrs. Harrelson was distraught and nearly out of breath. There was no room for the pleasantries that usually accompany the start of a phone conversation.

"Rochelle, how far do you live from your mom's house?"

"About thirty minutes," Sharon's eldest daughter answered.

"You've got to go up there and be with your mother."

"We're going up there anyway. Why the sudden need?"

Mrs. Harrelson's fragile composure began to slip further and she let the words rush from her lips. "You've got to go tell your mom Glen died this morning in a fire at the house."

Rochelle was overwhelmed. She could barely think of a response. "What house?"

But Mrs. Harrelson was gone. The line was dead.

Rochelle and Bart made it to Round House in record time, probably less than fifteen minutes, though they didn't time the drive.

Danny and Misty were in the front room playing when Rochelle and Bart went inside.

"Bart and Rochelle are here!"

"I'm so glad you're here," Sharon said. "Come and sit down. We'll eat supper and watch a movie."

"Mom, I think you better sit down," Rochelle said, tears running from her eyes.

"What's wrong?" Sharon asked.

"Mom, Glen's mom just called . . . Glen died this morning in a fire at the house."

Sharon stood perfectly still for a moment and started to cry, before words came to her lips.

"Oh my God, how did this happen?" she finally asked.

Rochelle held her mother, feeling her shuddering body convulsing with grief.

"How did this happen . . ."

She collected herself enough to tell the children the terrible news that their new stepfather was dead.

Danny Nelson stood in the front room, his eyes wide open and his mouth agape.

"Mommy," the nine-year-old boy said, "why do all our daddies have to die?"

Something snapped. Her crying shut off like a tap run dry.

"Oh," she said, as she fumbled with her shoelaces, tears obscuring her vision. "I've got to make a phone call. I've got to find out what's going on."

Bart, who stayed out of most of the conversation, told his young wife to take her mother down the mountain to the pay telephone at Robinson's Mill. He would stay at the house with the little kids. It was all he could think to do. Everyone had been so shaken by this tragedy. Imagine the poor guy dying in a terrible fire like that. What could be worse?

Way up north, near the scene of the crime, Thornton Detective Glen Trainor was called out to the crime scene at the fireman's house. A bit later, Elaine Tygart also received news of the suspicious death. Within a few hours, the two would be heading for Trinidad. Driving down the freeway to solve not one murder, but two.

28

SNOW WAS THREATENING, TURNING THE SKY OVER Brighton, Colorado, into a leaden lid. Lorri Nelson Hustwaite's knotted stomach rolled inside her and her knees nearly buckled as she walked the long corridor to the visiting area of the Adams County Jail. She was there to see Sharon Lynn, the woman who had been arrested following the Pizza Hut confession of her involvement in the murder of Perry Nelson. Lorri, pale and wan from the trip and the anxiety of the pending confrontation, had arrived from Montana to ask the question to which everyone had sought an answer.

Directed over to a seat separating visitors from prisoners by a wall of glass, Lorri spotted Sharon before her former stepmother saw her. As she moved closer, the woman who killed her father stretched forward as a delighted smile rushed over her face.

"Lorri," Sharon called out with the kind of exaggerated excitement one uses to demonstrate to a long-lost friend a sense of joy for a reunion.

Lorri did not return the look. She did not match Sharon's smile, nor was her greeting given with any semblance of friendliness.

"I want to know one thing," she said. "Why did you kill my father?"

The happy look long gone, Sharon shook her head sadly. "I never meant for it to happen," she said. "I can't possibly explain it all. It is far too complicated. My feelings. My feelings were all mixed up.''

As Lorri listened, Sharon trashed her father's memory. Sharon shifted blame and said Perry had cheated on her. He had an affair with another woman and it broke her heart.

"You don't know what I was going through with his affair. It hurt.''

"You've had many, many affairs,'' Lorri snapped. "And you're not dead.''

Perry Nelson's favorite youngest daughter fought her tears and tried to keep her composure while Sharon went on about how no one could understand her. No one could understand the pain Perry had caused her by his betrayal.

Her father's betrayal? *What betrayal?* Sharon had slept with a half dozen guys and murdered Perry. Betrayal? Lorri had heard enough. She realized at that moment that she had come to *say* something, not to *listen* to the woman behind the glass. The woman behind the glass could say nothing that would undo what she and her lover had done.

"I want you to know that you not only killed my father,'' Lorri began, her voice breaking into a million pieces, "you also killed my children's grandfather and my grandparents' son. You killed your own children's father . . . and they say you paid a man fifty thousand dollars to do it.''

Sharon looked down as a preschooler does when caught misbehaving.

"I would gladly have paid you ten times the amount you paid Gary, if you would have spared Dad. But it doesn't work that way, does it?''

"No, Lorri, it doesn't,'' Sharon answered, now irritated by her visitor.

Lorri stood up. "I hate you. And I will hate you forever.''

"I know,'' Sharon said.

With that, Lorri turned to leave. How she found her way out of there, she would never quite know. A man offered help as she sobbed her way down the hallway, but she declined. Outside, she realized she had not returned the plastic-laminated visitor's tag that had been affixed to her blouse when she was processed for the visit.

She could think of nothing but her father and the lies her stepmother had told her.

On the way back to the Springs, the snow came down like talc. Lorri could barely see as she drove along the freeway, remembering Sharon and her father. Remembering the encounter she had had with evil. Between the tears and the falling snow, Lorri would later wonder if only the hand of God had assured her safety.

After her sister was picked up by Tygart and Trainor and taken away to jail, Judy Douglas tried to figure out what had gone wrong and how it could have been stopped. *When could it have been stopped?* She knew whatever role Sharon had in the deaths of her second and third husbands, it was the result of a seed planted long ago. Sharon had been on a selfish course to disaster since she was a child. Sharon was a speeding train that could not be stopped. And though she had not allowed herself to believe that Sharon was capable of murder, Judy became consumed with guilt and worry that if only she had told Glen that things were not so great between him and his wife, that Sharon was a woman who could never settle for just one man at a time, things would have turned out differently. Maybe he would have been alive if Judy had told him to leave Sharon.

Judy also wondered if well-to-do Buzz Reynolds hadn't been an intended murder victim a couple of years before.

"Maybe it just didn't work out for Gary and Sharon at that time," she said later. "I'm still not sure that Buzz and she were legally married, but I suppose that wouldn't stop Sharon."

But there had been money involved, though Sharon insisted that Gary took their love to the extreme and killed Glen so the two of them could be together. Killing Glen, she said, was never about money.

But it had not been for love, after all. As Andy Harrelson figured it, Glen's murder would have resulted in a bloody windfall for Sharon and Gary. She would have picked up half of the house, with equity of more than $100,000; life insurance of $30,000; balloon payments due from the businesses Glen had sold that would have been tens of thousands in proceeds;

his house on Columbine Court; and his pension—which would have paid her $1,200 a month for the rest of her life.

Not to mention any life insurance polices that she might have taken out herself. Unless the brass-balled widow made a death benefit claim, such policies would likely never surface.

Grandma Nelson's neck had never healed properly after a nasty fall. It left the elderly woman with a stooped appearance, causing her to tilt her head upward to see straight ahead. Doctors told family members Perry's mother should have recovered more fully from the fall, but for the stress and devastation of losing her son. A broken heart, the doctor explained, can affect the body's ability to heal.

Yet every morning, as she had done for her whole life, the nearly eighty-year-old woman would wake before dawn to kneel by her bedside and pray. Her hands were weathered and the veins rose to the surface as they often do in older people. After her son disappeared, Mrs. Nelson prayed he would be found safe and sound. After his body was discovered in Clear Creek, she prayed her boy had not suffered long.

It was after Sharon confessed to murder that Mrs. Nelson pressed her shaking hands together and prayed for answers.

"Why, Lord, why did You take our son away? Why did You let this happen?"

One time, as clear as a whisper in her ear, Mrs. Nelson received an answer. It came to her as if spoken by the Almighty.

"It was the only way I could save him," the voice told her. "It was the only way."

Epilogue

HAVING CONFESSED TO THE MURDERS OF PERRY Nelson and Glen Harrelson, Sharon Nelson and Gary Adams are now behind bars in "his and her" prisons in Canon City, Colorado. There had been no trial, no public stoning of a woman who stopped at nothing to get what she wanted. Sharon pleaded guilty to two counts of first-degree murder, telling the world she had forfeited her right to a pair of murder-trials to spare her children. Others speculated that she feared the death penalty. Gary Adams held out longer than his lover, insisting through his attorney that he was not guilty of anything.

But in the end, he also pleaded guilty to two counts of first-degree murder when it was confirmed love-of-his-life Sharon would testify against him. He also made one last mistake concerning the whereabouts of the gun used to kill Glen Harrelson. Gary told a jailhouse snitch where he had hidden it. Authorities returned to the Dude Ranch and found the firearm under the porch steps. Ballistics proved an exact match.

Both Sharon and Gary took the easy way out: plea-bargains spared the state the expense of lengthy trials and ensured the lovestruck pair would never face the executioner.

And yet it wasn't over. The obsession that led the two to kill for passion and money still lingers.

Sharon continues to wonder if Gary had ever loved her enough to divorce Nancy. It is a question she still asks, a decade after her arrest. She now says her confession was a big mistake, a manipulation by the authorities. She is a battered woman who had feared for her life. She is a victim.

Gary says he still loves Sharon and remains surprisingly blunt about his involvement in the crimes. While Gary concedes that he killed Glen Harrelson, he remains less forthcoming about his exact role in the murder of Perry Nelson. Yes, the ice blue–eyed killer admits, he tried to drown Perry that night in Clear Creek. Yes, he smashed his head with a rock.

"But he was alive, when I saw him last. He was alive," he said.

Neither Gary nor Sharon will be eligible for parole until they are in their mid-eighties.

And while the pair were picked up and put in jail within hours of Sharon's Pizza Hut confession, the road to justice for others was a slow one. The surviving Nelson children—including Misty and Danny—filed a claim against the insurance companies that paid off Sharon, the killer of their father. As more information came to light, it appeared that insurance investigators were quite suspicious of Sharon Nelson. They held their cards to their chests, however. They never informed the police about what they had uncovered: that Perry had not left Trinidad alone the night he disappeared; that Sharon had purchased five of six policies within six weeks of the murder; that Gary moved in within days after Perry's disappearance; that she immediately sold off many of her husband's belongings and assets. If the insurance companies had been more forthcoming with the authorities, Sharon and Gary might have been prosecuted years before and Glen Harrelson's life might have been saved.

"This isn't a case of twenty-twenty hindsight, piecing a murder together six years later," said the Denver attorney representing Perry Nelson's children. "These facts are so obvious and transparent it would have been like pulling on a loose end of a ball of yarn. The only people who knew all these facts and these patterns were the insurance companies."

The fight for the insurance benefits that should have never found their way into the killer's hands was drawn out for almost a decade. There were several reversals, culminating with the original verdict finally being upheld in the summer of 1996.

The payout, plus interest, was divided equally among Perry Nelson's five children. For Lorri, of course, it was never about money. No mountain of dollars could replace her father. No cash could compensate her son and daughter for the absence of their grandfather.

No money could ease her broken heart.

And yet life goes on down in Trinidad and the surrounding Colorado communities touched by Sharon Lynn's selfish kind of evil. Her children, her neighbors, her friends . . . and her men . . . none can forget her.

Though they try. God, they try.

Acknowledgments and Notes

IT IS IMPORTANT TO SAY HERE THAT THIS BOOK would not have been possible without Rod Colvin. Rod, a fine author and skilled journalist, had a passion for this story for many years. I am so grateful he entrusted his voluminous research material to me, much of which is the basis for this book. Rod, many thanks for your incredible research and the support you gave along the way. You are a great writer and an even better friend.

Others to whom I am indebted for their support of this project: literary agent Susan Raihofer of Black, Inc., New York; Charles Spicer, editor at St. Martin's Press, New York; Lucy Stille, film agent at Paradigm, Los Angeles. Also, thanks to readers and friends Paula Bates, Tina Marie Schwichtenberg, James Glenn Schwichtenberg, June Wolfe, Daniel Leonetti, Cliff Cernick and Patti Soloveichik.

While many of the sources in the book were extremely helpful in reconstructing the Nelson saga, it would be remiss to omit special thanks to Blanche Wheeler, Andy Harrelson, Judy Douglas and Julie Nelson for the photographs from their personal collections. Many of their images appear in the photo insert.

Even though it goes without saying, it must be mentioned here: None of my books could have been written without the support of my family. This is no exception. Thanks to my wonderful wife, Claudia, and my daughters, Morgan and

Marta, for putting up with the long hours when phone calls come and I never leave the glow of my Mac.

Since most of the events described in this book took place several years ago, I have elected not to identify certain individuals featured in this true-crime account. Therefore, some names and personal characteristics have been changed. And while it happened long ago should not be forgotten, neither should the dredging up of it impact lives today. The perpetrators' names, however, have not been altered.

Sharon and Gary cannot run. They cannot hide. Like shadows on sticky summer afternoons, their crimes will follow them the rest of their days. Lorri Nelson Hustwaite and the others who loved the victims will see to it.

—*Gregg Olsen,*
Olalla, Wash.
Fall 1997